KU-387-308

PENGUIN BOOKS

The Dealmaker

Born in 1959, Guy Hands graduated with an MA in Politics, Philosophy and Economics from Mansfield College, Oxford, and then went to work for Goldman Sachs International, where he became Head of Eurobond Trading and then Head of Goldman Sachs' Global Asset Structuring Group. He left Goldman Sachs in 1994 for Nomura International Plc, where he established PFG before spinning out Terra Firma as an independent private equity firm in 2002. Since then, he has overseen the investment of €17 billion of equity in thirty-five businesses with an aggregate value of €47 billion. In 2012, Guy was named the 20th most influential figure in Private Equity International's '100 Most Influential of the Decade'. He established Terra Firma Capital Partners Limited's commitment to donate 10% of annual pre-tax profits to local initiatives in London, while Terra Firma Capital Management Limited supports numerous charities in Guernsey. He is also President of 'Access for Excellence', which promotes access to higher education. Additionally, Guy is a fellow of the Duke of Edinburgh's award scheme. In 2018, Guy was awarded Spear's 'Philanthropist of the Year'. He is also a member of the University of Oxford Chancellor's Court of Benefactors.

4 3 0054717 8

The
Dealmaker

Lessons from a Life in Private Equity

GUY HANDS

FOUNDER AND CHAIRMAN OF TERRA FIRMA

PENGUIN BOOKS

PENGUIN BOOKS

UK | USA | Canada | Ireland | Australia
India | New Zealand | South Africa

Penguin Books is part of the Penguin Random House group of companies
whose addresses can be found at global.penguinrandomhouse.com

First published by Random House Business 2021
Published in Penguin Books 2022

001

The permissions on pp. 329–333 constitute an extension of this copyright page

Text and plate section design by Peter Ward

Typeset by Jouve (UK), Milton Keynes
Printed and bound in Great Britain by Clays Ltd, Elcograf S.p.A.

The authorised representative in the EEA is Penguin Random House Ireland,
Morrison Chambers, 32 Nassau Street, Dublin D02 YH68

A CIP catalogue record for this book is available from the British Library

ISBN: 978–1–847–94057–5

www.greenpenguin.co.uk

Penguin Random House is committed to a sustainable future
for our business, our readers and our planet. This book is made
from Forest Stewardship Council® certified paper.

To Julia. You have been my rock, and I could not have survived without your unconditional love, unwavering support and limitless patience. Thank you, I love you and will do forever.

CONTENTS

PROLOGUE

I am strong, I am weak
I am everything between
I am proud to be me
I am human
I am weird, I'm a freak

Escape The Fate,
'I Am Human'

1977. It's the middle of a wet, miserable summer. The Sex Pistols, then signed to EMI, have tried to gatecrash the Queen's Silver Jubilee by performing their anarchic 'God Save the Queen' on a boat on the Thames. I'm a seventeen-year-old boy spending the afternoon with a group of girls at the municipal swimming pool in Tonbridge. Onlookers are no doubt wondering what charms I possess that make me such a centre of female attention. In fact, I'm there at the girls' request, in my capacity as an amateur photographer, to record them celebrating the end of their secondary school education.

I don't have much else going for me. I'm skinny, awkward and uncoordinated – a severely dyslexic outsider who feels constantly frustrated with the world. I can relate to the anger of punk, though I am very much a rebel without a cause. I am convinced I am a failure before my life has even really begun. Not surprisingly, most boys my age regard me as pathetic.

Like the girls I am photographing, I have also just finished my A-levels. Walking out of the school gates for the last time, I have vowed never to return to my school again unless I can majestically sweep through the gates in a Rolls-Royce.

1982. I am now twenty-two and my dream of opening a wine bar-cum-art gallery in the beautiful Cornish coastal town of Fowey has died under a mountain of debt, debt which claims the career of my friendly and supportive bank manager. I realise that I am going to have to secure a well-paid job very quickly if I am to avoid bankruptcy. A career in Wall Street suggests itself. I fear that this will involve selling my soul, but I also know that I stand to make eye-wateringly more money than my Fowey venture could have ever brought me. Successful in my application to Goldman Sachs, I embark on twelve years with the most successful investment bank of the twentieth century.

1995. I'm now working for the Japanese investment bank Nomura. We're negotiating an oil offtake deal in Russia, and have hit a problem. The company that is supposed to be supplying the oil cannot provide even the most basic information about their legal rights to it – they seem to believe that introducing me to their political connections in the Russian White House in Moscow should be sufficient. Big Peter, the wannabe oligarch I am dealing with, invites me and my two colleagues, Jenny and Richard, to a meeting in a military camp some 50 miles outside Moscow where, he says, he is going to 'lay his cards on the table'.

Leaving Richard behind in Moscow – sensibly – I arrive with Jenny and we are taken to a room where the concrete walls are splattered with bloodstains and bullet holes. We are kept waiting for over an hour and a half without explanation. When Jenny needs the loo, the male guards follow her to the cubicle, where she has to shout at them to let her use it in privacy. Finally we are frogmarched to another room to meet Big Peter, who is sitting at a large table, armed gunmen on either side of him, with his translator, Little Peter, standing beside him.

Little Peter quietly explains that Big Peter will have us shot unless I agree to do the deal. Knowing that there is no way that Nomura will simply say yes, I find myself having to explain that my employer will need a lot more than my say-so before they agree to release several hundred million dollars into Big Peter's Swiss bank account. A lot of screaming and shouting in Russian follows.

We're finally led outside, put in a black limousine and sent back to Moscow. Two days later I receive a mysterious call inviting me to breakfast at the Hotel Metropole. There I am welcomed by a soft-spoken man in an understated suit who reveals himself to be a KGB officer. He suggests I leave the country quickly as I am dealing with some 'very bad people'. I take his advice. Later that year I receive a Christmas card 'from your friends in Moscow'. It includes a photo of my children.

1999. I'm still at Nomura, where I am preparing to buy a portfolio of North Sea oil wells. When negotiations start, oil is averaging $16 per barrel. The price soon falls, however, and as it approaches $10, Nomura's Tokyo office loses its nerve. We do the maths and calculate that if oil drops to $6 we stand to lose $200 million. We pull out.

As it happens, oil doesn't end up at $6 that year, but bottoms out at $9. If we'd held our nerve, done the deal and then sold later at $100 – the price crude oil reached in February 2008 before peaking at over $140 – I would have made $9 billion for myself and Nomura would have made $36 billion.

2002–2007. I leave Nomura's protection and on 1 April 2002 start my own company, Terra Firma. I am completely independent, and completely alone. I own 100 per cent of the new enterprise, and everything I have is committed to it. If it works it will be the biggest and most successful deal of my life. If it goes wrong, the downside is frightening – I could lose everything and would need to start again. An Inland Revenue inspector has told me that for several years, when I was at Nomura, I had been the UK's largest individual taxpayer. If I quit now, my wife Julia and I would be able to enjoy a lifestyle way beyond our wildest dreams, and I could spend far more time with my children, or if Julia agreed, go into politics. I'm also aware of the view held by some of my oldest friends and my doctor that continuing to work as hard as I have been will kill me. But I feel I have another deal in me. In Terra Firma I want to create a private equity firm to rival – and surpass – the greatest of the US giants.

To achieve my dream I need to hire the best dealmakers in the world and turn them from guns for hire to people who are incentivised to work for me. Our shared aim is to become bigger and bigger, and for all of us to earn more and more. As 2007 dawns, this strategy seems to have worked. Terra Firma has eight successful businesses under its control, and one, Deutsche Annington – of which I personally own over 10 per cent – has become the largest housing company in Germany. I have grown a staff of just over twenty, who stayed with me when I left Nomura, to over 140. Owning the ninth largest private equity company in the world – and the best-performing of the large ones – I am gaining ground on the Americans.

2007–2021. The rollercoaster years. At the outset I am the sole owner of one of the top ten private equity firms in the world – the smallest of which today is worth tens of billions of dollars. In 2007 I successfully raise a €5.4 billion fund, the largest second-time independent European buyout fund. And I'm named 20th in the 100 most influential figures in private equity of the noughties.

Yet, by 2009, I am technically bankrupt. Over the next decade I experience further financial worries and several health scares.

These setbacks alter the course of my life and force me to rethink my priorities.

Looking back on my life today, I recognise that I have often been extraordinarily lucky and – just a few times – unlucky. I recognise, too, that being born a white male has provided me with a degree of privilege denied to many others. Sometimes I've been good at making the best of the opportunities I've had. Other times I've been pretty awful. And I've come to experience at first hand the eternal truth that in business no one is as good as they think they are.

What follows is the journey of a dealmaker – the steps that an unpopular, unhappy, angry boy who felt he didn't belong anywhere took that led him to remote North Sea oilfields, cut-throat boardrooms, shady meetings in hotel rooms, opulent parties in royal palaces, moments of triumph, hours of despair and finally to an island off the coast of France: a place of unexpected peace where he rediscovered a sense of purpose.

I hope that you'll find something in my story that will strike a chord with you. I also hope you can learn from my mistakes and be a more rounded individual than I have been. For those of you reading this who don't have a finance background, I hope the next time you hear about a private equity sale or purchase in the news, you have a better understanding of what really goes on in the world of deal making. But above all, I hope you have as much fun reading about my deals as I've had doing them.

And in case you were wondering: yes, I could have driven up to my old school in a Rolls-Royce if I'd wanted to. But while I owe my old school a lot and have even given money to it, I've never felt the urge to go back.

CHAPTER 1

The First Deal

Day after day, alone on a hill
The man with the foolish grin
Is keeping perfectly still
But nobody wants to know him
They can see that he's just a fool
And he never gives an answer

THE BEATLES,
'The Fool on the Hill'

When people ask me what the most important thing about any deal is, they're usually expecting me to say price. Obviously I want to buy at the lowest possible price, and I spend a lot of time and effort finding out what the sum should be. But actually that's not what ultimately interests me. For me, it's all about 'the Story'. The Story is what makes each deal unique. Understanding the Story is what gives me the edge. The Story consists of people, companies, pressures, technology, global factors, micro factors and a myriad of other things – some of which can be analysed, while others simply evoke a gut feeling. This book is the Story of my business life, the Story of the deals I've done and the Story of the lessons learnt.

If you were to ask me what my favourite musical is, I would say *Hamilton*. I hasten to add that's not because I'm claiming to have had the same life experience as the legendary founding father of the US. It's because I have always seen myself as an immigrant who has struggled to fit in. I've been brought up in Britain, I love Britain, but culturally, in many ways, I'm an alien and I feel like one.

My parents, Chris and Sally, were white South Africans who, like most white South Africans growing up during the Apartheid years, enjoyed a very privileged lifestyle. Both had grown up in Durban and had even gone to the same nursery school.

My father's father ran one of the major law firms in Durban and after attending one of the most expensive private boarding schools in South Africa, my father went on to study law at Natal University. My mother, meanwhile, went to the University of the

Witwatersrand, an institution founded on the principle that universities should know no distinctions of class, wealth, race or creed. Both then had a spell in England, my father at Oxford where he completed his master's in law, my mother in London where she studied at the Maria Grey teacher training college situated in Twickenham and Kilburn.

They got married in South Africa, but because both loathed the Apartheid system they took the decision, soon after I was born, to move to the British colony of Southern Rhodesia (as Zimbabwe was then known) – a beautiful country that had a considerably more liberal government than its neighbour. My father practised as a barrister; my mother ran a nursery school in the capital, Salisbury. Photos of me at the time show a happy, smiling, blond-haired, blue-eyed, energetic boy. I had my adored nurse, my beloved dog Kim, and I could play outside in the sun every day without a care in the world. On top of all that, from the age of two my mother let me join in with the nursery school children, who were aged from four years up. She says that being able to play with children who were substantially older than me kept me happy and distracted, while she could get on with the task of running the nursery school. Since I was always happier with older children, she tells me, there was an indication that I might find getting on with my own peer group more difficult.

Soon, however, the attractions of Rhodesia faded for my parents. In a continent where Black majority rule was starting to take hold, Zimbabwe joined South Africa in trying to stem the tide. In 1964, Ian Smith, soon to be elected prime minister, was to declare his intention to resist Britain's demand for majority rule and make a unilateral declaration of independence. 'I don't believe in Black majority rule ever in Rhodesia – not in a thousand years,' Smith said.

Both my parents objected to Apartheid. While a student, my

mother had heard Nelson Mandela give a speech and was so impressed that she went out of her way to meet him afterwards. She told her parents that she thought he would be a future prime minister of South Africa. Their response was typical of the time – 'Don't be so stupid Sally, and keep that sort of thought to yourself.' As a barrister, my father had a few run-ins with the judiciary over the laws that governed the Black population. My parents tell me that during my time in Rhodesia I became terrified of the police, having witnessed for myself as I was being driven through Salisbury the beatings they administered to members of the Black African community.

My parents decided they needed to leave Rhodesia. But they had no desire to go back to South Africa. That left England, where both had studied. A decision needed to be made swiftly: South Africa had left the Commonwealth in 1961 leaving only a short window for would-be émigrés like my parents, so they took the plunge. In 1962 the family moved from sunny southern Africa to a country that, a few months later, was in the grip of its coldest winter since 1740.

At first my parents rented a small cottage in Burnham Beeches, near to where my mother's aunt and uncle lived. It was pretty basic – my father had to feed coins into the meter to keep it even remotely warm, and it was far from dry. My mother, who was pregnant at the time with my brother, Philip, suffered from the damp. When she went into hospital to give birth, my father and I briefly moved in with my mother's Aunt Phyllis and Uncle Arthur in their pebble-dashed bungalow in Colnbrook, near the end of Heathrow's main runway. Old-fashioned British eccentrics, my great aunt and uncle left covered food outside under a tree to keep it cool and still cycled to the shops every day, even in their nineties, on bicycles they'd bought before the Second World War for a tour of France.

Meanwhile, my parents put all their savings together to buy a semi-detached house called The Retreat in the middle of the high street in Cookham in Berkshire, which we moved into when my mother came out of hospital. It couldn't compare with what my parents had been used to in South Africa, but at least they now had their own home and at least it was dry. To help make ends meet they took in an elderly lodger, and when she left, my mother did some teaching to bring in some cash.

It wasn't an easy transition for me. I had been upset by the brutality I had witnessed in Rhodesia (my mother tells me that when I was given toy soldiers for my third birthday, I buried them in the garden with their swords). But the fact is that I had been blissfully happy there: the country was warm and sunny and I had children to play with in the nursery school. To be honest, I felt we had been cowards to leave. And now here we were in this cold, wet place, where, because my father was having to pay to requalify as a solicitor, we were under incredible financial strain.

I blamed my parents for my unhappiness. It wasn't until I had children of my own that I appreciated how difficult it was for them to make such a momentous decision: to move from a country that they loved to one where they knew they would have to struggle. Back then all I knew for sure was that somehow I had to survive in what to me was a very alien environment.

Once I turned five, I started at the local village primary school, Holy Trinity in Cookham, where I found myself in a class of forty five- and six-year-olds. My prim and proper elderly teacher initially told my mother that I was the most remarkable child she had handled in her teaching career. I had very broad general knowledge, she said, and enjoyed debating all sorts of topics – political, religious and scientific – that don't normally engage five-year-olds. However, my precociousness did not go down so well with my classmates. In my first week I had my teeth knocked out and, away from the safety of the classroom and Mrs 'Prim and Proper', I was constantly bullied.

Cookham was one of those places where there was a huge mix of ability, wealth and social status. At home time, farmworkers in their tractors parked alongside rich professionals in their Rolls-Royces to collect their respective children. But it swiftly became apparent to me that my family was much poorer than any of my friends' families, not least because when better-off families in Cookham invited me over to play with their children they quite often gave me gifts. It felt like charity, and it probably was.

A further discovery that I made was that not all children stuck to the rules in the dogged and obstinate way that I did. I had joined the chess club, mastered the game and had even reached the final of the school tournament. But here I was confronted by a kid who cheated; he kept trying to place his king next to mine so that he could call a stalemate. Other kids said, 'Guy, just don't let him,' while I wiped out his pieces one by one. Then, of course, he made the illegal move. 'Your king's touching,' he said, and threw the board on the floor. I was bewildered and hurt to an extent that still registers with me today.

The problem, I now realise, was that I lacked the ability to be flexible, shrug my shoulders and move on. Once fixed on a course of action or behaviour, I found it difficult to alter it even if things clearly weren't going my way or weren't working. I remember around this time dressing up as a scarecrow for the local fancy dress competition and remaining in character for several hours. When people spoke to me, I didn't say anything – after all, I was a scarecrow. But while I might have been convincing in the role, it wasn't a performance guaranteed to make me any friends. Indeed, my mother was asked if I was 'all there'. I won the prize, but I think it was more out of sympathy for my poor mother than anything else.

It was my first form teacher at Holy Trinity who realised that something was wrong. I was very precocious when it came to talking about world affairs, animals, birds, astronomy, chemistry, stocks and shares, business and maths, the last of which I had learnt about from Uncle Arthur. But I couldn't read or write. My teacher called my mother – who was pregnant with my sister Alison – in for a meeting. Standing outside the classroom looking after my brother, in his pushchair, I could hear raised voices. Then my mother tearfully emerged.

Apparently, she told me on the walk home, the teacher had said she couldn't understand how I could talk about incredibly complex subjects and yet be illiterate, or how my maths could be excellent even though I rarely wrote things down. Perhaps, said the teacher, the problem lay with my mother's South African accent. If my mother didn't speak English properly, how could I be expected to?

My reaction, according to my mother, was to say that I was going to teach myself to read. Once home, I disappeared upstairs, clutching a collection of word-and-picture books, and spent the weekend poring over them. I refused all offers of help from my parents. Mrs 'Prim and Proper' was my problem, not theirs. I was five and already keen on fighting my own battles. By Monday morning, I could read three- and four-letter words: cat, dog, car and boat. It was sufficient to get Mrs 'Prim and Proper' off my mother's back.

My mother, however, who had studied psychology, realised that something fundamental was amiss. She asked around and got me referred to various people, who did countless tests on me. Nothing seemed to help.

And then, when I was eight, her former psychology lecturer at

Maria Grey, Ms Bailey, put my mother in touch with Margaret Branch.

Margaret Branch had lived a remarkable life. She had served as an ambulance driver during the Spanish Civil War and later helped smuggle Jews out of occupied Prague during the Second World War. At one point she had been captured and tortured by the Nazis, but escaped and made her way back to London. After the war she worked at Guy's Hospital as a psychotherapist and helped co-found, along with her life partner Camille Ruegg, the National Association for Gifted Children.

When I met her, she came across as strict but kind. And she got to the root of the problem straightaway. There was a gulf, she said, of 100 points between my visual perception and my verbal and mathematical reasoning. She decided to refer me to the Word Blind Centre in London, one of the first organisations in the UK to focus on what is now referred to as dyslexia. The centre in turn referred me to Dr MacDonald Critchley, a well-respected neurologist and a meticulous observer of human behaviour.

In his light and airy consulting room in London, the avuncular Dr Critchley set various tests for me: reading, writing, maths, brick stacking, memory exercises, sound repetition and a bewildering assortment of other physical and mental tasks. In some I scored so poorly that Critchley joked that my dog would have performed better. 'But don't worry,' he said, 'dogs don't rule the world.'

He tested my verbal and mathematical reasoning and also gave me an abstract reasoning test normally reserved for children over eleven. I answered each question confidently. At the end he told me the results were impressive. I might not have scored anything on the spelling test, and I had the reading age of an eight-year-old, but when it came to abstract reasoning and maths, I was up there with sixteen-year-olds. I was very bright, he concluded. And I was very dyslexic.

Dr Critchley's view was that trying to get me to read and write at anything like my intellectual potential would be impossible and hugely frustrating for me. Instead, I needed to develop a way of coping. He knew I would never perform well at school. What I should therefore do, he said, was to get through my education as happily as possible and then plough my own furrow. Whenever I saw him over the next fifteen years he didn't spend any time asking about my academic progress. All he worried about was my well-being. His positive attitude – and total faith in me – meant a lot. When, despite my terrible A-levels, I got into Oxford I wrote to him to share the news. He wrote back to say that he wasn't surprised because if anyone was going to get in with such bad exam results, it would be me.

I was lucky. The Word Blind Centre had opened in 1962. Just thirty years earlier, the standard method of getting the brain to work better was to administer electric shocks. Had I been diagnosed earlier, that would have been my fate.

Describing dyslexia to those who are not themselves dyslexic is very difficult. Most people are so used to the written word that they don't give a second thought to how they actually interpret it. But for a dyslexic child such as myself even the simplest word on the page might just as well be written in secret code. My brain simply couldn't make a link between what the squiggles were and what they represented. Word blindness is a pretty good description of what I experienced. Even today, my spelling level is only that of a seven-year-old and I can't read any better than a thirteen-year-old.

People often speak of dyslexics as having unique skills. While that's true for some who, like me, have been fortunate enough to be born with sufficient raw intelligence to devise ways of coping, the majority of dyslexics find life a struggle. It's no coincidence that 30 per cent of prison inmates and 70 per cent of those on death row in the United States are dyslexic. The criminal justice system (and the legal system in general) tends to be strongly biased against those who are not literate.

The issue with my brain, as Dr Critchley explained to me at the time (without the benefit of more recent research), was that one side wasn't connecting properly with the other. He said this was also the case with a number of other conditions – some of which I had (such as dyspraxia) and others I didn't (such as autism). While most children would have found being told that they had these conditions depressing, I still remember feeling exhilarated when I finally understood what the problem was. I would have to deal with my dyslexia and dyspraxia myself, but now I knew what they were I felt I could cope with them.

As a child these conditions often caused me to behave erratically. I had no sense of direction, for example, and so would run the wrong way on the football pitch when I had the ball. Once on holiday in Ireland I went for a walk with my brother Philip and got so hopelessly lost that a search party had to be sent out for me. Philip, even though he was only four years old, found his own way back to the farmhouse where we were staying hours before I was found. I struggle even today. Car GPS systems are a challenge because I often can't work out which way I'm facing. I have to rely on the audio function to tell me when I've gone wrong or, more often, on my wife, Julia. My solution is simple. I switch on the audio, turn the volume up and either discover I'm going in the right direction or get told to turn the car around.

Then there was my poor pronunciation. A lot of the kids at school couldn't understand what I was saying. I had to attend speech therapy sessions for years. Even today Julia suggests I only use words I can clearly enunciate – which I try to do. But sometimes I have to resort to words I find difficult, and I constantly have to learn new words and jargon that have recently entered the language. It's a source of great amusement and annoyance for my children.

Back in my schooldays, my struggles with language contributed to making me a target. It didn't help that I and the other children perceived me to be physically weak. I had grown upwards but not put on weight, was hopeless at football and the youngest in a class of forty. It really was no surprise that I was badly bullied.

My classmates could be cruel and vindictive. Quite often, I would be attacked in the playground or forced to be by myself. At home, I tried to cope with my unhappiness and frustration by using an inflatable dummy my mother had for drying clothes on as a punching bag. Although for a while I was fortunate enough to have two extremely good teachers at Holy Trinity who looked out for me, it didn't last. The two good teachers were followed by two bad ones, and the bullying carried on. Two of the older kids – a brother and sister – decided to attack me while I was taking Midge, our Labrador, for a walk on Cookham Moor. They chased me and cornered me under a bridge until Midge leapt to my defence, running at them, snarling and growling. They backed off and we fled. As with most of the other struggles I had at school I didn't mention anything to my parents, although possibly my parents knew more than they let on as my mother described me to Mrs Branch as very stoic and not willing to ask them for help. Eventually they saw the bruises and went to the headmaster, who told the kids off for treating me badly – which only encouraged them to treat me far worse.

Finally, one day, I snapped. I was in my fourth year at Holy Trinity and the bullying had, if anything, got worse. I was being regularly attacked and was covered in bruises. When a group of children turned on me just as we were coming back into the classroom from break, I lashed out. I knocked a desk down between us, but they kept coming. Eventually, with what strength I had, I picked it up and pushed it down on one of them. At exactly the same moment, a teacher charged through the door, saw what I'd done and told the headmaster I was totally out of control.

With the help of Margaret Branch, I gained a scholarship to Ravenscroft Preparatory School in Somerset, a 'special school' for children with severe learning or social difficulties or both. The student body was a very strange mix. It even included a few local children, ranging from a farmer's daughter to a boy whose father was a professional gambler.

I arrived as a boarder halfway through the spring school term. I was nine and a half. The headmaster, Mr Gillam, had been told that I had a great interest in politics and the stock exchange, beat my father at chess frequently and loved swimming, even though my strokes were uncoordinated. He had also been informed that I was untidy, couldn't do up shoelaces or tie a tie, had boundless uncontrollable energy and talked non-stop. Since the school did actually take me, I assume they must have seen my test results too.

Not surprisingly, my early experiences of Ravenscroft were not good. I felt isolated and a long way from family and friends. To make matters worse, since my mother didn't drive, I had to stay at school during the half-term holidays. It's perhaps no surprise that although I dutifully wrote regular letters to my parents and asked them to pass messages on to my brother and sister, whom I missed greatly, I felt disconnected from them. Indeed, throughout the remainder of my childhood, even when I was back with the family, I never quite felt 'at home'.

In the classroom I still found basic skills such as reading and writing a huge challenge. The teachers used phonetics and colour-coded cards – where each sound would be represented by a colour – to help me with my reading. But my spelling and writing obstinately refused to improve. On the other hand, I had a real understanding of numbers. I could iterate very complex equations in my head and think through complex mathematical questions and ideas, sometimes for hours, before going to sleep. When I got it right, I knew I had. The headmaster – whom we called 'Gilly' – encouraged this love of numbers. He proved a real friend. Whether or not he had spoken to Dr Critchley, I don't know, but his focus also seemed to be on watching over my mental health and not worrying about my academic success. He taught me to focus on what I could do well and find ways to cope with what I couldn't.

Despite Gilly's support, there were still obstacles to overcome. There was one teacher, for example, whom we called the 'Colonel' and who was responsible for teaching me Latin and French, who seemed to hold the view that kids will always learn if you beat them hard enough. Once a week, we would have a French test which involved writing out a hundred words. The penalty for each mistake was a slap with a belt. Needless to say I didn't get a single word right.

Eventually, the Colonel, despairing of me, sent me to Gilly, who told me not to waste any more time on French. He moved me into his class of thirteen-year-olds, let me drop subjects he knew weren't essential and encouraged me to take up any hobbies I liked to fill the leisure time my new, lighter timetable created. At a stroke, French and Latin disappeared and everything from acting to photography took their place. Photography became a particular obsession. I would wander around the school grounds taking pictures. Early results were hopeless. But eventually I improved.

The other kids in the year didn't take kindly to me or my unorthodox timetable. Back in the dormitory, on the evening of the day I was transferred from the ten-year-olds' class to the thirteen-year-olds' class, they took the centre springs out of my decrepit, metal bed frame, causing the mattress to collapse around me as I climbed in and trapping me so I couldn't move. Once they had me at their mercy, they pelted me with whatever was at hand. One boy threw a tin can, which split my head open and produced an awful lot of blood. Mr Gillam had to drive me to the nearest hospital.

Once my injury had been seen to, the headmaster drove me back to school in his ancient Citroën DS. It was clear he meant to give my tormentors a caning. But I begged him not to. I remember sitting in his car and panicking, then standing in his office and trying to persuade him to change his mind. I told him that if he caned them, they'd just bully me more and I'd end up having to leave.

Eventually we made a deal: he wouldn't cane them, but he would tell them that if I ever complained about them in the future he would flog them to within an inch of their lives, regardless of whether they had or hadn't actually done anything wrong. It was my first real deal – and it proved successful. From then on, the other boys in my dormitory and I got on wonderfully well and stood up for each other.

Of course, part of the reason why I was able to persuade Gilly was that I talked things through with him very carefully. Unfortunately, I didn't adopt the same approach with my French teacher, hence the reason he continued to torment me for the rest of my time at Ravenscroft. It was a useful life lesson.

It is inevitably the case in any school, and particularly in a special school that takes boarders, that undesirable things will happen and that these undesirable things tend to go unnoticed by the powers that be or get swept under the carpet. This was particularly so in the 1960s when behaviour that would cause a scandal today was – if not exactly accepted – at the very least inadequately policed. I can recall an occasion when a friend and I were staying in a dormitory away from the main school and decided to sneak out one night, and we came across some of the older boys dancing naked and playing games in the housemaster's study. My friend told his father and, after we'd been interviewed by the headmaster, the teacher was removed. I also had personal experience of unwanted attention from a teacher. Because it was believed that repetitive physical exercise that involved one's fingers helped connect the right and the left hemispheres of the brain, I had taken up the piano. Unfortunately, my piano teacher used my lessons as an opportunity to touch me. I didn't complain about him to the headmaster – it would be the teacher's word against mine – but I did take revenge occasionally by pouring salt in his coffee or letting the piano lid fall on his hands. I suspect that many boys of my generation who went to boarding school can speak of similar experiences.

I won two academic prizes at school. For my success at maths I was given a book about the South Sea Bubble – presumably either because Gilly wanted to point out to me that making money in the stock market was not a sure thing, or because he was amused at how much of a tongue-twister 'South Sea Bubble' would prove for me. He was right on both counts. I still struggle with the words South Sea Bubble and while I've continued to take an interest in the stock market, I am wary of the elements of gambling and hysteria that go with it. Today Benjamin Graham's book *The Intelligent Investor* is more my scene than speculative bubbles.

The other prize I won at Ravenscroft provided me with an unlikely inspiration and a talisman that has stayed with me ever since. When I was ten, I won an English prize. That may sound absurd, given my dyslexia and atrocious spelling, but one thing I could do, since it wasn't bound by the usual rules of grammar, was write poetry (provided it was short). And for my efforts in this field Gilly presented me with a book on Shaka Zulu. Quite why he did so remains a mystery. He knew that my parents came from South Africa and perhaps thought that I would identify with Shaka as a loner, if one with potential. And yet, it does seem a strange choice to give a ten-year-old boy a book that included detailed descriptions of the contraception methods used by Zulus in the early nineteenth century.

But the fact is that it was an inspired choice. I identified with Shaka. It wasn't just that he came from the same part of South Africa as my parents – he lived between the Drakensberg plateau and the Indian Ocean – it was that he, too, was bullied as a child. The book's author, E. A. Ritter, described how Shaka, the illegitimate son of the ruler of the then small chiefdom of the Zulus, was thrown out along with his mother by his father and then picked on and humiliated by the boys of his mother's tribe, the Langeni. Even when the two of them moved to his great aunt's home among the Mthethwa people, he was tormented and teased. Yet, through diplomacy and conquest, he went on to take the Zulu nation from just 1,500 people to a tribe that controlled 12,000 square miles of territory. For a child who had experienced what I had experienced, I found this both consoling and inspirational.

One story struck me in particular. After Shaka had become chief of the Zulus he trained his army to use a short, heavy, stabbing *assegai* instead of their typical, light, throwing one. And he toughened them up by making them take off their sandals and stamp large three-pronged 'devil thorns' into the ground with their bare feet. He then took this army on a night march right into the heart of Langeni territory where he surrounded the capital and demanded that the chief surrender. Having done this, he singled out all the boys who had inflicted misery on his family, reminded them of incident after incident and called each one forward for judgement. Before he passed sentence he asked if they could recount a single act of kindness that they had shown him, his mother or his sister. Only one was able to do so, and he was released and given an ox as a present. The others were divided into two groups – the cruellest on the left, the least vindictive on the right. Shaka had the former impaled on stakes driven into the ground, with fires lit underneath them as evening fell. The latter were dispatched more mercifully, with a single club blow to the head.

So yes, identification with a man who could be cruel and who was ultimately betrayed and murdered was, in some ways, strange. But for a ten-year-old boy who had few friends, was constantly bullied and lacked conventional skills, the thought of power and revenge was immensely consoling. I identified with the fact that Shaka managed to succeed in spite of everything. And he succeeded by refusing to compromise.

Not even Shaka's example, however, could shield me from everything that was thrown my way. One day, my mother received an urgent call from the school, asking her to come as quickly as she could to Bath Hospital. An older French boy, who resented that I was close to his younger sister, had pushed me under the water with such violence that I required emergency resuscitation. I remember coming to in hospital and experiencing piercing head pains, caused by damage to my sinuses and eardrums. I also recall being greeted back at the school by my dormitory friends as if I'd returned from the grave. But because the incident itself was such a blur in my mind, I accepted the explanation that Gilly gave me that my hospital stay was down to bad sinusitis, not a near-drowning. Even so, I became unhappy, withdrawn and terrified of water, convinced that if it got into my sinuses, I would suffer agonising pain or have to go back to hospital.

By now my family's fortunes had improved. My father had

secured a good job as a lawyer at British Steel and even had a company car. I was very proud of him and I was particularly proud of the fact that he worked for the company that sponsored Sir Chay Blyth, the first person to sail single-handedly the 'wrong way' around the world, which was seen as impossible at the time.

At the same time I was very aware that the steel industry in general, and British Steel in particular, was in decline. My father spoke positively about the company, but it was constantly making cost cuts and redundancies. These upset my father and they worried me, even as a young boy.

The fact is that the experience of even a few relatively tough years as a child creates a deep paranoia about it happening again and provides strong motivation to avoid it. I've had a deep fear of losing everything for as long as I can remember, which perhaps helps to explain why self-made millionaires like me so often tend to remain focused on creating wealth long after the average person feels rich beyond their wildest dreams. I describe it as the fear of the 'Under Toad', a phrase I've borrowed from John Irving's novel *The World According to Garp*. The book provided me with a visual metaphor for the deep fear of having no control and losing everything, a metaphor I've lived with for as long as I can remember. Those occasions when I've let that image slip from my mind have been when I've found myself drowning and in real trouble.

CHAPTER 2

Finding My Calling

I'm a-gonna raise a fuss
I'm a-gonna raise a holler
About workin' all summer
Just-a trying to earn a dollar

Every time I call my baby
Try to get a date
My boss says 'No dice, son
You gotta work late'

Sometimes I wonder
What I'm-a gonna do
But there ain't no cure
For the summertime blues

EDDIE COCHRAN,
'Summertime Blues'

So shocked were my parents by the near-drowning incident that they started looking for another school. In theory this should not have been too great a challenge. I had passed my eleven-plus exam and there were some good grammar schools in Kent, where my parents had recently moved. In practice, my dyslexia counted against me.

Eventually, the Kent educational psychiatrist arranged for me to have an interview with Mr Rendall, the headmaster at Judd, the grammar school nearest the new family home. He agreed to give me a go but, because he was worried I might struggle, said I would have to stay at Ravenscroft an extra year. I can remember feeling a mixture of relief and anxiety – relief that Judd was prepared to take me, anxiety about going to a new school where I knew no one and where I might well be bullied. In the meantime I had to sit out an additional year at Ravenscroft with nothing to aim for and no exams to do. Lonely and worried, I became emotionally withdrawn.

My first week at Judd in September 1971 was a disaster. The teachers couldn't make out anything I'd written and sent me home at the end of the week with a book of spellings and letters to copy out. And although I wasn't bullied, I was a year older than the rest of the boys in my class, taller (and skinnier) than them and had reached puberty during the summer holidays. This meant that I was the only kid who had to shave, and I felt self-conscious and awkward. I took refuge at the back of the class with the intellectual misfits, the disruptive kids and the bullies. It suited me. I quickly learnt that it was the kids at the front of the class – along with those who wore glasses – that got bullied. If you sat at the back and dumbed down your conversation, you were fine.

At the end of the year, our academic rankings were posted on the school noticeboard. Out of 100 children, I came second to bottom. My best friends were all in the bottom ten. I don't think they were intrinsically any less bright than many of their more successful peers, but because they somehow didn't fit the education system – and because they could be disruptive – they were ignored and then spat out by it. None of them got through to the sixth form.

The second year started out even worse than the first. Only the headmaster and one other teacher had sympathy for my dyslexia. The others thought I was lazy. One used to throw a board rubber at me every time I answered something incorrectly. He very rarely missed. My English teacher took a mark off for every grammar or spelling mistake I made. It didn't help that I won a special award in a Kent poetry competition for the most promising young writer. If anything, my success made things tougher for me, especially when it was covered in the local press and my school wasn't mentioned.

With my third year looming, nothing going right and the prospect of having to take up German, yet another subject that I knew would be a struggle, Mr Rendall decided to refer me to the Kent educational psychiatrist. I spent nearly an hour with him. He could see straightaway that I wasn't in a good place either emotionally or academically. I was also starting to argue with the teachers and becoming increasingly disruptive. 'What do you want to achieve?' he asked. I said I wanted to miss the third year. He laughed. 'You're not going to miss the third year unless you can give the school some reason to jump you a year,' he said.

By the end of the session we had struck a deal that the psychiatrist then managed to sell to Mr Rendall. If I did very, very well indeed and achieved an average of above 70 per cent in all subjects, excluding Latin and French, I could skip the third year and drop languages altogether in the fourth so that I could focus on English, especially my pronunciation and my spelling.

With that promise as an incentive, I worked really hard at those academic subjects that I knew I could do well in. My teachers didn't notice any difference in my behaviour in class: I still sat at the back and avoided them as much as I could. So, when the results of the exams finally came through I shouldn't perhaps have been too surprised that my form teacher hurled my papers at me in front of the whole class and shouted that I was the laziest boy he had ever come across. After he stormed out, however, and I had read the red scrawl on my physics paper complaining about my inability to hand in homework, I noticed that there were two circled numbers at the bottom: 1 per cent and 92 per cent. I had come top in the year with 92 per cent. Actually, I would have got 100 per cent had I not reversed my drawing of a pulley system and put the correct weights on the opposite hooks. Overall, I came fifth in the year with an average of 72 per cent, having done well enough in my good subjects to compensate for the ones I had struggled in.

From the fourth year onwards, things got better. English may have remained a struggle, though I continued to write and read poetry (I loved Rudyard Kipling's 'If') and enjoyed jotting down my thoughts on philosophy and the appropriateness of different political systems (on re-reading these notes recently, I was intrigued to find that I was sympathetic to the aims of the South African Communist Party). But being allowed to drop languages transformed my life. Although the additional speech therapy, spelling and reading lessons that took their place didn't help much, I was able to indulge my love of photography and also, for the first time in my life, take on paid employment.

The job was with Lansdowne's, a local newsagent opposite the railway station in Sevenoaks and close to two Victorian pubs – the Farmers and the Railway and Bike – that became the centre of my social life. Lansdowne's was run by a short, slightly tubby man who wore button-up cardigans that didn't quite cover his stomach and that tended to burst open. His family were Jewish immigrants who had fled from Nazi Germany in the 1930s. Mr Lansdowne himself worked incredibly long hours and saw his staff as a second family. Aged fourteen I joined him as a junior shop assistant, filling the shelves, carrying stock up from the basement, stacking newspapers and marking addresses on those earmarked for home delivery.

When I was on paper mark-up duty, I had to be at the shop at 5 am to ensure the papers would be ready for the delivery boys just after 6 am. That left me just enough time to get home, wash the ink off my hands and arms, get changed and go to school. Gradually, as I proved I could work hard, I was allowed on the till, then given stock-taking jobs, then till reconciliation and eventually put in charge of a shift. The pinnacle of my career at the shop was being placed in charge of the work rota and the task of checking that the till money balanced at the end of the week. I loved the job, despite the low pay (twelve and a half pence an hour), though this did go up as I became more senior. And I particularly loved interacting with customers. I was fascinated by what they bought, even if it was nothing more than a few sweets or a magazine.

I also learnt some useful lessons. The first was the unsurprising one that you have to run a business for profit. Mr Lansdowne was good at arranging his displays and providing for his customers. But he was arguably too sentimental. He hated to let any customer down, so ended up stocking lots of things that sold only in tiny numbers. I realised that there always needs to be an appropriate balance between giving the customer what they want and making a profit, and that management – and indeed owners – are not always the best people to determine what that balance should be. The brutal fact is that businesses that get it wrong in either direction fail.

I also learnt the importance of displaying goods in a way that encouraged sales. Here Mr Lansdowne was a master. He knew that people do not necessarily purchase what they mean to buy when they go in, so he would display appealing goods in a prominent position. And when he was talking to a customer, he'd always prompt them about something else they might want to buy. It was extraordinary how many people who'd just come in to buy a newspaper would say yes to the question, 'Would you like any cigarettes today?' and leave with a newspaper, twenty Marlboros, a chocolate bar and a packet of condoms ('Something for the weekend, Sir?').

Mr Lansdowne's employees were an eclectic bunch of kids, ranging from ages thirteen to nineteen. Quite a few came from difficult backgrounds. The time they spent at the shop gave them the stability they needed, and it wasn't unusual for an ex-employee (sometimes a bowler-hatted City worker) to stop by and thank Mr Lansdowne for having helped them trust themselves. But inevitably there were those who took advantage. I vividly remember the day Mr Lansdowne, who had just returned from a holiday, called me into his office to say that he was going to fire almost everyone. 'I had an audit done before I went away,' he said, 'and I've had an audit done now. People have been stealing from me. It's very sad, because . . .' He couldn't finish.

I later found out that they had been taking whole boxes containing cartons of cigarettes and selling them at school. I think to some extent Mr Lansdowne blamed himself for this. He had treated everyone who worked for him almost too much like family and he had been too trusting. Those he had been closest to, it turned out, had taken the most. If his experience showed that one of the tough aspects of business is that trust can be betrayed, it also demonstrated the need to put in systems and controls to try to ensure as far as possible that trust is not put to the test.

After the staff thefts were detected, the shop changed. It became more businesslike and profitable. Electronic stock-checking was introduced. But Mr Lansdowne's relationship with me and my co-worker Andrew remained unaltered. He even let me indulge in a little entrepreneurship on my own account. The tight margins involved in my repackaging of bulk purchases of camera film meant that particular venture didn't make much (teaching me an important lesson about the necessity of doing deals where you clearly add value). But my move into 'pobbles' – little animals made of semi-precious stones that I put together myself – proved both profitable and popular with local schoolgirls (my sister Alison acted as my wholesaler).

Gradually I found that although my unhappiness (which since Ravenscroft had replaced my anger) didn't disappear, it was dampened. Mr Lansdowne valued me, Andrew was a good friend and I had things to do that I enjoyed doing.

All that compensated, to some extent, for the fact that school remained a series of uninvolving classes held in dark, dusty rooms dominated by huge blackboards on which teachers scribbled notes at breakneck speed while talking at us as quickly and loudly as they could. For someone with a mind like mine none of this was ever going to work. I couldn't copy things down quickly enough, and if I tried to copy things down I found I couldn't listen at the same time. It took me years to realise that my memory is the best tool in my mental workbox. At the time, I endured the lessons and poured my energies into my job, putting in forty hours a week. I regularly fell asleep in class. My teachers put it down to laziness. I put it down to my work commitments.

The one thing that improved in my fourth year at school was that I went from being the oldest kid who sat at the back of the class to one of the youngest who sat at the front. I acquired new friends among the brightest boys in my year. My tribe became four or five strong. We got on well and we supported one another against the inevitable bullies.

When one particular bully picked on my friend Peter, I decided for once to step in. As other boys encircled us, egging us on, I closed in on him and within a short time managed to hold him down, my anger compensating for my relative weakness. Then I tried to negotiate. 'Look, why don't we forget about this?' The bully agreed and we stood up. As soon as I turned the other way, he hit me on the back of the head with both fists so hard that I briefly lost consciousness and crumpled to the ground. I'm not sure what lesson I learnt, but I didn't regret my decision to get involved for a minute.

It was thanks to my tribe that I acquired a love for and certain skill at poker. We'd play during lunch break and, away from school, at various pubs, notably the Beehive in the nearby village of Chipstead, where we would take on men who worked in the local cold storage business. I could calculate the odds very quickly because of my ability at maths. But to get to the point where I could be a major contender I knew I had to be able to 'read' the other players, to know when to bluff and when not to bluff. Fortunately I found the cold storage people reasonably easy to read, so Thursday evenings turned out to be profitable.

With money coming in from my winnings and my earnings at Lansdowne's I was able to indulge my other obsession, photography. I have a very poor visual memory and an equally poor visual imagination – it's known as aphantasia. I memorise events, places and people, not as most people do, but via triggers, such as my acute sense of smell or lists of details. I can't, for example, form a mental picture of my wife Julia, but I know that she has blonde hair. Photography helps me because it enables me to keep a physical record of my life. In fact, over the years I've taken thousands and thousands of pictures – probably more than 200,000.

By the time I was sixteen, photography was not only offering me a helping hand with my aphantasia but was also the inspiration for a business opportunity. So, with an advertisement in Lansdowne's shop window, I launched a part-time career shooting weddings, portraits and, the bane of my life, people's yippy little dogs and unruly cats. I wasn't technically good at first but I had a reasonable eye and was quite creative and my skills improved over time. Various friends got me to take their photographs, as did some of their mothers.

Perhaps my most challenging – certainly my most embarrassing – assignment involved the forty-year-old mother of a friend who wanted me to take portraits that she could then give to her husband of her lying naked on a fur coat (apparently, she'd had similar pictures done for him when she was twenty-one). I had never seen a naked woman before, I couldn't get the lighting right and I was worried the end result wouldn't do her justice. It didn't help my mental state that there was a real sensuality to her. Eventually I decided to go for the 1930s starlet effect, with a soft-focus photograph of her naked in a modest pose. Since I didn't have the requisite lens and could only achieve the effect I wanted by smearing some Vaseline on the edge of a filter, I asked her if she had some. She roared with laughter. 'What d'you want to do with Vaseline?' I blushed a deep shade of red and explained. She went off to get me a pot. The first shoot was, not surprisingly, a disaster so I had to go back again. She paid me for both sets of photos. I am not sure she gave them to her husband.

Equally difficult but physically dangerous, rather than embarrassing, were the swimming costume model portfolios I shot for the girls I knew. The girls loved them. They saw them as a passport to fame and fortune. Their mothers were of the view 'if you've got it, flaunt it'. Their fathers, however, wanted me dead – or at least as far away from their daughters as possible.

My biggest financial photographic coup was an accident. I had been asked to shoot an entire school to provide school photos for the proud parents, but, thanks to the photo-processing lab, I ended up with badly underdeveloped rolls of film. As it was not possible to arrange a reshoot, I decided to offer the pictures at a knock-down price of £1 per child – as opposed to the usual price of £5. Usually I got a take-up rate of between 10 and 20 per cent. This time it was almost 100 per cent. Another lesson learnt: reducing prices (in this case by 80 per cent) doesn't always lead to greater profits, but it's surprising how often it can do so.

Many parents would have tried to clamp down on my teenage activities, but my parents didn't try to steer me down a particular path; they rightly believed in giving me moral pointers and hoped I would find my own way. Provided I didn't steal, didn't do drugs, didn't chew gum and got myself through school, they were content. I honoured the deal and worked as hard as I could at what I knew I was good at – business. I hoped that would give them some confidence that there was something in life I could actually do.

Even though the odds seemed stacked against me, I did well enough in my GCEs to get into the sixth form. Initially, I was going to do two maths subjects, chemistry and physics, which the school was confident I would do well at, but before the end of my first term in the sixth form I asked if I could drop one maths subject for economics. This posed a timetabling problem since economics clashed with chemistry. However, the conundrum was resolved when an unauthorised experiment in the chemistry labs led to an explosion, the summoning of the fire brigade and an offer from the headmaster of either a caning and a continuation of my chemistry studies, or no caning and the abandonment of chemistry in favour of economics. I reluctantly gave up chemistry and focused on economics.

My mother's belief in me and the fact that my father had gone to Oxford made me determined to apply there, and since my A-level studies were going well the school supported me. I therefore sat the entrance exam in my fourth term of sixth form, was invited to Oxford for an interview – and rejected. 'He would be an interesting student, but he needs to grow up,' was the verdict. The school, not surprisingly, wanted me to look elsewhere – the London School of Economics, perhaps, or Queen's University Belfast – but I was stubborn. It was Oxford or nothing. The LSE might be an intellectual powerhouse, but it hadn't produced twenty-three prime ministers. The headmaster took a deep breath and agreed that I could try again after my A-levels.

I worked all hours and things seemed to be going well. But one day as I was coming home on the train, I fell out of the door at Sevenoaks station and collapsed on the platform. The results of the initial medical tests were so alarming that it was thought I might have pancreatic cancer. After a spell in hospital, a rather less fatal diagnosis was reached. I had an extreme case of reactive hyperglycaemia, now known to often be a precursor of type 2 diabetes. My GP's prescription was that I should eat six meals a day and take sugar tablets whenever I felt hungry – not perhaps the best diet to recommend a pre-diabetic. But I obeyed and regularly got up in the middle of the night to chomp my way through sausages, bacon and eggs. I was consuming something like

5,000–6,000 calories each day – not to mention all the glucose tablets – as though I were a long-distance runner.

The impact of the health scare on my A-levels was little short of disastrous. Wildly fluctuating sugar levels and several physical collapses meant that I missed various papers, and while I fetched an A in economics, I achieved only an E in physics – and an X in maths. Unsurprisingly, no university was interested in me.

This setback, though, did not deter my Oxford ambitions. Even though Mr Rendall was very supportive (he wrote to Oxford on my behalf) I decided that I had reached the end of the road with Judd and vowed never to return unless I happened to be driving a Rolls-Royce at the time. Instead, I signed up to a cram college in Tunbridge Wells called Linden Park, which was a huge, old rambling house full of – to me – fascinatingly exotic Iranian students.

My first week proved a real baptism of fire and an education in the best sense of the word. I'd been given an assignment that involved undertaking a moral analysis of Nazism. I duly read out my essay, only to have it snatched from me, torn up, thrown on the floor and stamped on, while my teacher yelled that it was bourgeois and boring. He was harsh, but he was right. Given my terrible academic record, what chance did I have of getting Oxford's attention if I was boring, if I was trying to say exactly the same thing as every other student. I had to make a virtue of my difference.

As the weeks went by, I painfully learnt two important lessons. First, there was no point in trying to produce great volumes of material – I didn't have any more knowledge than the others and I wrote more slowly. Second, I had to start actually thinking. 'You've got a good brain,' I was told, 'but you've put it in this box called education, and it's currently completely wasted.'

With the help of an unlikely pair of teachers – one a

voluptuous, middle-aged communist woman; the other a stick-thin young man with fascist beliefs – I started to make progress. When writing an essay I learnt the importance of spending half my time thinking and the other half writing. And I also learnt that one good paragraph is far better than any number of OK paragraphs, and that one good argument is far better than three totally correct pages of recycled facts. By the time the exams rolled around again I had made sufficient progress to secure an interview at Keble College to read philosophy, politics and economics (PPE).

It didn't go well. I was asked about Paul Samuelson's economic theory and I floundered: it was very definitely not part of the Linden Park syllabus. Assuming that I had failed miserably, I rang Mr Rendall from a call box in despair. He was both sympathetic and practical. Sometimes, he said, colleges would take students who had put them down as their second choice. Keble had been my first choice because my father had done his postgraduate law degree there and applicants had been advised to apply to colleges where they had a personal connection. I had no connection with my second choice, Mansfield College, but it had to be worth a try. I duly rang the principal's secretary there and asked for an interview.

She was polite but firm. If they wanted to interview me, they would call me. Extreme measures were clearly called for. I'd spent the autumn following the Oxford entrance exams selling encyclopaedias door-to-door so I knew all about doorstepping. I therefore haunted Mansfield for the next few days, parking myself outside the principal's secretary's office, the porter's lodge, the junior common room or the library – anywhere that was warm and dry. My war of attrition lasted for two whole December days. Eventually the principal's secretary took pity on me. 'There's a space coming up,' she said. 'I'll get you an hour but will you promise me if it doesn't go well, you'll go home?' I promised I would.

My written papers were still sitting somewhere in Keble. However, or perhaps because of that, I shone. I wasn't constrained by my record with the written word. Instead I could go inside my head to construct complex mental models to answer questions about supply and demand, and the relative competitiveness of economic trading partners. I could engage in freewheeling discussions about freedom of expression in a general interview with the chaplain, the principal of the college and the geography don. I drew comfort from the fact that the academics ended up challenging each other as well as me. Mansfield would be somewhere, I felt, where I could finally be happy.

But, of course, I knew my grades stood in my way. And I didn't have a second language, which was then a precondition for a place. It was very kind of Mansfield even to agree to give me an interview. I tried one final gambit at the end of my economics interview, when the inevitable question came up as to why somebody with terrible grades who didn't read books would want to go to university.

'Because I'd like to study to find an alternative solution to left-wing and right-wing politics and if you accept me, I promise I will,' I answered.

I returned to Sevenoaks, where my parents had converted the garage into a bedroom with its own door so that I could slip home without waking everyone else up at three in the morning after the pub and poker games. On Friday 23 December, on what was almost the last post before Christmas, an envelope with an Oxford postmark arrived. My mother charged into my bedroom and pressed it into my hands. I threw it gently across the room and turned over to go back to sleep.

'Aren't you going to open it?'

'I know what it says. I'm going back to sleep.'

'How can you possibly know? What does it say?'

'It must be an acceptance because why on earth would they be writing to me if they weren't going to accept me? They'd just tell the school and Rendall would phone me.'

Under pressure I opened it and handed the contents to my mother. Seconds later she was on the phone to everyone – family, friends, Mr Rendall – screaming each time, 'He's got it! He's got in!' I rolled over and went back to sleep.

It's a strange thing with me. While failure hits me hard and hangs around, I register success very briefly, if at all. Indeed, with success comes a feeling that I'm getting into deeper and deeper water, and that the 'Under Toad' will be more difficult to spot and harder to escape. The sensation of pride when I have done something well is so temporary it virtually doesn't exist.

Having secured my place at Oxford for the following autumn I went back to earning money. I worked at Lansdowne's during the day and at nights I worked at a data transfer company located on a cold storage estate. My brief foray into selling encyclopaedias door-to-door had confirmed the taste I had developed at the newsagent's for dealing directly with customers but I enjoyed little real success even when trying to sell windows door-to-door, which I thought I would be a natural at. Eventually I spotted and answered an advert in London's *Time Out* magazine, placed by a gallery in Kingston-upon-Thames, for someone to distribute 'young artists' work'. The gallery itself was a small two-up, two-down shop with a wooden and white interior, so close to the river that there was just a path separating the back of the shop from the Thames. They used the upstairs rooms for storage and their framing shop, with the downstairs used as a gallery.

The three artists I met had no sales pitch. One of the three, Anthony, had a few years earlier been on holiday in Canada and taken a job in Toronto selling painted velvet pictures door-to-door to finance his trip. Today, these pictures from the 1960s and 1970s have a marvellous retro feel to them, but back then I felt they were truly ghastly.

I agreed to take two sample portfolios of their work, excluding any velvets, home with me and started to put together my own pitch. In my mind I had an image of sitting on someone's living room floor, plucking out images from a giant portfolio to a rapturous reception. Unfortunately, I hadn't thought through how I would get into these living rooms. And when my friend Peter Nixon, whom I had roped in, and I descended upon an unsuspecting Brighton one evening, the failure to have a practical plan of attack was painfully exposed. Trolling around the streets between 7 pm and 10 pm looking like a cartoon burglar with an oversized black bag, I was lucky not to get arrested. Peter was not so fortunate. He was reported to the police three times, and on the last occasion was told by a kindly officer that perhaps carrying black bags up to people's houses and knocking on doors wasn't the best idea. Peter quit our partnership and I went back to the drawing board.

I went back to the artists to get them to frame some samples for me (watercolours of street scenes seemed the most promising) while I set to work on developing my script. The first part of the new strategy worked well: having a framed picture, rather than my foot, to prop open a door massively improved my chances, and I found I was getting into two or three living rooms each evening. But even my revised script let me down. I was so enthusiastic about each picture in the portfolio that my pitch took ages. And sometimes it proved too successful for its own good. People would want to buy all the pictures and, not being able to afford them, would end up purchasing none.

The answer came to me back in the Kingston gallery when, observing a customer asking to have a picture framed, I noticed that the artists responded by taking out two frames and asking her which one she liked best. She chose, they measured, they framed, she paid. Clearly, I was giving people too much choice. That was why I wasn't closing. From now on I limited the selection. And when potential customers asked me the inevitable question whether the pictures I was selling were a good investment, I kept my answer short and honest. I had no idea if they would be worth more in the future, I said. People should buy them simply because they liked them.

This art-selling venture was a turning point for me. My confidence blossomed. The product, the sales patter and the reception from customers – it all came together. Now I started to advertise for salespeople and put together a team of four. All of a sudden, we were selling ten paintings a night. Soon, I had two teams of four. Each night, when everyone had completed their door-to-door sales trek, we'd gather in the pub and exchange stories about our successes and failures. I'm not quite sure what other drinkers made of the regular sight of seven or eight dishevelled girls, often wet from the rain, handing over piles of cash to the young man in their midst.

Our operation spread from Sevenoaks to Tunbridge Wells, Orpington and further afield in Kent. Within six months, I had four teams on the road selling paintings door-to-door right across the south-east. Whatever the individual quality of the paintings, we'd come up with a brilliant delivery system and a great sales pitch. We knew how to market art.

Harnessing the power of the spoken word, designing a sales pitch, learning to read people's reactions, discovering what makes a sale and what destroys one, and, above all, recognising just how much in sales comes down to emotional connection and how little is to do with intellect, was a revelation. No one likes to admit they bought something because they liked the salesperson's banter. But I have a pair of powder blue crocodile shoes sold to me in Harrods by a very flattering sales assistant, who challenged me to go a 'bit wild' and express myself, that prove how persuasive a great salesperson can be. Academic 'cleverness' has nothing to do with it. I employed ordinarily smart people who proved outstanding and supposedly brilliant Oxford undergraduates who didn't make a single sale. Many years later, at EMI, I found an entire company staffed by clever people who didn't know how to make a sale. I had to let the majority go.

While all this was going on I met my future wife – at a New Year's Day party in 1977, to be precise. 'That's the woman for me,' I thought. But I was too shy to act and Julia didn't notice me. At the time I was seeing a lovely girl called Elizabeth, who was going to go to Oxford to read classics. Her father didn't approve of me (he thought my dyslexia meant that I would never get a job) and he bundled her off to Germany for a while to be an au pair, a job she hated. A year later, at another New Year's Day party hosted by the same mutual friend, I encountered Julia again. She was dancing to ABBA. Afterwards, I asked her for a kiss. For some reason – to this day she doesn't know why – she agreed and she also agreed to go on a date. I was eighteen, she was seventeen. Rather bizarrely, on the day we set off for the Mermaid Theatre in Blackfriars to see *The Point* with Davy Jones and Micky Dolenz of the Monkees, Elizabeth came to the station with me (we were still meeting clandestinely, but she was quite relaxed about my going out with someone else given her father's opposition to me). And that date with Julia became the first of many. Elizabeth faded into the background. Julia became my girlfriend. Like me, she was planning to head off for university, but to Cambridge, not Oxford.

There's a photograph of us together at her eighteenth birthday party that I keep on my phone. Julia is looking at me as though asking, 'What has he done wrong, how do I care for him and how do I keep him in line?' I, however, look like the cat who has got the cream. She showed a very strong, and at times very strict and firm, loving tenderness towards me right from the start of our relationship. I began to realise that I could be happy.

My success at business had shown me that I could express myself, be creative and use my emotional and negotiating skills. My relationship with Julia gave me stability. I knew I was with someone I loved and respected and who shared my dreams. I could completely rely on her. She was not just the love of my life, not just the friend of my life, but she was the talisman of my life as well. She kept me grounded. Now, as I left my childhood behind, I had found a calling and a soulmate.

CHAPTER 3

Oxford University Politics

Mammas, don't let your babies grow up to be cowboys
Don't let 'em pick guitars and drive them old trucks
Make 'em be doctors and lawyers and such
Mammas, don't let your babies grow up to be cowboys
'Cause they'll never stay home and they're always alone
Even with someone they love

WAYLON JENNINGS & WILLIE NELSON,
'Mammas Don't Let Your Babies Grow Up to Be Cowboys'

When I drove up to Oxford alone in my 1968 Mini Cooper I was leaving behind the comfort, warmth and support of Julia, her family and my family to enter an utterly alien environment and meet a largely alien people in the knowledge that I probably had the lowest academic results of anyone entering that learned establishment. I drove doubting I would be able to cope at Oxford and wondering why I had ever wanted to go. Perhaps I should return home and focus on my picture-selling business. Only Julia's promise that she would come and stay with me in a couple of weeks stopped me from turning the car round.

Mansfield College is a mid-Victorian Gothic edifice built from Cotswold stone. Unlike all the other Oxford colleges, which are entirely closed off from the road outside and accessible only via the porter's lodge, Mansfield has a large gap in its external wall along Mansfield Road – meaning that people have always been able to come and go as they please at all hours of the day and night.

This touch of the informal is of a piece with Mansfield's heritage. It was the first nonconformist college to be founded in Oxford, opening in 1886, just a few years after the prohibition on non-Anglicans taking degrees was lifted. You could say it has rebellion at its heart, which suited me down to the ground. Oxford as a whole seemed very traditional to me. Mansfield definitely wasn't. And for someone who at that time was obsessed with the Stranglers and the anti-establishment vibe of punk music, it seemed the perfect fit.

I was allocated a small, stark bedroom with a study attached in the new, 1960s accommodation block. It was pretty basic stuff, but then Mansfield was as poor as a church mouse, as indeed were most of its alumni who, up until the late 1960s, had virtually all become nonconformist clergy. There was a small, two-bar electric fire in the study that provided some heat but as the cold Oxford winter descended it proved hopelessly insufficient and barely kept the room much above the temperature outside.

We were housed in alphabetical order, so my staircase was full of people beginning with H. My neighbour, Rupert Hill, was the son of a prep school headmaster and had spent his childhood in boarding schools. He was slightly surprised to learn that I had been to a grammar school, while I, for my part, found myself having to adjust to the mindset and habits of someone who came from a completely different background. Like many of the private school types at Oxford, he would drink huge amounts of beer, go rowing at odd hours, play rugby and field hockey at any opportunity and delight in dorm-room-style practical jokes. He once shimmied up the wall outside my room and jumped in through the window on top of Julia and me when we were in bed together. We were not amused. Otherwise, Rupert treated me very well. I discovered very rapidly I couldn't match his and his friends' beer intake either in volume or speed, so I switched to vodka. I could drink a lot very quickly – although I was more than likely to pass out about half an hour later.

At Rupert's school the hygiene facilities had been communal, so he had no problem adjusting to the set-up on our staircase with its two bathrooms shared between eight people. In fact he thought the ratio luxurious. Not being used to one person having a bath while another sat on the loo, I found it alarming. I quickly worked out that I needed to be either an early riser or a very late riser, if I wanted to be able to use the bathroom in peace. I became a very late riser.

In the first year students were expected to eat at least

breakfast, possibly lunch and certainly dinner in the main hall. It rather resembled the dining hall at Hogwarts, with pictures of the past principals of Mansfield decorating the walls. Breakfast was served cafeteria-style, through a hatch where the food was laid out. The prospect of limp, tepid sausages and semi-congealed eggs just wasn't inviting and I skipped most of the breakfasts that term. Dinners in hall, however, were good in a somewhat 1970s culinary way, particularly the weekly 'formal hall' meal where people were expected to wear gowns, the lights were turned down and candles were put on the tables. It was thanks to formal hall that I first encountered pheasant stew and duck à l'orange and became obsessed with roast potatoes. The fact that you could bring your own wine and invite a guest added to the sense of conviviality.

As I soon discovered, formal hall at Mansfield was very different from formal hall at other colleges. At Mansfield, although you had to don an academic black gown, no one cared whether you wore a tie or turned up in jeans. At other colleges, though, I was amazed to discover that some people wore their public school uniforms, complete with tailored three-piece suits and Eton, Harrow or Winchester ties. This sense of exclusiveness extended to clubs and societies where some students wore smoking jackets and carpet slippers straight out of Evelyn Waugh's *Brideshead Revisited* or smoked cigarettes in extended holders, trying at the tender age of eighteen to look like the movers and shakers of industry and politics that they hoped to become. The more self-assured, who belonged to such clubs as the Bullingdon, indulged in champagne-swilling and restaurant-trashing and other forms of outrageous behaviour.

What so many of the privately educated students had in common was incredible confidence, poise, charm and wit. The most arrogant and articulate pupils at my grammar school didn't even come close. Fortunately for me, the students at Mansfield were, for the most part, cut from a rather different cloth. There, public school kids rubbed shoulders with grammar and state school kids and various students from abroad.

All the same, my first term was as melancholy as I had feared it would be. I couldn't find anything that floated my boat, regardless of the number of clubs I joined. I didn't have the confidence for acting, my public speaking was below par and I was overwhelmed by a great feeling of disconnection from my peers and tutors. To make matters worse, I had given up the day-to-day management of my door-to-door business to Julia and my mother. That they continued to be as successful as I had been but with far less drama wasn't really a consolation. I was missing them and it. I was confident about my ability to run and set up small businesses, and business had given me a sense of purpose, but navigating Oxford's political, social and academic worlds was a challenge I was struggling to meet. I couldn't see what relevance it had to my future life.

I succumbed to the heavy drinking culture. The initiation ceremony at most colleges involved huge amounts of alcohol. I refused to down the six pints of beer that were laid up on the bar for me. Instead, someone poured out 24 shots of vodka, which I necked in less than a minute and passed out almost immediately. At least I was never challenged to another drinking game: I'd earnt my spurs. But as the term went on, I drank more and more, and – not surprisingly – depression set in. My shelf was full of empty vodka and port bottles – vodka from when I woke up through to late evening, and port from then through to the early morning.

The only bright points in the eight-week term were Julia's visits. She came to see me a couple of times and helped me with my essays. My tutors had quickly discovered that my writing was unintelligible and, even if they could penetrate that, my spelling might as well have been in code. They therefore allowed me to read my essays out loud. Julia, who was a far better academic than me, read the books on my reading list and prepped me on the subject I was meant to be writing about. With her help, I managed to bluff my way through tutorials. But it was tough, and I returned to my parents' house for Christmas stick-thin, looking terrible and smelling of booze and wondering whether to quit.

Julia had found out that she had got into Cambridge a few days after I returned to Sevenoaks. While she had been forbearing up until then, she made it totally clear that she was going to Cambridge regardless of what I chose to do. With no Julia around, the idea of moving back to Sevenoaks and returning to running my business was not so attractive. I also worried about how well I would be able to compete with the bright young men who would surround Julia at Cambridge. I vowed to sober up, eat properly, find a way to survive Oxford, meet its academic demands and graduate.

The second term saw me adopt my new policy of sobriety, just as some of my fellow students were beginning to admit to themselves that they wrote better essays when they weren't high on pot. But I realised I needed something to boost my confidence, so I relaunched my career as an entrepreneur. I paid a student artist called Judith Slough to produce line drawings of birds, animals and street scenes, had them silk-screened by an Oxford printer, colour-washed by a girl I knew back in Kent and finally framed by my sister Alison. My plan was to go from being a commission salesman to having my own business. If it worked, I calculated, my profits would be far higher.

The new business initiative gave me the lift I needed, but my academic achievements remained patchy. I found I was good at economics even if I didn't buy into the standard view that 'economic man' is rational and predictable. Today I still hold that macroeconomics is of little use unless you also understand behavioural science, and that in business you can't communicate with people if you don't understand something of their background. In politics, I struggled with the history but was intrigued by the psychological element. In a tutorial on Russian politics, I can recall my fellow students devoting their energies to the structure of the Politburo as we debated whether Russia would ever become a democracy, while I argued that since the Russian people had been conditioned to suffer for hundreds of years they would always choose an autocratic leader. It was a kind of national Stockholm syndrome, I suggested, and since a Western-style democracy was not what they expected it wasn't one they wanted. My tutor became tearful and, when I finished, he sat there silent for a moment. Finally he said, 'It's so sad, but you're right.' He then dismissed us. I found out later that he had escaped the Gulag in the 1930s.

My record in philosophy was mixed. I fell out with my philosophy tutor completely over the concept of pleasure (not least because I suggested that in the future people would derive sexual pleasure from plugging themselves into a machine, like the Orgasmatron in Woody Allen's 1973 film *Sleeper*, and that this would have as much value to society as all the opera ever written). But while he tried to get me kicked off the course – and I did indeed drop this part of my degree – I actually did rather well in the end of year exams. My tutor had been a visiting fellow from another university. The fact that Oxford's philosophy dons were prepared to view my exam essays favourably suggested that they had a tolerant view of eccentric ideas. Had I dropped economics rather than philosophy I suspect my final degree would have been better.

*

Meanwhile the art-selling business I had established at home was continuing to prosper under Julia, with my mother doing the books, my sister Alison framing the pictures, while Philip and my father tried to keep the sales teams' second-hand cars going at minimal expense. I, for my part, was good at training the salespeople. Julia was happy to work alongside me but not for me, and once she went up to Cambridge I took total control of the business again. I knew in my heart of hearts that business was where my passion and skills lay.

But if Oxford confirmed my desire to go into business, it also awoke a political consciousness. For the first time in my life, I found myself surrounded by people who had inherited privilege, who assumed they had a right to do so, whose life goal was to use that privilege to secure jobs in politics, the law and so on, and ensure that their children would go on to enjoy a similar life of privilege.

Later in my university career, I was invited to one of the more secret clubs – a debating society named after some Conservative MP from the 1800s. You were only allowed to attend if you promised not to reveal the club's existence to anyone. I suspect you're not even supposed to allude to it in a book. At the one meeting I attended, held in a dimly lit set of rooms in Oriel College (the last all-male Oxford college to admit women), an ex-Winchester boy, who couldn't have been more than twenty, gave a forty-minute talk on an obscure aspect of eighteenth-century political history in a voice that sounded like that of a sixty-year-old lecturer. When he finished, glasses of port and plates of cheese and biscuits were handed out and we were all required to comment on what we'd just heard and ask a question. The others spoke volubly about the British Empire and the rise of the Whigs and Tories. They seemed to know an enormous amount about the past, perhaps because they were still living in it. I, by contrast, was tongue-tied, felt humiliated – and was never asked back.

But I knew instinctively that my peers had no connection with or understanding of the contemporary world or what the past could teach us. And I was convinced that, while they might well end up running the country, they had nothing to offer when it came to dealing with the various problems and challenges it faced.

The 1970s is romanticised today for its kooky fashion, its sexual liberation and its wonderfully creative music and arts scene. For me as a teenager, though, it was an era when everything was going wrong. There was civil strife in Northern Ireland. There were endless strikes. The lights went out with alarming regularity. And in the long, hot summer of 1976 there was even the prospect of water rationing. Add to that an 83 per cent top rate of income tax and an emergency bail out by the International Monetary Fund and it was hard to take an optimistic view of Britain's future. Even switching on the TV made me miserable. Programmes such as *The Benny Hill Show* depressingly revealed the racism and sexism of the time, while *Till Death Us Do Part*, which sought to parody them, merely served to show how deep-rooted they were.

Given my dislike of the privilege I saw around me at Oxford, it may seem surprising that I ended up a Conservative. But conservatism at the time was being reinvented. I can recall being impressed by a speech I attended by staunch left-winger Tony Benn. But I know that I was even more impressed to hear one given the very next day by Margaret Thatcher's political mentor Keith Joseph. I despised the old right wing of the party with its casual racism, sexism and sense of entitlement. Ultimately I would turn against much of the social agenda that Thatcher came to stand for but, at the time, and certainly as represented by Keith Joseph, she seemed to be a breath of fresh air. She wasn't smug and complacent. She had a sense of energy. And she valued the things that I, too, valued: individual merit, effort and enterprise.

With Mrs Thatcher as my inspiration, I threw myself into the Conservative Association from the start of my second term, ignoring those right-wing elements of it that I cordially detested. I galvanised myself to campaign for the Conservatives in the 1979 election, an election that came in the wake of the three-day week and that, for me, represented Britain's last chance to escape the downward spiral of increased taxes, inflation and devaluation. If Thatcher didn't win, I told myself, I would leave the country as soon as I had my degree.

I spent most of 3 May driving my beaten-up 1966 beige Mini Cooper through the streets of Oxford to carry elderly men and women to the polling booths. It was colder and rainier than usual for the time of year, so it was imperative to get the vote out. I was worried but excited. The city had been held by Labour for more than a decade. I had been leafleting for the two weeks leading up to polling day and felt that if Oxford turned blue, the country probably would too.

Oxford was then, and still is, a city of three parts that seemed to mirror the make-up of the nation. East Oxford had the Cowley car plant full of unionised manual workers and a large community of immigrants who were mainly employed in small businesses – the Indian restaurants and open-all-hours shops lining the Cowley Road. This part of Oxford was strongly left wing. Central Oxford, where the university resided, leant towards the soft left. The wealthier areas of Oxford town, plus the surrounding countryside, were solidly right wing, but weren't necessarily pro-Thatcher.

Having spent twelve hours a day selling encyclopaedias and pictures, my pre-Oxford days had trained me well to knock on doors – only now I was selling the Conservative Party. I had a sense of how the campaign was going in Oxford and I thought it was going to be very close. Two things cropped up on the doorstep over and over again. First, in the wealthier parts of Oxford, many of the people I spoke to said that while they normally voted Conservative, they didn't know whether they could vote for a woman to lead the country. Second, students and those from the poorer parts of Oxford made it clear that they didn't just dislike Thatcher, they were violently against her. Part of this hatred was caused by her 'Thatcher the Milk Snatcher' image – a legacy of her time as education secretary when free milk for junior schools was abolished.

Oddly, many on both the left and the right hated her for the same reason: Thatcher was not from the establishment and she was now independently wealthy. It wasn't difficult to understand why the left should dislike her for this. But the reason for the right-wing loathing was more complex. Part of it, I suspect, was down to misogyny and snobbery because she was a woman and came from a lower-middle-class background. But I suspect much of it had to do with the fact that she scared them. She was radical and she was independent. There was no chance of her being controlled by those members of the Conservative Party who wanted to protect the status quo.

Our local candidate was John Patten, a fellow of Hertford College and first-time candidate, who was later to be voted 'Dishy Don of the Year' by *Cosmopolitan* magazine. He was from the left wing of the Conservative Party and was known more for his looks, his intellectual prowess and his Catholicism than his ability to doorstep electors. When I took him round East Oxford I wasn't sure which surprised him most: the kids smoking cannabis right out in the open, the burly manual workers from Cowley or the two-up, two-down terraced houses crowded with people. While I could hardly claim close kinship with these various groups, I was a bit more in touch with them than John if only because I loved the food they ate: exotic Jamaican food served to the sound of reggae, wonderful Indian dishes from Bangladeshi-run restaurants and substantial fry-ups from the British Leyland workers' Cowley café. What the car workers thought when I took Rupert Soames, Winston Churchill's grandson, to the Cowley café early one morning while he was still dressed in white tie from a ball the previous evening probably doesn't bear thinking about.

Thatcher, of course, won. In the summer term of my first year, inspired by her victory and emboldened by the confidence my business had given me, I decided to throw myself into the university's political organisations. For the Conservative Party, Oxford student politics centred physically around the Oxford Union, a large collection of Victorian buildings bang in the centre of Oxford, and a 'playground of power', according to journalist David Walter's 1984 history of the institution. The Union was like a junior House of Commons, complete with debating table. It was a nursery for future leaders who wanted to practise their oratory, listen to eminent guest debaters and master the political art of doing deals in the shadows: 'If your people vote for me, mine will vote for you,' followed several weeks later by the backstabbing: 'Oh I am sorry, they just got confused and didn't vote.'

If the Oxford Union was the House of Commons, the Oxford University Conservative Association (OUCA) tried to operate like the parliamentary Conservative Party. I wanted to debate political ideas. Most of the others had no interest in philosophy. Their key concern was: 'Who's succeeding in the Conservative Party and how do we get ourselves one rung up?'

At the time, the Monday Club was the organisation for those

on the far right of the Conservative Party. When I arrived at Oxford, they had given up fielding candidates in the OUCA elections and the right-leaning, though reasonably moderate, faction at the centre of things was now the 'Magdalen Machine'. To the left of them were the Tory Reform Group of 'wets', who identified with Edward Heath and regarded the European Union positively. Bitterly divided over Europe and immigration, the three factions fought each other endlessly. I think it would be fair to say they hated each other more than they hated the Labour Party.

The various sides had largely held to a truce to allow candidates to concentrate on helping John Patten win the seat. But when it came to that term's OUCA presidential elections, the gloves were off. I myself rejected the compromise candidate, Viscount Clive Mackintosh, in favour of Charlie Williams, an Etonian who believed that we needed to jettison the Tory Reform Group and Edward Heath's ideas if we were going to move forward and change Britain. He mocked the truce cabal as 'piss poor' and in his manifesto even had a photo of him and his team apparently pissing on a tree to underline his point. He was a maverick, highly intelligent, very quick-witted and an outspoken spirit of nature. In his inevitable donkey jacket he looked more like a socialist trade union member than a public schoolboy. He challenged everyone and everything. Inevitably he lost.

In that election, I was elected to the committee for the Oxford University Conservative Association in the second-to-last position. At the same time, the Oxford Union election saw me elected to the most junior position on the most junior committee of the Oxford Union in the term that Philip May, Theresa's husband-to-be, was president.

I had managed to perform the manoeuvre of working hard to get John elected, while not compromising my own views. So, when the Conservative Central Office got in touch to say that William Hague, who as a sixteen-year-old had stormed the party conference a couple of years earlier with his 'roll back the frontiers of the state' speech, was coming to Oxford that autumn, I was tasked with looking after him and making sure that he didn't fall in with the 'wrong', non-Thatcherite branch of Conservatives. Within an hour of Hague's arrival at Magdalen College, I tracked him down to his room where he and his girlfriend were unpacking and quickly started work on persuading him to join the Magdalen Machine.

We got on well from the off. He'd come straight from a Yorkshire comprehensive and knew almost nothing about life outside the North of England. He told me that he had thought the South of England was flat and was shocked to discover Kent had hills. He'd also never eaten an Indian meal before, something I remedied as soon as I could by taking him to my favourite curry house on the Cowley Road. He loved it, and thereafter we'd pitch up several nights a week. He'd always order a chicken tandoori – or, as he called it, 'chicken done in an Indian way' – with chips. I did try to get him to try other Indian dishes, but he wasn't having it.

Once I got to know William reasonably well, I linked him up with two other state school Thatcherites at Oxford, Gary Jackson and Richard Old. The four of us would meet, well away from prying eyes, at the British Leyland workers' café in Cowley, to discuss how we could set about dominating Conservative politics at the university. With my sales background, my role became that of a political operator.

Richard was the charismatic leader who could persuade people to follow him and delivered amazingly powerful speeches, although when you thought about the words you realised he hadn't said very much. Gary was the brains and our conscience, he kept us down to earth and on the straight and narrow.

For his part, William was the one we all thought would become prime minister. He was solid, decent, thoughtful, good company and amusing. His lack of pretence made him a breath of fresh air in the viper pit of university politics and his accent helped him cut across the class divide. He was also incredibly clever; he seemed to have a photographic memory and could finish a book in the time it took me to read the first twenty pages. It was no surprise to me that he achieved a remarkable holy trinity – president of OUCA, president of the Oxford Union and a first in PPE. We became good friends and went on to share a house later in our university careers.

Along with Richard and Gary, I assumed the task of keeping him safe from scandal, calling on the services of a Conservative Central Office press officer to tip me off when photographers were descending on the more rowdy dinners and events so that I could ensure that William didn't attend. At times he objected to us acting like his older brothers. The fact remains, though, that – unlike many other politicians – William has no inappropriate photos to worry about from his student days.

At the time, as now, the links between the Conservative Party and Oxford were strong. Theresa May, who graduated from Oxford in 1977, often returned to visit friends and drink at the Oxford Union. Three years older than me, she was intelligent, self-assured, sophisticated and glamorous. She also seemed to know everyone who mattered, while simultaneously taking note of even a minor player like me. Her future husband Philip became president of the Oxford Union, but while ambitious he never struck me as particularly political.

From time to time, rich Tories would sponsor weekends away for aspiring student politicians. One I remember vividly was held in a beautiful country house just outside Oxford. There were about thirty of us there, including the son and daughter of the then chancellor of the exchequer, Nigel Lawson, who was regarded by both his supporters and himself as totally brilliant. His son Dominic, who had been at Eton and Westminster, and who sensed my social and intellectual unease, was unfailingly kind. His sister Nigella, not then the woman-of-the-people TV cook she is today, proved somewhat cutting when I made a particularly poorly expressed point. I soon realised I couldn't hold my own in such company, and spent the rest of the weekend longing for it to be over. I remember wondering why, instead of talking about major social issues and the future of Britain, the assembled company seemed interested only in discussing politics past and how to win future elections. Not for the first time, I was made to feel acutely aware of the huge gulf that existed between those who had been privately educated and those who'd been to a grammar or state school. William, by contrast, was unfazed. Like others in the room, his focus was on winning, but unlike me, he did not have a chip on his shoulder, and felt totally self-assured. So far as the others were concerned, the fact that he chose Churchill as his role model – even down to his style of speaking – certainly helped.

Despite my social and intellectual unease I did manage to make it to the top of university Conservative politics at the beginning of my final year when I became president of OUCA. I embarked on a robust programme of speaking events by such Conservative luminaries as Nigel Lawson and Geoffrey Howe, all listed on a black-and-white brochure simply known as 'the card'. Non-Conservative partisans were invited, too: for example, Erin Pizzey, then chairperson of Chiswick Women's Aid. Visits to the House of Commons, jazz bands and numerous dinners were organised. I even encouraged the Oxford University Conservatives to get up at 5:30 am to be bussed to Cowley to canvass workers at the Cowley factory. OUCA's term card, funded by adverts for local restaurants, featured a soldier holding a machine gun and the Polish slogan 'Na Zachod!' ('To the West') but with a question mark at the end rather than an exclamation mark. Ten years later, of course, Poland would move into the ambit of Western-style democracies. On the back I had put the following quotation: 'Democracy is rule by the uneducated, while aristocracy is rule by the badly educated' (my truncated version of the G. K. Chesterton remark: 'Democracy means government by the uneducated, while aristocracy means government by the badly educated').

I found I was good at the machinery of politics, good at negotiating its factional element (I ended up serving on both left- and right-leaning committees) and good at securing support from individuals and small groups. However, I was terrible at public speaking. I always found the prospect of having to address the debating chamber of the Oxford Union terrifying, not just because I knew my speech would be awful but because the dress code demanded that I wear a bow tie, and I couldn't tie one. I just prayed that no one detected that I always wore a clip-on.

One encounter gave me some hope. Ahead of one debate I found myself in the urinals of the OU standing next to former prime minister Harold Macmillan. I noticed he was desperately nervous, so much so indeed that he confided to me that he was fearful that with his hand shaking so much he would end up splashing my shoes. Macmillan was known to be a brilliant public speaker, so I asked him why he wasn't more confident. He couldn't explain why but noted that many of the best speakers he had come across – Churchill and Lloyd George included – had similarly found public speaking intimidating.

If public speaking left me nerve-racked, the nastier side of university politics left me saddened and depressed. During one particularly nasty OUCA election, my car was covered in concrete. I tried to scrape it off but had to reconcile myself to the fact that most of it would fall off when it dried. At about the same time a magazine titled *Private Guy* was distributed throughout the university, accusing my friends and me of all sorts of sexual shenanigans – most of which I'd never heard of – and a host of other antisocial activities.

I wasn't the only person to be singled out for attack (a previous Oxford Union president and future member of the Cabinet, Damian Green, had been thrown into the river from Magdalen Bridge in a row between the left- and right-wing factions). But I wasn't prepared to stand for it. I never did discover who the concrete-car culprit was but I did some detective work on *Private Guy*, and this led me to the Cherwell typing centre, where most pamphlets and publications were produced. The same typing ribbon had been used to produce *Private Guy* and 'Sincerity Not Cynicism' – the slogan of the Tory Reform Group. I established who had booked the typewriter and threatened to issue a libel writ. The guilty party crumbled. The next term an enormous apology was posted on every student noticeboard in the university and the culprit exited Oxford politics.

Having won the election for president of OUCA, I tried for treasurer of the Oxford Union but lost by a single vote. Traditionally, seeking the treasurer role meant that, unless you had been defeated by a large margin, you would stand for president the following term. But when I discovered that William was planning to enter the fray, I stepped aside. He was a better candidate and my best friend. Instead, I settled for the unpaid office of Oxford Union bursar.

The impact of this decision was twofold. By introducing an annual subscription for lifetime membership of the Union (previously membership had been automatic) I put the Union on a far more secure financial footing (today such standing orders generate £1 million a year). And by taking a year out, I was able to ramp up my art business.

On the back of the profit I had so far made, I managed to buy a house on Nelson Street in Oxford's Jericho area – then a distinctly run-down part of the city. And from there I trained hundreds of undergraduates to become door-to-door salespeople and earn from £20-£30 an evening in the process. By early 1980, this business was going so well that I decided to open my own art gallery. I bought a vacant launderette on Little Clarendon Street on the corner of Walton Street, which was then an up-and-coming, distinctly Bohemian area. I cleared out the washing machines, painted the walls, named the gallery 'Artsake' and opened for business.

At first I tried selling art produced by artists from South America and the Middle East. But I swiftly discovered that while passers-by might have liked what was in the window, they didn't have the confidence or the money to purchase it. The venture might have worked in London or New York, but in Oxford in 1980 it stood no chance. I therefore rapidly switched my focus. I had noticed that the picture-framing part of the business was doing well and that what most people brought in to have framed was posters, particularly those produced by Athena, a highly successful company that ran the gamut from arty to slightly naughty (perhaps their most widely purchased – certainly their most famous – creation was the picture of the girl on the tennis court in a very short tennis skirt with the curve of her bottom exposed).

So now Artsake became an art poster and framing shop. Much of my stock, which I mounted on racks, came wholesale from The Poster Shop in London. Other posters were sourced from museums and galleries all over the world: Israel, the Netherlands, the US, France, South America and Australia. Some came from art galleries that were closing down. The margins were fantastic and, to bring in extra income, I let out the flat above the shop and converted the launderette's boiler-house into a little shop run by a lovely young woman whose nude self-portraits we also sold.

It was all going very well, and I was settling down to two lives: my Oxford life, mixing with would-be politicians; and my small-business life, mixing with artists, bohemians, restaurateurs and craftspeople. I loved the contrast and could see my business growing before me.

But then Artsake was hit by a bad case of subsidence. I had made the naive assumption that because the building dated from 1820 and was still in one piece 150 or so years later, I didn't need to commission a structural survey before I bought it. That was unwise. It needed substantial repairs and extensive underpinning. What had been a nicely profitable business now became a millstone. I found myself owing £40,000 – six times the average wage at the time – and, in addition, paying 20 per cent per annum in interest on the debt. I faced bankruptcy.

I had two options. One was to open a second business to increase my earning power (I briefly considered partnering with a woman who had worked for me and who had a master's in design to start a lingerie business). The other was to do something that had most definitely never been part of my grand plan: get a 'real' job. But what choice did I have? I had to pay off my debts. My life as a political operator and entrepreneur was no longer sustainable.

When I talked to the university careers adviser about my situation, he pointed me towards the employer that paid the most: Goldman Sachs. With his next breath he asked me what I thought my degree grade would be. On hearing me optimistically say a third rather than a fail, he told me I had absolutely no chance. Goldman Sachs only took graduates with first-class degrees: 'Well, I've got no choice but to get them to take me,' I retorted.

I walked out of his office and started my journey to the dark side.

CHAPTER 4

Really, Really Greedy

Something's happening and it's happening right now
You're too blind to see it
Something's happening and it's happening right now
Ain't got time to wait
I said something better change

THE STRANGLERS,
'Something Better Change'

While clearing my debts was essential, the idea of joining the world of finance worried me. When I was sixteen, I had gone on a depressing school careers trip to visit some merchant banks. One of the senior people at Hill Samuel had described his day – he was picked up by his chauffeur (who was paid by the bank) in a car (that was paid for by the bank) from his farm out in Kent (also subsidised by the bank). I had been left wondering what he thought it was all for. Where was the British hunger to succeed through what one did rather than through who one was? Where was the drive to compete internationally? I promised myself that I would never join the British banking system.

Five years later I was a scruffy, art-loving graduate and determined would-be entrepreneur. Unfortunately, I was an entrepreneur who owed the Midland Bank £40,000. If I carried on along my current path I would paying off that loan for the rest of my life.

At least, I thought, Goldman Sachs was a bit different. I had read about it in *The Economist* when I was doing my A-levels and had immediately been struck by its unorthodox culture. It was clearly a trader's investment bank with a hungry, entrepreneurial culture that didn't exist elsewhere in the City. The problem was that my CV was not going to get me an interview. I therefore got my mother to type a letter for me on Artsake-headed notepaper that boldly stated five basic facts and carefully omitted two others: I was a student at Oxford; I didn't speak any languages; I had my own art gallery; I had a clean driving licence; I had sold encyclopaedias, double-glazed windows and paintings door-to-door.

The two facts I omitted were my academic record and my dyslexia. The letter concluded with a request for an interview for a sales role in their equities division.

It was the impertinence of youth writ large. But something must have caught the bank's attention. To my surprise I was offered a lunchtime slot with one Jamie Kiernan during his day of recruiting interviews at Oxford. Equally to my surprise, Jamie was from the fixed income division, not equities.

The interviews were held at the Randolph Hotel in very plush meeting rooms. But whereas my fellow students were subjected to the usual intensive bombardment of questions by two interviewers arranged behind a desk, I found that I was apparently meeting Jamie – a big, friendly Irish American – for lunch. I suspect he was bored and didn't want to eat alone.

From an etiquette point of view, the lunch wasn't a success. I made the mistake of ordering soup, which arrived in a tureen along with the most enormous soup spoon and which I proceeded to dribble everywhere. But amid our discussion of picture selling something about me must have clicked with Jamie, because he put me forward for a series of interviews in London with the fixed income and equity divisions, which dealt with bond underwriting, bond trading and bond sales. He patiently explained that bonds are basically a debt security sold, or issued, by governments and corporations when they need capital. Goldman underwrote the issuing, sold the bonds and had a team that traded bonds on the secondary market. He also told me that the salespeople and the traders were two very different tribes and that the relationship between them could be stormy. Bond underwriting, he said, was for experienced people. Trading involved a level of risk and trust that ruled me out. But a role in fixed income sales, which meant dealing with institutions and getting paid a salary with a potentially large annual bonus, was a possibility.

The Goldman people I met in London were all very bright and very different from one another. Those in the equity division were cultured, sophisticated and well-dressed. Those in fixed income were, for the most part, a strange collection of highly intelligent misfits, who shared little in common except for an unbelievable determination to succeed.

There was Eddie, for example – an Anglo-Greek socialist waiting for the revolution whose father ran a hotel in Pimlico. And then there was John Keogh, who ran Goldman Sachs' London bond trading desk, and whose keen native intelligence and gut instinct made him a contrarian with an opinion on everything. Interviews were conducted by John, Eddie and Eric Sheinberg, the head of corporate bond trading in New York, who had flown in specially. 'If we hire you,' Eric said, 'there are three rules: don't steal, never lie to me and don't stick your pen in company ink.' And he offered some advice, too: buy some decent clothes (he even offered to lend me the money). I did as I was told.

Summoned for another round of interviews to New York, I found that I was being put up in a glitzy five-star hotel. Fortunately, the bank was paying. I then made my way to the Goldman Sachs offices. It proved a bizarre world of contrasts. On the one hand there was the bustle of the huge trading floor with its salespeople, traders and banks of screens that showed flickering green numbers that constantly changed. On the other, clustered around the trading floor, were the management offices, where everything was serene. Each Goldman Sachs tribe could be identified by the amount of noise they made. Management was quiet. The salespeople were loud. And the traders in the centre were the noisiest people I had ever encountered. Their lungs, you felt, could give out at any moment and their faces would go so red that I was sure someone was going to have a heart attack. Every now and then one of the salespeople would gingerly approach the traders and be screamed at. They'd then run back to their desks where their team would either commiserate with them or high five them.

Quite early on I discovered they already had a nickname for me – 'the truck driver'. Owing to an administrative error I had been issued with an HGV licence when I'd finally passed my driving test and had shown it at reception as a form of identification. Clearly, word had got around. I was then subjected to a battery of interviews. The head of fixed income (the management tribe), having tried desperately to find something we could connect on, finally discovered that we both liked eating and proceeded to regale me with stories of his favourite New York restaurants. At a subsequent interview he took me through the bonus scheme that could increase my earnings to the princely sum of £42,000 in my first year. 'What does your father earn?' he asked. At the time my father was earning about half as much. 'How do you feel about the fact that your father has worked all his life, he is better qualified than you and in your first year you could make more than he earns? Do you think you deserve it?'

'That's not really a question for me,' I said. 'It is a question for you. You've offered to pay that amount. And you need to decide who is the person deserving of the job.' I had no idea whether that was the right answer but it certainly set the tone for my Goldman Sachs career there and then: answering back and speaking my mind.

My last interview that day was with a trader called Chuck Davidson, whose nickname, I later discovered, was Chuckles. He was a big man, an extraordinarily successful trader and very entertaining. When I walked into his office, he was reclining on a swivel chair behind a telex machine. He asked me just one question: 'Truck driver, could you drive me to the airport in a really big truck?' When I nervously answered yes, he opened the door and screamed to the trading floor, 'He really is a truck driver!' Then he turned back to me and said it was my turn to pose questions.

'What makes a good trader?' I asked.

'Greed,' he instantly shot back. 'You've got to be really, really greedy.'

I thought this was worth a follow-up: 'So what makes a great trader?'

He rolled his chair backwards and pointed to his groin. 'These. You need great big brass balls.' He burst into thunderous laughter.

I got the job and joined the London office of Goldman Sachs with three other trainees the day after finishing at Oxford. Two weeks later I was sent on Goldman's training course in New York. I quickly learnt that as long as you worked hard, displayed some common sense and showed a greater aptitude for the job than the next person it was as close to a licence to print money as one could imagine. But that licence came with responsibilities. John Whitehead and John Weinberg, the firm's co-heads, explained to us that while we had been selected for our talent, our role was to serve the client. Our clients, they said, should always make more money than us. If we did a good job for them, we would get paid very well, but if we ever stopped working for our clients the firm would no longer want to work with us.

In 1982 Goldman's London office exuded the atmosphere of a scrappy start-up: it was very small, unassuming and, telex machines apart, pretty low-tech. It traded in government bonds, equities and money markets. And its trading goals were twofold. One was the obvious one: to make money. The other was to avoid paying tax on the money it made – not perhaps surprising in an era when the top rate of tax was 83 per cent. Payments in kind would frequently turn up, giving the office the feel of a market stall. One day it would be a huge delivery of toilet paper, the next it might be boxes of lingerie. Such consignments would be sold on to friends running stalls in places like the Old Kent Road. I wasn't earning enough to worry about my tax rate, and I learnt not to ask.

I was placed at the centre of the cut and thrust of buying and selling international bonds. It was the days before PCs and broadband, so my colleague Patricia had to co-ordinate the information from thousands of telexes every night, setting up orders to be executed during the day. I would get in at about 6:30 am to make my way through the bond sheets left on my desk from the night before, using a Hewlett-Packard hand-held calculator to work out the impact of any changes in the US government treasury market that had taken place since then and moving the bond prices up or down depending on the yield needed to attract a buyer and a seller. The HP calculator was the latest thing in technology – faster and more accurate than the huge desk calculators with wheels of paper that were still used in some banks. When Eddie and John came in, we could start quoting prices based on my numbers and begin that day's process of buying and selling bonds on the phone.

For me, words on a page often looked like a polar bear in a snowstorm. But numbers were easy. I grasped the essentials very quickly and found that my instincts on bond valuation were usually right. I also mastered the financial and legal complexity of debt obligations. Soon I developed an interest in highly illiquid bonds, particularly in the most esoteric, high-yielding versions with unpopular credits or those with warrants attached. If I found bonds which I felt the market undervalued, I would accumulate as large a position as possible in the hope of being able to sell for a large profit. I was, in other words, seeking to find value where others didn't see it – an approach I have stuck with ever since.

We worked hard and we socialised just as hard. In the early 1980s, most of the City seemed to be in a permanent state of hangover. Lunches were largely drunken affairs, which went on late into the evening. At Goldman we imbibed much less than at most other banks, but even so I would always have a few glasses of wine with lunch if I was eating out. The office itself was a no-alcohol zone.

From my first day I was intrigued by just how wide the variation was between the levels of returns that different investors hoped to achieve and how the investors seemed to be driven by emotion not logic. At that time, companies were regarded by most investors as being more stable than just about all countries except the US. France, for example, was seen as a huge credit risk and had government bonds trading at above 19 per cent, whereas Disney theme parks were trading at around 9 per cent. Investors clearly felt that Walt Disney would repay its debt on time but were far more sceptical of the French government.

I learnt some other key lessons, too. The first was that intellect has huge value, and huge limitations. Sometimes stamina and just being there is all it takes to get a trade done. I found the best traders would still be working in the late afternoon, preparing for the next day's trades, long after most of their competitors had called it a day. Inspired by them, I would work into the early evening.

I also discovered that you only need a little more information than everyone else to make a lot of money. Just studying the prospectuses of the companies whose bonds I traded in was sufficient to give me an edge, not least because a lot of the companies had strings attached to the debt they issued. I was staggered that some very bright people could trade on price without trying to understand the value. They didn't read the prospectuses and they didn't ask any questions. In the world of the blind, even the one-eyed 23-year-old can be king.

Finally I discovered that in trading, and indeed in all aspects of buying and selling, a strong personality is well-nigh essential. My boss John, who could smell a seller or buyer down the phone on another continent, and who at one point was making more money than anyone else trading in London, would pulverise salespeople to get the market he wanted. There was no particular intellectual process involved here: he would use his personality to change the market, treating international bond trading as one huge global poker game. Like Jon Corzine in New York, who went on to head up Goldman Sachs before a career in politics as a US senator and then governor of New Jersey, he didn't wait for the markets to buy or sell. He projected his will on the market and others cowered in his wake.

Having cut my trading teeth in London, I was soon posted to Tokyo. It wasn't easy for me. Julia and I had become engaged in 1983 and fixed 1 September 1984 for our wedding, largely because I knew I would find it an easy date to remember when it came to anniversaries. Reluctantly, therefore, we had to spend most of our first few months as a married couple apart as I found myself going almost straight from a honeymoon in Italy, where I'd gained fourteen pounds in twenty-three days, to the Hotel Okura, one of Tokyo's grandest and most traditional hotels.

Goldman's fixed income office in Tokyo was a large room consisting of four people: Hiro, a local Japanese salesman; Willy, a Hong Kong Chinese salesman covering the rest of Asia; one Japanese bilingual secretary; and one very young, very inexperienced Englishman who was missing his home and his wife. As Goldman's overnight bond trader, I was responsible for running the London and New York books while the traders slept. In short, I was a glorified clerk under strict instructions to keep my book flat and avoid risk. Serve the customer, I was told, but don't try to make any money for the firm and definitely don't lose any.

All was fine for a few weeks – on a good night, the business I did probably just about covered the cost of my phone calls, accommodation and a meal. Then one evening, the market underwent a substantial rally. I sold off my position, balancing the book as usual and was pleased to end the night around $40,000 up. What I didn't realise, though, was that had I hung on to my position I would have made a fortune, certainly in the hundreds of thousands, if not millions. The person responsible for the London book was livid and I felt compelled to ring Jon Corzine to explain what had happened. I also mentioned that I had been balled out by the government trader in London. Jon listened sympathetically and then said, 'Just go out and spend some money, and T&E [travel and entertainment] it. Don't worry about the cost, I'll sign it off.'

It was a classic Goldman response: splash the cash and you'll feel better. I chose to console myself at the white-tie dining room at the Okura where, for the first time in my life, I ordered caviar. Two waiters duly turned up with a large, round, black pearl of beluga caviar encased in an enormous ice oyster shell with clouds of dry ice curling from it. Everyone was staring at me. The waiter offered me vodka or champagne. I chose Krug champagne and realised it looked to the entire world as if I was drowning my sorrows after being stood up on a date. The one upside was that Jon came to the conclusion that I would be more useful away from Tokyo rather than in it. I found myself back in London for Christmas after just three months.

The mid-1980s witnessed a technological revolution in the world of finance. People barking down phones and waving slips of paper started to give way to computers. The old-timers saw technology as a hindrance. But it was clear to me that it was the future. When we imported from the US a value-based spread-trading program that could evaluate trades almost instantaneously, we were the only firm in London, apart from Salomon Brothers, to have one. The pace of decision-making became ever faster, punctuated by embarrassing moments of silence when the computers went down – as they frequently did in the early days. At such moments – as the air turned blue with expletives from brokers, salespeople and clients – John, Eddie and I would tell the sales force to pretend we were all in the loo.

Over the next few years, senior salespeople and traders at Goldman Sachs who had once commanded earnings in excess of $1 million a year were fired and replaced by a computer and a smart MBA graduate earning $65,000, doing far more and much faster trades than the old-timers ever could. Soon computers became more than vehicles for information and communication, they became a way of creating new products aimed at particular types of investors. Goldman Sachs and a few other firms on Wall Street, for example, began buying US government bonds and then separating the principal payment from the interest payment. They would then sell the two separately for a higher price than they would command as a single unit. Often, we sold the principal payments to individuals who wanted the capital gain for emotional and tax reasons, and we sold the interest payments to insurance companies who needed the current income to meet medium-term liabilities.

Over time, what Goldman started became common on Wall Street and the profit margins went down. But I was always looking for deals that would give me an edge, so in 1986 I started exploring the possibility of adapting similar techniques to low-quality credits. The strategy required someone prepared to take a long-term view, and here I was fortunate enough to come across a smart and endearing Hong Kong businessman, V-Nee Yeh, who was about my age, had come over to London to learn more about the markets and came from a family that had thrived on taking a long view of things. I put together securities where he took the principal as much as thirty years out, with no interest payments and often guaranteed by a poor-quality bank. Then I sold the coupon payments to institutions. The margins I made were extra-ordinary and I'm glad to say that V-Nee, years later, got his principal payments. By my calculation, he would have made close to $500 million for his investment of just a few million. Such is the power of compound interest on high-yielding bonds over thirty years.

These were some of the happiest days of my working life. I felt I had been spinning a thousand plates in the air at Oxford so, to begin with, becoming an employee at Goldman Sachs was like a holiday. Whereas everyone else was complaining about how hard they were working, I was enjoying a decent (if short) night's sleep, a predictable pay cheque at the end of each month, my lunch paid for, an annual bonus and paid holiday. Now, I had less responsibility and less stress than I had ever known.

To balance this charmed situation, I got my adrenaline flowing by focusing down to the smallest detail on the positions I'd taken. It was a lovely feeling of freedom. But it couldn't last for ever.

The first intimation that things were going to change came when I acquired a new boss from the New York office. Luke assumed that the London traders who took him to lunch and dinner liked him. They for their part saw him as a schmuck in a poker game and couldn't resist ganging up on him. He started to lose heavily, argued with me about the best way to trade the London bond markets and became increasingly less friendly. Our relationship ended up being distinctly fraught.

While all this was going on, I had accepted an invitation to attend an international bond dealers' conference in Singapore. On my third day there I was summoned to meet Luke's boss, Nelson Abanto, at the glitzy Shangri-La hotel. I was shown out to the swimming pool – which looked like something out of a James Bond movie – and there found Nelson, who looked as though he could star in one. He was an incredibly fit man who taught martial arts to the British Army at Aldershot, had two Purple Hearts, could dance like an angel and was extraordinarily good looking. He swam over to me.

'Guy, I just wanted you to know I fired Luke this morning.'

I was stunned. 'Oh . . . So who does that leave in charge of the Eurobond desk?'

'You. Good luck,' he said, before dropping back into the water and swimming off.

And that was it. I was twenty-six, and in charge of the Eurobond desk. I had made it not just in Goldman but in the London financial markets.

Becoming management started to change my view of Goldman and it also started to change the way my colleagues saw me. I was no longer Mr Nice Guy. To Luke's friends – and he had many – I was Mr Bad Guy.

My influence may have increased with my promotion, but some friendships were severed forever once it became official. Everyone assumed that only one person in the London fixed-income team would make partner and now I was a potential contender for this dream position. Being partner not only brought with it a share of the profits but a stake in the company and a voice at the table (true, in bad years you could be called on to cover losses but this hardly ever happened). More than one person informed me: 'Guy, you realise that you are no longer a friend while we are competitors for partnership.'

Making partner was an intensely competitive business. I am

(almost) certain that no aspiring partner ever had one of his competitors killed, but I know that many wished their rivals a short life. As one investment banking partner put it to me: 'There are three of us up for partner this year in my area. I think they will make two. If you work out how much it is worth to me to make partner versus how much I'll make if I don't, the logical thing would be for me to hire a hitman to take one of the other two out. I am such a coward I won't do it,' he added as I gaped at him. 'But still . . .'

While all this was going on, both Goldman and the City were undergoing seismic change. Goldman's London operation went from what felt like a start-up to a major concern that employed 400 people. In such an environment and under such pressure sustaining office friendships – indeed any friendships – proved a challenge. Instead, I focused on my career, on Julia and on starting a family.

At the same time the City experienced the Big Bang. At a stroke the fixed commissions paid to brokers disappeared, along with a whole range of practices that had enabled the City of London to function as a public school 'old boys' club' for years. At a stroke, too, the shortcomings of the British merchant banks were exposed. They didn't have the capital, they didn't have the systems and they didn't have the people needed to compete in this brave new world.

Smelling blood in the water, American investment banks circled the City, waving their chequebooks and buying up firms from senior partners who, with rare exceptions, recognised that the new world was not for them and who were therefore happy to cash in and retire to their country estates. The environment quickly changed as trading screens replaced open outcry trading. And so did the City's culture and work ethic. It became less clubby, less old-boy-network, less drunk and marginally less sexist and racist. At the same time it became more egalitarian, self-righteous, competitive, aggressive, conceited and greedy. Intellect and technology combined to make money and those who survived felt they had earnt it. The government, meanwhile, applauded the ever-increasing tax contribution that the City made to the British economy.

I prospered by putting in long hours and casting my net widely. One of my most successful trades involved buying a bond called Euratom, issued by the European Atomic Energy Commission. It was viewed as a ticking time bomb because of its name. Everyone was convinced that if there were a nuclear accident, Euratom would somehow be on the hook. But for anyone who understood how the company worked, this was complete nonsense. Euratom was guaranteed by a number of countries through the 1957 treaty that established it. It was effectively a supranational like the EU, the World Bank or the Atomic Energy Commission. Its bonds were issued and guaranteed by a combination of countries. Its credit rating was thus very high – the same as bonds issued by the European Economic Community.

Having studied the prospectuses and gained an understanding of the opportunity they promised, I started buying as many bonds as I could. Eventually there were none left to purchase, so I put together a sales presentation for potential buyers across the globe and eventually did a deal with an insurance company in Florida. It picked up around 150 basis points a year of extra yield over the life of the bonds. I made several million for Goldman Sachs. There was nothing difficult about this. It just involved hard work.

By late 1988, the bond markets had become far more competitive. We needed to do something different. As we put together the budget for the following year Jon Corzine told me that he needed a business plan that would aim to make twice as much in 1989 as

I had in 1988. I explained to him that that would be quite a stretch because, after all, margins had fallen by 50 per cent. 'Fine,' he responded. 'We'll raise your trading limits fourfold, which means you can hold four times as many bonds and overall make twice as much money.' His maths was correct. As long as the markets held up and we could increase our turnover by fourfold, our profits would double.

Unfortunately, the reality wasn't as good as the maths and 1989 became the one year during my time at Goldman that I made a loss. By August, when I went on holiday, we were sitting on over $1 billion of illiquid bonds, including $100 million of US bank bonds that looked cheap but were going to get a lot cheaper. By September, when I returned to the office, the book had gotten bigger; now we had nearly $250 million worth of US bank bonds. My worry was that we weren't the only ones in such a mess. By November, my paranoia was proved justified.

Over recent years, in what became known as the Zaitech bubble, Japanese companies had been borrowing against corporate balance sheets and investing in foreign bonds, which paid more money. By 1989, the Big Four – Nomura, Daiwa, Nikko and Yamaichi – had a staggering 40 per cent share of the market. Once Japanese banks and second-line brokers were included in the mix, that share was closer to 50 per cent. Japanese banks had even taken 100 per cent of the bonds in some deals I had done.

And then in 1989 the Japanese government raised interest rates. It also quietly urged Tokyo banks to avoid risky foreign deals. In August all potential Japanese investors withdrew from a proposed bailout of United Airlines. The writing was on the wall. Once the Japanese stopped buying, no one else wanted to buy either. Deals that relied too much on debt fell from favour and the market effectively died for low-quality bonds. Some issues dropped 40 per cent. It proved almost impossible to find anyone who would take the risk on individual junk credits. American and European buyers were interested only in investment-grade ratings.

I knew that most of what I was handling was high quality and would come back in time. But Goldman overall had a huge junk bond inventory. We therefore marked our position down and took a heavy loss. We had to find new ways to get back in the game.

The answer we came up with was collateralised bond obligations (CBOs), which were a way of pooling a large number of different bonds and selling them together that offered considerable flexibility. By repackaging them into different, discrete tranches in a process known as securitisation we could cater for different investor requirements – be it the return on the tranche, its rating or its expected duration.

Until then, securitisation had been used almost exclusively for good-quality mortgages or pools of credit card payments. We, by contrast, wanted to employ it to divide the pool into many pieces to get it sold. We structured the CBO so that the top piece, which had first rights to the cash flows, got a triple-A rating and had a short duration, while the bottom piece was effectively equity and got paid off last. Fear drove the buyers of the triple-A piece and greed drove the buyers of the equity piece. Our job was to arbitrage both impulses. I proved extremely good at understanding where to price them.

In 1990 I underwrote this first CBO, which we dubbed Pearl Street (so named both because the street is located close to Goldman and is home to the famous Fraunces Tavern, and because one bright analyst likened what we were doing to finding a pearl in an oyster). Pearl Street took a portfolio of junk bonds, securitised them (i.e. split them into tranches), directed their cash flows in different directions and then had them managed by someone on behalf of the securitisation's investors. In this case, the manager was Goldman's Asset Management Division.

From the jaws of disaster, we had snatched victory. We made a profit on the bonds that went in, we made a profit selling the bonds that came out and we got paid management fees for managing the portfolio. The collateralised bond obligation market was born.

The deal's success meant I earned my first Tombstone. Made out of Perspex or glass, and often very elaborately designed, a Tombstone is given to someone who has worked on a major bond or equity transaction. My Pearl Street Tombstone, which sits on a shelf in my boardroom in Guernsey, is a Perspex block that tells a story that begins with a picture of a rubbish bin – representing the junk we started with – and finishes with a real pearl, to illustrate the conversion we achieved in investors' eyes.

With the success of my securitisation venture under my belt, I started looking for another challenge and found it in Saks Fifth Avenue. This flagship retailer, where rich New York families came to splash their wealth on clothes, shoes, cosmetics and accessories, was in trouble. It had been sold to Investcorp, a Bahrain private equity firm, for $1.5 billion, partly financed by a total of $500 million in high-interest loans. The problem was that Saks had a poor credit rating, which made borrowing in the traditional manner prohibitively expensive. And Investcorp was finding the loans hard to refinance. It faced the very real prospect of seeing the entire cash flow of the company being diverted to pay interest on the debt – or, worse, the company going under.

My plan involved persuading Financial Security Assurance (FSA), a monoline insurer (a company that traditionally has a single line of business as an insurance provider against a borrower's default), to guarantee a loan to Saks based on the collateral of Saks' flagship store in New York and other properties in Beverly Hills, San Francisco and around the US. The collateral package added up to far more than the debt and FSA felt it was taking little to no credit risk in return for a substantial fee. Having FSA's guarantee was enough to convince the credit agencies that the transaction could be rated triple-A. Saks would therefore be able to raise money cheaply and pay off the $500 million.

Inside Goldman, there were doubts that I could bring all parties to the table, doubts that I could persuade a big American corporation owned by a Bahraini investment firm that refinancing was worth pursuing and doubts I could sell the debt down. Alongside the doubts was a sense – and a certain resentment – that I was ranging off my turf.

I remained confident. But then came 17 January 1991 and the launch of Operation Desert Storm by coalition forces, led by the US, against an Iraq that the year before had invaded neighbouring Kuwait. At a stroke I witnessed investors taking fright and Goldman Sachs was left holding $500 million in bonds with no one to sell them on to. I continued to believe in the deal. I also felt that we had to stick with our client – that it was the honourable thing to do. But among my colleagues there was real disquiet.

The next thing I knew, I was taking a call from the then head of Goldman Sachs, Steve Friedman. 'Guy,' he said with undisguised menace, 'I want you to imagine I am holding a gun to your head and that I'm telling you you've got to sell the position or I'm going to pull the trigger. What are you going to do?'

I hesitated for a moment before replying, 'I'm going to ask you politely to pull it as slowly as possible.'

Steve slammed down the phone.

Although I knew that my response was career-threatening, I

was also convinced that unless we hung in there and waited until the markets recovered we faced taking a huge loss. At the time, there was no other game in town. Fortunately, the Gulf War ended in February and we were able to sell down the Saks debt in March. Goldman Sachs recorded a healthy profit on the transaction. I remember being asked what my underwriting fee would be on the deal. The client suggested it should be the usual 1 per cent, or $5 million. I made the flippant comment that I wouldn't get out of bed for 1 per cent and told them I thought 2.5 per cent was the minimum they should pay me. They didn't argue. Goldman got 2.5 per cent: $12.5 million. I would live to see another deal. But Chuck Davidson had been right: in difficult times you definitely needed balls of brass.

Securitisation was really the same thing that I had been doing for a number of years: separating out the promises to pay from different elements of security and re-bundling them. The difference now was that I was no longer doing it with a single security, but with a portfolio of securities and other assets. My objective was to securitise as broadly as I could.

With my recent successes under my belt Goldman Sachs allowed me to set up a business area called GAS – Goldman's Global Asset Structuring group. To make it work, I found, I needed three things: good legal advice, good analysts and the latest computer systems. When Andy, my favourite lawyer, told me I couldn't do something, I had two stock replies: either, 'Is there another jurisdiction where we can do it?' or, 'If we can't do it, what is the closest thing to it we can do?' When the analysts insisted that they couldn't produce the particular model I needed, I had just one stock reply: 'Get a better computer.'

Of course, once I found an area to securitise, others inevitably copied, so I was constantly having to move on to securitise assets that others hadn't considered. I loved what I was doing. It was intellectually stimulating and I really liked my little team of three. I was also making a lot of money for Goldman – and for myself.

But as time went by I found myself becoming increasingly distant from Goldman. Bob Rubin, who became co-chairman of Goldman Sachs before serving as US treasury secretary in the Clinton administration, had once said to me, 'Guy, you're good and you should make partner. Just keep your head down. Don't ruffle too many feathers.' But while his advice was good, I didn't follow it. I turned down an opportunity to transfer to Tokyo in 1988, in a move that would have seen me made partner, because when Jon Corzine put forward the proposal at dinner with Julia and me, Julia's response was, 'Guy can go to Tokyo, but I'm not going.' The man whose wife turned down his potential partnership became an infamous tale at Goldman, but I was proud of Julia for her refusal to be 'a good Goldman wife'. And I found it difficult to be 'a good corporate citizen'. My new boss, Mike Mortara – 'Pizza Face' in the book *Liar's Poker* – once took me out for a wonderful meal at an expensive Italian restaurant in New York's Little Italy and tried to get me to swear undying loyalty to him and to Goldman. But I realised that my loyalty was to the business I did and to my clients. It wasn't really to Goldman.

If Goldman became frustrated with me, there was one deal that really sparked my frustration with them. I had received a call from a man called R. J. who wanted the bank to help him do a mobile home park securitisation in the American South. It seemed a good deal to me. But it caused diplomatic problems. Mike was furious that the call had gone to London for a piece of business that, in his view, should have been handled by his 200-strong team in New York. And I was then deeply frustrated to learn that when the New York people did actually meet R. J. they laughed him out of the room when he explained what he wanted to do and how he thought the deal might work, and that he ended up going to Morgan Stanley instead. A few years later, he sold the business for a profit of over $400 million. When I heard I called up a senior real estate investment banker who had been particularly negative about my doing business with R. J. 'Hey, it's R. J. here,' I shouted down the phone. 'You're still not partner – and I'm worth $500 million. Fuck yourself.' Then I hung up.

A year or so later, I bumped into the hapless investment banker at a drinks party. I innocently asked him if he'd ever heard again from R. J. after he'd rejected the deal and he told me about the extraordinary phone call he had received. 'Is it true that R. J. really is worth $500 million?' he asked. I took great pleasure in saying that R. J. was probably worth closer to $1 billion these days, and that his new businesses were going from strength to strength.

The frustrations increased. My team and I had noticed that management teams of traditional companies tended to use their capital very inefficiently. They would use it to become conglomerates or to diversify pointlessly into unrelated fields (water companies buying hotels, for example) when they should have been reinvesting in their core business. We became convinced that there was money to be made by restructuring such companies, making them more efficient and employing their capital more wisely.

This appealed strongly to the entrepreneur in me, and so by April 1994, after eighteen months' hard slog and with Julia doing most of the typing (since I couldn't produce such a document at work), I had come up with a sixty-page business plan. The core concept was simple. Rather than use the bank's balance sheet to underwrite the securities that came out of a securitisation or debt restructuring, my proposal was that we should buy the assets themselves, even if those assets were whole companies. The bank was taking most of the risk, underwriting most of the securitisation, so why shouldn't it take most of the profit by doing the deal as a principal? Instead of bringing in tens of millions in fees each year from a securitisation department, it could earn hundreds of millions each year from a principal finance department.

I took my plan straight to Goldman and was referred upstairs to Jon Corzine, now Goldman's head of fixed income. I was excited. He was the man most likely to run the firm after Steve Friedman, and his word was law. We arranged to meet in the departure lounge at Phoenix Sky Harbor International Airport in Arizona. He glanced at the presentation, turned it over in his hands and gently slid it into the brown leather folio case he was carrying that day.

'Guy, the politics is just too much,' he said. 'I'm not going to have a battle with the rest of the firm over this.'

'Jon,' I replied. 'If I can't do this, I'm probably going to leave.'

My stomach was churning. My mouth was dry. I felt faint. I had raised the stakes and didn't know what to do if Jon called my bluff. Would I become a self-employed entrepreneur again, in which case I'd have to sell the house, move somewhere smaller and take the kids out of private school? Would I try to get another job at another investment bank? Should I run around Wall Street seeing if someone else would back me? Should I stay at Goldman, becoming increasingly unhappy and disenchanted until they fired me? Perhaps we could move to Hawaii and start a small boat hire business, or move to Italy and buy a vineyard.

I turned for advice to a former potential client, Mort Fleischer, who lived in Phoenix, and who ran the Franchise Finance Corporation of America (FFCA), which owned restaurant chain real estate across the UK (surprisingly, he didn't own a single McDonald's). Two years earlier, I had tried to persuade him to appoint Goldman to take FFCA public. In the event he went with Merrill Lynch, but the fact that I turned up at our meeting with one eye heavily bandaged following an encounter with a golf ball had at least made me memorable. The would-be client had gone on to become a friend.

Over steak and red wine at a local restaurant Mort told me I had to leave Goldman Sachs. My heart was clearly no longer in it, and it was not good for me nor fair to them for me to remain. It was a difficult thing to hear. But he was right. I owed Goldman a lot, they had given me a fantastic education. The fact was, though, that I needed to move on, even though branching out on my own inevitably involved a risk to the comfortable family life I had carved out for myself.

But I wasn't happy. I still desperately wanted to be a principal and an entrepreneur. I still wanted to work for myself, to build businesses, to identify problems, solve them in ways others might think crazy – and then make those solutions work. I was regarded as brilliant but trouble to manage.

I was well off but not rich enough to say get lost. And I had my children and Julia to think of. Our eldest son had been born in 1987, followed by another son, then two daughters, the youngest born in 1997. Goldman gave me a company car, we took foreign holidays on my frequent flyer miles and, in 1990, bought a house in Sevenoaks on a road that, when I was a kid, I assumed I'd never be able to afford to live on. Things were pretty idyllic materially. Julia and I had all we had ever wanted.

Was I willing to risk everything for my one shot at guts and glory? Of course, it came with the possibility of a massive pay cheque. My business plan assumed I'd make around 10 per cent a year gross on equity employed and that over five years we'd employ around £200 million per year. If things worked out, I could see a pay cheque of roughly £10 million – an incredible sum.

Goldman was becoming an elite institution and rather than

being an underdog trying to break into the markets, it was starting to own the markets. Instead of trying to disrupt the establishment, it was the establishment. Mort was right. It was time to leave the nest and spread my wings.

CHAPTER 5

Forming, Storming, Norming and Performing

Everyone around me is a total stranger
Everyone avoids me like a cyclone ranger
Everyone

That's why I'm turning Japanese
I think I'm turning Japanese
I really think so

THE VAPORS,
'Turning Japanese'

I had my business plan, but I had no track record outside of Goldman and I knew it would be difficult to raise an independent fund by myself. Mort recommended I meet with Nomura, the Japanese bank. The Tokyo-based group had no investment banking business to speak of outside of Japan, he argued, so there would be no one for me to rub up against. Nomura's very weakness in international investment banking might just give me the opportunity I was looking for.

Mort introduced me to Rick Magnuson, the Merrill Lynch banker who beat Goldman for the deal with the Franchise Finance Corporation of America. Magnuson now worked for Nomura with blue-collar, Yonkers-born Ethan Penner, who was developing an aggressive real estate business in New York for the Japanese bank. Ethan's upbringing was modest, but he liked to entertain so much that he hired the co-founder of a fashionable restaurant as a marketing executive to ensure his team and its clients could always get a table at any restaurant.

At Nomura he operated effectively as a non-bank aggressive commercial mortgage lender, at a time when US banks and insurance companies had all but abandoned traditional commercial real estate lending amid steep losses. Basically, he borrowed at the rate Nomura could borrow at and then lent at a substantially higher rate with the intention of selling down the risk through the securitisation model. He was doing what I had been doing at Goldman but as a principal and on a far larger scale.

When the Japanese stock market boomed in the 1980s,

Nomura became the biggest securities firm in the world. At one point it was four times the size of Merrill Lynch, America's largest brokerage firm. In 1986 it was one of the first foreign-owned members of the London Stock Exchange and had a market value of over $100 billion when Goldman was worth just $1 billion. Its share dealing had accounted for up to 15 per cent of turnover on the Tokyo exchange.

But the bank was having problems. Although Nomura still had a lot of money, the Japanese equity market – the bank's largest client base – had crashed. In addition, Nomura had been rocked by scandal. It had reacted to the Japanese stock market crash by bailing out its biggest clients' losses while letting its smaller customers sink. It had also lent $100 million to a known gangster who had used the money to manipulate the stock market. The chairman, Setsuya Tabuchi, was forced to resign in July 1991. It needed to restore its image and rebuild itself. With the Japanese economy showing no signs of recovery, that meant developing its international business.

And that consideration is what underpinned Ethan Penner's business and gave me my opportunity. His real estate operation was one of four new ventures, including one trading in emerging markets business, a proprietary trading business in London and a debt trading business in New York. Nomura's Tokyo-based management's master plan was to roll out new ventures in New York, London, the Middle East, Singapore and elsewhere using the strength of their Japanese balance sheet to give top traders and entrepreneurs the ability to make money as they saw fit. This, they hoped, would make a lot of money for Nomura. Equally importantly, it would allow management to learn the business from these successful *gaijin* – the Japanese word for foreigners – so that they could go on to establish spin-off versions run by Japanese teams worldwide.

Ethan wanted me to work for him. He offered a very high salary as well as a handsome bonus – 50 per cent of the earnings I achieved for him. It was tempting, not least because he was happy for me to be based in London and willing to underwrite my success. But I also had reservations. Handing over 50 per cent of the profits I made on a business I had set up didn't, on reflection, seem that attractive. And I was also acutely aware, from my time at Goldman, that superficially similar as Americans and Brits may seem, their cultures are very different.

I turned to a friend at Nomura in London – Jerry Melchionna, a former New York punk I had met in my Goldman days – who suggested that the person I needed to see to 'get money' was Takumi Shibata, the head of investment banking for Nomura in London. Duly brushing up on my Japanese etiquette (including the correct use of the honorific suffix *san*), I therefore began a series of clandestine meetings with Shibata-san, hoping that news of my meetings would not get back to Ethan. I didn't want to end up working for him, but I also didn't want to risk upsetting him, particularly when I wasn't sure how things were going to turn out.

Ethan had shown little interest in my business plan. But the intellectual and well-read Shibata-san went over it again and again, analysing it in microscopic detail while making extensive notes in the series of notepads he brought with him to our meetings. As the days became weeks and then months, I wondered how many more cups of Japanese tea I could take and started to worry that Shibata-san was interested only in stealing my idea for himself. One day, however, quite out of the blue, he made me an offer.

By a strange coincidence the offer came at almost exactly the same time that a headhunter called me about a potential role as the fantastically well-remunerated head of European capital markets at Citigroup. Shibata-san's offer was infinitely less generous.

He proffered an £83,000 salary, no shares, no loan and no bonuses. He did, however, offer me a share of any profits made. Far more importantly, he was offering me my own business within Nomura and a real opportunity to control my own destiny. We agreed on a profit share that constituted an extraordinarily good deal for Nomura, but on a job that we both knew my heart was set on.

At one of my early interviews with Nomura, I had asked them if they would be willing to pay for a business coach to advise and mentor me if I were to join them. I felt this was essential if I was going to make a successful transition from the distinctive culture of Goldman, where I had been a technical expert with entrepreneurial instincts, to Nomura, where I would need to be a business leader with entrepreneurial instincts. They agreed and I found myself a coach. In terms of personality, Patrick Allen – an older, highly refined and cultured man – was about as different from me as it was possible to be. But his patient wisdom in guiding someone who threw ideas around like hand grenades was invaluable.

That said, our first encounter came as something of a shock. Patrick immediately made it clear that he didn't think I should take the Nomura job. They might be footing the bill for our conversation, he said, but he worried that they would chew me up and spit me out – and all for a pay package that was less than 3 per cent of what Citi were offering. I had already turned the Citigroup job down. He advised me to go back to them to see if it was still available.

Having someone methodically tear one of my ideas apart is something I find extremely valuable. Quite often, it will cause me to change my mind or at the very least, change direction slightly. But sometimes it helps convince me that I am right. I use the expression 'I hear you' several times each day. It means what it says – not 'I agree', or 'I disagree', just 'I hear you'. I said 'I hear you' to Patrick, travelled home and told Julia what had happened. 'You should listen to him,' was her reaction.

What Patrick's challenge helped me to do was to unpick the reason why my gut favoured the Nomura job. At Goldman I had thought I was an insider but it transpired that I was an outsider. At Nomura, I knew from the start that I would be an outsider but that knowledge would actually make life much more straightforward. The key thing was to be respected, and I knew that at Nomura I would be.

When I told Patrick what I had decided he introduced me to American psychologist Bruce Tuckman's 1965 theory of the stages of group development. It's informed my thinking ever since. According to Tuckman, there are four phases any team needs to go through: coming together, tackling problems, finding solutions and delivering results. He called these four stages forming, storming, norming and performing.

Forming, Tuckman's theory has it, is the stage where people get to know each other, and try to grasp the task at hand. They discover each other's strengths and weaknesses and learn who to rely on. At this point they avoid conflict and 'play nice' because they want to be accepted. Their leader's job is to help the team figure out objectives, roles and responsibilities.

Storming begins as people feel safer and start pushing the boundaries. There may be clashes as different personalities and working styles rub up against each other. The leader needs to keep the team focused and resolve conflicts.

Norming is where the plan comes together. Team members begin to benefit from others' strengths and accept their weaknesses. They'll help each other out and start socialising with each other. At this stage, the leader should be asking questions rather than issuing instructions, and even organise social events to encourage team-bonding.

At the performing stage, the team is stable and the goals are clear. People get the job done with minimal supervision and conflict. A good leader will encourage creative disagreement, help celebrate achievements and – crucially – step back. High-performing teams are largely autonomous. A good leader will delegate and focus on the vision.

With Tuckman's theory rattling around my head, I began work at Nomura in London on Monday 5 December 1994. Day one was full of surprises. Shibata-san, who had been so enthusiastic to recruit me and who I was keen to work for, had been promoted to a new role in Hong Kong the week before. In his place was Kozo Yamazoe, who had been at the same level as me in the corporate pecking order during the interview process. I had assumed we'd be peers, but he was now my boss – although with none of Shibata-san's power and influence.

In Tokyo Shibata-san was seen as someone who might end up running the firm. Yamazoe-san, on the other hand, was seen as too unconventional to be a leader; it was rumoured he had been a left-wing student in Japan in the late 1960s and left the country in the early 1970s after the government clamped down on socialists. He had lived in India for a while, before arriving in the UK and working as a travel agent, with Nomura as one of his accounts. His history meant he was unlikely ever to return to Tokyo, let alone rise to run the firm. As a result, Yamazoe-san was not taken particularly seriously by the Westerners in the London office.

Over time, I realised how wrong the Westerners were and how much they had underestimated Yamazoe-san. Apart from anything else, he had two great skills. He had an intimate grasp of how to tailor presentations in a way that the Japanese audience in Tokyo would understand them, which made him indispensable to me. And he had a wide knowledge of Europe's best restaurants, which made him indispensable to Nomura's head office.

I would soon learn from Yamazoe-san that the Japanese view the written word in a different way from most Westerners. Long, complex, English sentences full of difficult spelling and odd pronunciations are frowned upon. Statements that are entirely self-contained pictures are favoured. The job of the written word in Japanese is to bring the listener on a journey, explaining everything as simply as possible. At Nomura any senior *gaijin* attempting to bamboozle the Tokyo bosses with complex words received short shrift.

As a dyslexic, I was delighted. For the first time in my life, I wasn't embarrassed to say, 'I don't understand that word,' or 'Please could you spell that for me?' I was free to use short sentences and simple words. For me, joining an organisation where simplicity was prized had huge advantages. At Nomura, I learnt – and still firmly believe – that it should be possible to write down good ideas so that a fourteen-year-old could understand them. If that's not possible, then the ideas probably weren't good ones in the first place.

That first morning, however, as I spoke to my team of sixteen fresh-faced Brits and Japanese who were earning on average £35,000 each, I found my words – simple or otherwise – weren't sufficient to motivate them. I gave what I thought was an inspiring speech. We were all getting in on the ground floor of something exciting, I said. It would be challenging but I guaranteed we would learn a lot and earn a lot. I confidently declared that over the next two years we would invest over £1 billion of the bank's capital in asset-backed businesses.

My team, however, only became enthused when talk turned to their travel and entertainment expenses (T&Es). There was a hiss of annoyance when I explained that Yamazoe-san was now the managing director and that it would be his responsibility and not mine, as deputy managing director, to sign off on T&Es. To check that they were still entitled to charge lunches, they disappeared to the pub as soon as I finished speaking and didn't return for the rest of the day.

Yamazoe-san, a generous-spirited man with a large smiling face and a big heart, felt sorry for me. Seeing me all alone at 6:30 pm, he asked if I would like to go out for dinner with him and the head of equity capital markets. I therefore ended my first day at Nomura consuming sake and sushi in a multi-floored piano bar in Soho. It hadn't exactly been an auspicious start, but at least the day had ended well.

A week or so later I went to a Christmas party thrown by one of the ratings agencies and found myself at the centre of a group of people interested in knowing more about the securitisations I had been working on at Goldman. At that moment a newcomer pitched up. 'Hi Guy, how are you finding Nomura?' they said. The crowd looked at me, shocked, as I explained I had just moved over from Goldman Sachs. It was as if I had just announced my own death. 'Oh my God, what did he do?' I heard one person whisper to another as the crowd melted away. I found myself standing alone and resolved, not for the first or the last time in my career, to lay off social events.

I threw myself into my work. Over the Christmas break I pondered what to call the new business. Nomura didn't want us to include the words 'private equity' or 'asset finance' – one sounded risky and the other sounded boring. We compromised on the Principal Finance Group, or PFG. Simultaneously I took time to work out what to do with my new team. At Goldman I had noticed that the quality of the management teams of the businesses we helped raise money for varied enormously. Many failed to grasp who their customer was and proved incapable of adapting to changing markets. As a result, although their foundations might be solid, they were viewed as risky and therefore tended to be undervalued. That's where our opportunity lay and that's where, I decided, I should focus my team's energies. I took time to review a list of some thirty possible businesses to invest in, acutely aware that I needed to secure a quick win. My team had never experienced a big success and my bosses didn't really understand the possibilities of what we were trying to do. We had to succeed at something just to prove we could.

I was also very much aware that I hadn't actually pulled off one of these deals before. I had worked out the overall plan, seen undervalued businesses, understood what they needed and was convinced that my approach would work, but I had yet to prove myself. The only way I was going to climb Everest was to do it myself. I decided to choose one business and put all my resources into it. I knew that if I failed, I'd be fired. It was risky, but I told myself that if something's worth doing, it's not going to be easy.

The most promising opportunity seemed to lie in the pub sector. I had a reasonable understanding of what pubs were about, having visited them regularly since just before my fourteenth birthday. I knew that the sector was undergoing dramatic change, and that the industry's management teams were struggling to keep up. And I had very strong views about what could be done to improve their performance.

Once upon a time, the brewing industry had been a licence to print money. Beer was, and still is, incredibly cheap to produce and if you could achieve scale then you could reduce the cost of its distribution and marketing. It therefore made sense for brewers to own pubs throughout the country, and over time the six leading firms had achieved what amounted to a monopoly. Each year they produced millions of gallons of beer that beer-drinkers had no option but to consume. Quality and service inevitably suffered because they were not critical to profitability, hence the consumer backlash represented by the very vocal launch of the Campaign for Real Ale.

But by the 1990s the easy money-making days were over. In 1989 the government had introduced legislation, known as the Beer Orders, that was intended to loosen the brewers' grip by capping the number of pubs each could own and allowing landlords to sell other brewers' drinks. Thousands of pubs had been put on the market as a result. Compounding the sector's woes was a shift in drinking habits. Supermarkets selling cheap alcohol were on the rise. Whereas once the pub had been the social centre of the community, now an increasing number of people were opting to stay home in the evening with a takeaway, a bottle of wine and a video. Across the country between 1987 and 1993, ten to twenty-five pubs a week were closing their doors for the last time.

Although the customer was changing, the pub industry wasn't. Pub businesses were still focused on selling beer. They weren't trying to maximise different revenue streams by offering food or entertainment as well as drink. They were closing their eyes and ears to what was happening, focusing on beer gross revenues to such an extent that they preferred to keep unprofitable pubs open rather than review their estate and their business plan.

Despite a definite lack of enthusiasm on the part of my new Nomura staff, I zeroed in on Phoenix Inns, a collection of 1,800 pubs jointly owned by the drinks and leisure conglomerate Grand Metropolitan and the Australian brewer Foster's. It was 100 per cent backed by assets, but strategically seemed stuck in the past. I arranged to meet Lord Sheppard, the chairman and chief executive of Grand Metropolitan. He was an East End boy made good, who had started out as a junior financial analyst in the motor industry but long ago switched to brewing. He'd taken charge of the group in 1986. He had a reputation for being very old-school – and for not suffering fools gladly.

At the start of our chat, Lord Sheppard treated me like the investment banker I had been just two months earlier. We even discussed an appropriate fee for selling the pubs, which were collectively valued at £250 million (Lord Sheppard admitted that if he didn't sell to me his only option was to sell each venue individually to the resident publican). Thinking like a banker, I was initially going to suggest £10 million – but realised that as I was a principal not an agent, I was taking all the risk and should therefore demand a higher fee. I asked Lord Sheppard what he thought that should be. He said £25 million. I said that didn't seem very much for taking the risk of the downside. 'Well,' he said, 'if things work out, you'll have all the upside. I could charge you for that upside opportunity and increase the price.'

In our game of chess, he'd made a good move. I decided to go for a draw. 'OK then, they're valued at £250 million. £25 million off is £225 million. That's what I'll pay you, subject to due diligence.' We shook hands. He said he'd like me to sign in the next four weeks. I said, 'I hear you,' explaining that I still had to persuade Nomura to back the purchase.

That turned out to be a very slow process. Every month, for five months, as I checked in with him without any definitive news to share, he became increasingly irritable. Our meetings got shorter and shorter. Fortunately for me, the sector's unpopularity at that time meant that he had no option but to wait.

While he waited, I was learning about *nemawashi* from Yamazoe-san. It's a Japanese word that literally means 'going around the roots', although it's best translated as 'laying the groundwork'. It's an informal process you go through when arguing for a proposed new project that involves preparing the way for the ultimate decision by talking to everyone involved to gather their support. If people find out about a new idea in a big meeting, they feel sidelined and are more likely to vote against the plan. If you gently seek their buy-in from an early stage – and that means securing the buy-in of everyone from the most junior to the most senior – you're ultimately more likely to win their support.

Nemawashi is a good but time-consuming way of achieving consensus. At Goldman I had been frustrated by the lack of support I received. At Nomura, the support was there, but I had to gather an awful lot of it both in London and in Tokyo before I could take another step.

Shuttling between the UK and Japan became a regular occurrence and I became very familiar with Nomura's head office, with its white-gloved and polite doormen-cum-security guards, its traditional ground-floor bank hall and its hushed, heavily carpeted upper corridors lined with priceless artworks, largely by French impressionists. I could not have been treated more graciously or politely. Nomura might have been my employers, but they treated me as a guest.

Some meetings went well, others not so well. But I was fortunate throughout in having the enthusiastic support of Yamazoe-san, who I spoke to several times a day. And it was Yamazoe-san who came up with a way to move things forward. 'Why not invite a group of senior Tokyo executives over to do a tour of the pub estate?' he suggested. That would be the best way to secure their backing.

I assumed, given my experience at Goldman Sachs, that a 'tour' would involve a meeting in the office, a visit to the pub and dinner in a smart restaurant. I was wrong. Before Nomura's senior management team would even consider coming to London, they had to believe it was a deal they would be happy to recommend and to ensure this they said that a middle-ranking team would have to do due diligence on a site-by-site basis. A quick visit to a local pub or two wasn't on the cards. Instead, I would have to oversee visits to all 800 of them.

Nomura's insistence on what I initially saw as needless back-covering actually proved to be invaluable. As I swiftly learnt during the long boozy process that followed, there is no substitute for first-hand knowledge. Seeing so many pubs and gaining an understanding of their locations and the demographics of their clientele allowed me to review every aspect of my business plan, from how to maximise the real estate value to working out what the operational opportunities might be. We went from pub to pub, colour-coding as we went: grey for pubs that catered to the over-fifties, pink for the gay community, blue for pubs with strippers and table dancers, and so on, through to family-friendly pubs, coffee outlets and gastropubs. As we did so, ways to maximise their value rapidly presented themselves to me.

Since that elaborate pub crawl, every deal that has gone well for me has involved my team conducting extremely granular site-by-site, customer-by-customer, product-by-product due diligence. The two deals that have gone seriously wrong did so because we took short-cuts. These days I insist that the team physically see what they want to spend money on. Many senior executives don't do this, and the consequences can be expensive.

With Phoenix we ended up imposing very tight spending budgets so any expenditure above £1,000 had to be approved by the stakeholder. It's a discipline we've since applied elsewhere. For instance, when Julia, as chairperson of Hand Picked Hotels, receives a request to replace a carpet, she visits the hotel to see if it's actually needed or not. A couple of years ago we found that within our German hotel business, the senior management was intending to approve redecorating expenses of €2 million to €3 million. Julia personally visited all the hotels involved and went through the architectural and interior design drawings. As she did so, she spotted savings that could be made and had the whole process redone and retendered. Ultimately, the hotels ended up with better quality products with a far greater life expectancy at a cost getting on for half the original proposed budget. Such an approach, which can involve something as simple as rejecting white carpets in favour of tight pile natural weaves, is hardly rocket science but cumulatively it can have a transformative effect. To adopt it, though, requires a particular mindset. You have to think like an owner and not like an agent. It took me six months to make the mental transition once I'd moved from Goldman to Nomura. Soon I was only flying airlines that offered generous air miles and had abandoned five-star hotels if there were good, cheaper alternatives.

As we made our way round every single Phoenix pub we discovered that the vast majority weren't making much money relative to their costs. That might have worried Nomura but for me it indicated an opportunity. Take, for example, a large pub in Holborn that we looked at. As a business it was valued at £40,000 – ten times the amount it earned. But it had a real estate value of £400,000. It would have been hugely expensive and difficult to improve it to the point where it would pay its way, but, sold off for alternative use, it offered the promise of a substantial return that would help us get cash back to Nomura very quickly and repay the equity we'd borrowed. It turned out that 60 per cent of the pubs we looked at fell into this category. At the same time, I also planned to apply the securitisation skills I had learnt at Goldman by bundling the income that came from the long-term leases to back the debt we issued. That would mean that the interest payments we owed were lower than on the underlying leases, generating a positive cash flow.

There were times during this elongated exploration that felt like I was on a perpetual stag night. We would turn up en masse at pub after pub, all in suits and half of us speaking Japanese. Since we felt we couldn't simply march in and out with clipboards we generally stopped for a drink. I will always remember my colleague Shu Matsuura trying to order a tonic and lime in a biker's pub in Catford, South London, where he was the only one at the bar not dressed head-to-toe in leathers, studs and chains.

As we neared the final sign-off, the senior team from Tokyo finally flew into London for three days of drinking, dining and observing pubs in the capital. We took them to the best in the portfolio, including one near Harrods that only served champagne. They demanded to see one of the pubs colour-coded blue, so on the final evening we decided to take them to Browns in Shoreditch, which billed itself as 'London's most famous strip pub'. Our large party was told the three house rules: contribute £1 to the jug before each stage show, no touching and no photos.

I paid for them and they clutched their pints as the pole dancer came on. Throughout her routine she was beaming in our direction. At the end of it she flung her G-string at us and shouted: 'Guy, what on earth are you doing here?' To this day, I still have no idea how she knew me. I had never been to Browns before. It didn't matter. My Tokyo colleagues went wild and the deal was approved. We paid £225 million for Phoenix Inns, becoming in the process the first non-strategic buyer of any scale in the pub sector. I felt vindicated.

Now we began the hard graft of hands-on management, with four members of the PFG team given the task of analysing each pub. Some pubs had resolutely stayed the same for forty years, while the community around them had changed completely. It wasn't uncommon, for example, to find a pub offering beer and crisps suitable for an all-male clientele of dockers or miners in an area now full of advertising agents, artists and accountants who wanted a glass of wine or a coffee with friends after work.

Our solution was to provide publicans with something more akin to a franchise model than the traditional tenanted pub arrangement. We encouraged them to study their customer base and choose what drinks, food and experience to offer accordingly. We didn't impose a one-size-fits-all solution. Instead, each publican was invited to develop their own business plan, playing to the unique character of their market and pub. As they proceeded to do so the old beer-orientated, bulk-selling, male-focused outlets gave way to a much more diverse range.

When it came to managing this part of the business, I realised that most pub companies were run by people who no longer wanted to get their hands dirty. They had run pubs but now they wanted to be managers – and they weren't necessarily suited for the role. I needed people who had the right attitude, rather than people who simply knew about the business. After all, skills and knowledge can be taught but attitude can't. I therefore put my own people into most of the senior roles, with Giles Thorley taking over the task of breathing new life into those pubs that we wanted to sustain. He proceeded to make an enormous number of very down-to-earth, sensible changes, the simplest being not trying to collect rents rigidly between 9 am and 5 pm. Publicans don't keep office hours, so it was not surprising that we had large rental arrears. We also instituted staff bonuses for rents being paid and improved performance.

For some pubs, though, it was too late. They ended up being transformed into car parks, flats, offices, restaurants or supermarkets. Some might claim that we were hastening the decline of the traditional English pub. I would argue the opposite. Had we not intervened, an awful lot more pubs would have ended up going to the wall. We ensured not just that the best survived but that their earnings were sufficiently boosted to safeguard their future. It's better, after all, to have one thriving pub in a village than two on the brink of collapse. Too little competition leads to high prices and excess profits. Too much competition leads to low quality and instability.

A lot of public companies talk about getting rid of the inessential parts of their business but take an inordinate time to do so. We identified what we wanted to get rid of in just a few months – aiming to be 90 per cent right in a short period of time rather than take forever to be 99 per cent right. I wish I had carried on with this approach through all the deals I have done since. On occasion, however, I've allowed an obsession with accuracy to leave me analysing to the point where paralysis sets in. As it was, our pub sales realised £200 million, recouping much of the purchase price from the weakest part of the estate.

The phone began ringing as soon as the Phoenix deal was mentioned in the financial press. The calls were a mix of congratulations, both sincere and insincere, offers of jobs and queries from old colleagues at Goldman who found themselves having to explain to their bosses how they had missed out on such an 'obvious' chance to make money. They'd all conveniently forgotten that I had gone to them two years earlier with my business plan. They were worried Goldman was passing up on something big. They now wanted to be my best friend.

We returned to Grand Metropolitan and Foster's two years later, paying £1.2 billion for another 4,300 pubs from their jointly-owned Inntrepreneur and Spring Inn subsidiaries. Not only could we borrow against future earnings once again, now we had the scale to negotiate beer discounts from the very brewers who had once called the industry shots.

There were several more pub deals that kept us busy and, for a time, Nomura was Britain's biggest pub landlord. We did not reach our goal of 10,000 pubs, but 8,500 at the peak wasn't bad going. I don't think that's what my Tokyo paymasters thought they had signed up for, but they couldn't grumble about the returns they were getting. In 2001, we sold the final portfolio of the Phoenix Inns pubs, generating a total of £406 million. The initial equity investment had been fully repaid within twenty-seven months and we achieved a total cash profit of £176 million.

And so, in true Tuckman form, the team was formed and we had reached the storming phase. We were impatient and aggressive. We loved the success and we wanted more of it. Accordingly, in late 1995, I started looking at a sector that couldn't be more different from pubs: railways.

At the time the British government was busy breaking up British Rail. Some of the smaller assets had already been disposed of. The next step was the sale of the rolling stock operating companies (ROSCOs), which were three businesses that between them owned all the engines and carriages used across the UK network.

The government assumed that, once privatised, these rolling stock companies would buy modern trains and lease them to such train operators as Arriva or Govia. Investing in a whole new fleet of rolling stock was an expense the public purse could do without. Better to get the private sector to finance the programme. And since everyone in the airline industry from Air France to Qantas was starting to lease aircraft rather than actually buy them, it seemed to make sense for railways to follow suit. A successful sale of the rolling stock companies would pave the way for the sale or flotation of Railtrack, the owner of the tracks and signalling.

Key to deciding whether to get into the ballpark was working out what the average life expectancy of a train was. The industry assumption was that it was thirty years. We soon realised that such a figure was very misleading. Some train components dated back to before the First World War. Other parts were only five years old. We concluded that we shouldn't be looking at thirty-year life cycles, but rather a programme of patching and mending trains so that they could last ninety years and longer. In any case, we reckoned that it would have been pointless even to consider spending millions on new models given the antiquated state of most of the track and signalling. We did not want to end up like Sir Richard Branson, with a fleet of shiny, aluminium, high-tech, tilting trains that couldn't run at full speed because the track had not yet been upgraded.

If we determined that the existing trains had a lot more life in them than the market thought, we discovered another potential upside too. The government might have been privatising the railways, but they weren't privatising the risk. If a train company – a customer for our stock – went bust, the government was legally obliged to step in to provide a replacement. This meant the credit risk was very limited and the rolling stock companies' future cash flow was more reliable than most potential bidders recognised. In effect, our bid would be underwritten by the government, which had a triple-A credit rating. We could afford to bid high to ensure we won. And we could securitise the remaining, very reliable lease payments to repay the capital invested and obtain a profit on the equity at no cost.

Hambros, who were advising the government on the sale, were convinced that there would be lots of bidders – up to 100 globally, according to the rumour mill they no doubt had a part in starting. We weren't convinced. We thought that, while the auction was competitive, only a handful of bids would be likely to come through.

We were right. When the bids were in, Hambros was left with

the management teams of the three companies that were bidding, with financial backers, for their own businesses – and us. So attractive did we regard this opportunity that we bid for all three of them. Because no bidder was allowed to buy more than one of the companies, all Hambros had to do was select whichever of our offers promised the highest premium above the management team's bid.

This proved to be our bid for Angel Trains, where our £700 million was far higher than management's £550 million. We were openly mocked in the press for our apparent extravagance. But we had done the sums and calculated the risks. Within three months we'd raised £720 million of debt, returned all of Nomura's money plus £25 million in profit and still owned 100 per cent of the equity. It was the first time that securitisation had been used to finance, as opposed to subsequently refinance, an acquisition in the UK. Once this became public, the financial press rapidly changed their tune and called our bid 'The Great Train Robbery'. The other two bidders rapidly copied what we'd done.

For the private equity industry, Angel Trains was a watershed. It made reputations and it attracted focus on the industry as never before. For us that proved a curse as well as a blessing. We'd pulled off a great deal, but in so doing we had given away our USP to our competitors. From now on imitators would appear left, right and centre – including Goldman.

We sold the equity in the Angel Trains company in 1997 to the Royal Bank of Scotland for approximately £600 million – a huge cash profit. Some might balk at the thought of all that money being made from public transport. I would point out how many public services the additional £150 million we laid out must have paid for, not to mention how much the business improved while we were running it. It is still operating as a leasing company twenty-five years later.

My relationship with Nomura changed. They still called the shots (they overruled me when I said that I thought we were selling Angel Trains too quickly and too cheaply). But they also made increasing efforts to accommodate me. If I was close to a deal, we didn't have to go through the full *nemawashi* process and a representative of the board in Tokyo would fly over to London at short notice to give the deal a hearing. And while Nomura still required granular detail, they asked the hard questions with total politeness and a razor-like focus that I appreciated. Their approach kept me on my toes.

It amazed me how these old Japanese men, often in their mid-to-late sixties, would snooze through most of a presentation and then suddenly sit up and ask the most insightful questions. On one occasion, my ultimate boss fell asleep three times during the meeting, which meant that we had to keep creeping out of the room until his secretary called us back. In this way a two-hour presentation that started at 2 pm turned into an eight-hour one. Finally, at 10 pm, when we were all done, my boss announced that he wanted to go out for sushi and sake. We obliged. The forensic cross-examination that ensued as we ate showed that while he might have been sleepy during the day, he now very definitely wasn't.

The next morning, feeling very chastened, I crept up to his office and asked his secretary if I could see him. He was jovial, fully awake and very friendly and, after I had apologised for the flaws in our presentation, he agreed that we could come back in a month's time. I assured him we would be better prepared. I sometimes wondered if the sleeping was just an act to test unwary Westerners' preparation and resolve.

The selling of Angel Trains marked the end of my honeymoon period with Nomura. Until then, the bank, my young team and I were all focused on the same goal: getting the pie to be as big as possible. But 1997 marked the point of divergence. That year my bosses asked if they could take money from my bonus pool to pay other people in Nomura London on the grounds that they simply didn't have the money to pay the contractual bonuses and were worried that if they asked Tokyo for the money, they might lose what little independence they had. I reluctantly agreed to cede £26 million of our profits to reward staff elsewhere, £30 million to buy themselves out of a deal they'd done some years ago with a San Francisco–based structured finance business called Babcock & Brown and keep £40 million for my own team. But as I quickly discovered, my act of corporate solidarity didn't go down well within PFG. They felt they had earned the money I was giving away.

For its part the bank made it very clear that even if I were to retain the £26 million I would not be allowed to use it to pay my people. The company believed that people paid too much too early would lose interest in the business and leave. They preferred to keep my team hungry. I didn't agree. I thought that paying more would mean that I kept my team and could hire more great people to build a much better business over the long term.

Sadly, I was proved right. The five most senior members of my team left collectively early one morning, along with our head assistant, to join Credit Suisse. They had burned brightly in PFG but felt they had not been rewarded appropriately. When richer pastures opened up, they seized their opportunity. Nomura saw them as ungrateful traitors who would have been nothing without my business ideas and Nomura's financial backing – and the bank might have been right. The fact remained, though, that I had just lost five skilled people who I liked, who understood the business and who worked hard. They had learnt alongside me and I relied on them. We didn't see each other again for seventeen years, until Terra Firma's twentieth anniversary party. When I met them again, I realised just how much I had missed them. PFG never felt the same once they had left.

Having passed through Tuckman's storming stage, this was the point I should have started the norming process with PFG, ideally as an independent business. But foolishly, I stopped paying attention to Bruce. I also stopped paying sufficient attention to my team. When my original tribal leaders left in 1997 I should have found replacements at the same level who could share my responsibilities and help my decision-making. Instead, I became too self-reliant. It wasn't until 2006, when I had been independent from Nomura for four years, that I finally started to hire people I could confide in and rely on. By then it was far too late.

If by now my successes had regularly become headline news in the financial press, it was my pay cheque that brought me national media attention. In January 1998, the *Guardian* ran a front-page headline that screamed: 'This man earned £40 million last year – things may even get better in 1998.' The reporter had been busy with her calculator and worked out that my salary and bonus were bringing me in £110,000 a day or £75 a minute – 2,500 times the national average wage or enough to pay the Cabinet's salary bill for the next seventeen years. Such wealth catapulted me into the ranks of Britain's richest people, according to the *Guardian*, alongside Pink Floyd's Nick Mason and Queen's Brian May. Every paper followed up on the story in the following days.

In the media's eyes, I was the ultimate city slicker. I was the Square Mile golden boy who had 'patented' a new form of financial engineering. I was the person responsible for moving securitisation from the back pages of the financial journals to the front pages of the tabloids. What still hurts is that the provocative but accurate number was almost certainly leaked to the newspapers by someone close to me at Nomura.

That all the ups and downs of my career over the following

years would be picked over by the UK press can be traced back to this single article. As a senior editor at the *Daily Mail* said to a PR man: 'It's not that we have anything against Guy and he's probably a perfectly normal, nice human being, but a financier with a name like that, hair like that and a fat stomach is the dream of sub-editors. He's just too easy a target and we wouldn't be doing our job if we didn't go for him.'

That *Guardian* headline left me feeling unsettled. That year, 1998, was the first year I could count in cold, hard cash the success I had achieved and know that, financially at least, I'd made the right decision in joining Nomura. But I didn't have the sense of pride I had experienced in my newsagent days when I totted up the hours I had worked and saw them translated into a pay packet of pound notes and shilling coins at the end of each week. Instead, I felt an overwhelming sense of acute embarrassment. The media coverage had changed the direction of travel not just for me, but also for my family.

CHAPTER 6

Maths Maketh the Money

> You've got to know when to hold 'em
> Know when to fold 'em
> Know when to walk away
> Know when to run
> You never count your money
> When you're sittin' at the table
> There'll be time enough for countin'
> When the dealin's done

KENNY ROGERS,
'The Gambler'

Back in 1982, Eric Sheinberg – then the partner in charge of trading at Goldman Sachs – asked me a straightforward question: what did I want to achieve financially in life? I told him I wanted enough to be able to afford a big house in the country, two Labradors, a Range Rover and foreign holidays.

His second question was – what sum would do that? I said I thought £10 million would be enough. He asked by what age I wanted to have that. By the time I'm forty, I told him. 'It won't be enough,' he said after a moment's reflection. 'Whatever you achieve will never be enough. It's not the money that's driving you but the need to succeed. If I'm right, you'll never feel you've succeeded.'

I think he was right. By 1998 I had made more money than I had ever thought possible, but I'm not sure I felt I had 'arrived'. I also found the success I had achieved far more difficult to live with than I had ever anticipated. If you win the National Lottery you can choose to remain anonymous. Most people do. But my wealth was a matter of public record and that seemed to change everything. The moment the *Guardian* article appeared, Julia and I started receiving begging letters and requests for investment ideas from people I had not heard from in years. At dinner parties, conversations no longer revolved around children or politics or food or television but financial schemes or friends of friends who wanted a job or a helping hand. Invitations flooded in from people we hardly knew. Julia and I had become a 'must-invite' couple.

For a while it proved very difficult to tell who our 'real friends' were – which people wanted to know us for who we were rather than for what we might be able to do for them. In time we discovered that just as the poorest in society tend to be those who give the largest share of their income to charity, so those people with the least asked us for the least. Our true friends, we realised, were not City moguls or plutocrats but came from such professions as teaching or nursing.

The sudden influx of wealth didn't lead to a similar transformation in our lifestyle. Julia still shopped for the cheapest offers in the supermarket and I saved the soaps, ketchup sachets, tea bags and shampoo bottles in the hotels I stayed in. We didn't buy the children expensive toys or clothes. I still wore the suits I had bought when I was at Goldman Sachs, and for the most part we still holidayed in timeshare resorts or stayed in modest hotels. The reasons, I am sure psychiatrists would say, were complex and no doubt stem from our childhood experiences. But there was also a simple explanation. Until 1997, Julia and I had worried that everything could go wrong.

I wonder, too, whether the determination to remain grounded arose from a sense that while the financial results I was achieving seemed miraculous, the processes that led to them were not. I'm not saying that it doesn't take a degree of skill and a lot of hard work to pull off a successful deal, but then that's true of a lot of other jobs as well. I remember once giving a speech to several hundred private equity practitioners, investors and advisers in which I explained the simple maths behind private equity. At the end of it a senior private equity partner took me aside and asked me never to give that speech again. 'If people actually understood what we do,' he said, 'they wouldn't pay us as much. We're probably in the best paid profession in the world. Let's not spoil it.'

If claiming that private equity isn't that complicated sounds like false modesty, it's perhaps worth saying a little more about the simplicity of the basic principles behind it. Essentially, doing a leveraged buyout is much like buying a house – except that you're using a company rather than a house as collateral for the loan and you have to ensure that you are borrowing from banks at a cost lower than the return on the deal you expect (a good relationship with trusted bankers is therefore absolutely essential).

Imagine you were to buy a company for £10 million at a price-to-earnings ratio of 10 – that is to say that if the shares are trading at £10 then the earning per share for an investor over a year is £1 – this would provide you with a 10 per cent yield each year. You then reinvest all the money the business gives you each year at a similar rate and you also gain, say, 2 per cent each year in earnings growth through inflation. After five years, you sell the business at the same price-to-earnings ratio. In the process you've made one and a half times your money.

Obviously, for this to happen you have to buy well, but there are also other weapons you can deploy to increase value. First, you can borrow, which will enable you to increase the return on your equity, as the debt is other people's money. In a typical leveraged buyout you use one third equity and two thirds debt. Let's say you borrow the debt at around 5 per cent interest for five years. Because the cost of your debt is much lower than the 10 per cent yield on the business, the return on your equity is supercharged. In this example, as you've paid 10 per cent (i.e. a price earnings ratio of 10) on your equity, which forms one third of your purchase price, and 5 per cent on your debt, which forms two thirds of your purchase price (and is someone else's money), at a stroke, your returns have gone from a multiple of 1.5 to 2.3: it is just maths.

Next, you can make operational improvements by increasing sales (which affects the top line) and increasing margin or cutting costs (which influences the bottom line). In the deals I look at, my objective in the first five years of owning a business is to achieve operational improvements of 4 per cent a year (we've usually done better than that, but 4 per cent over a longer period of ten to twenty years is ambitious). Now your returns – including leverage – have increased three times over.

Then there are mergers and acquisitions. Let's assume that you decide to merge your business with another business that trades on exactly the same multiple and that this merger occurs simultaneously with selling the combined business. It could be expected that the larger business will trade at a higher multiple (i.e. a lower yield). Say, for example, you increased the multiple from ten to twelve, and brought the yield down from 10 per cent to 8.33 per cent. The reason for a higher multiple is that you have created a larger business, which most would deem as being safer. By making the business safer, along with the other improvements, you have now increased the value of the business by four times its original value.

Finally, you can reposition the business, something I learnt during my securitisation days at Goldman that PFG and then Terra Firma specialised in. You might opt, for example, to change the business's profile, perhaps getting rid of its riskier parts to make the remainder safer. Or you might find ways to explain cash flows more transparently to give potential buyers more confidence in the numbers the company is producing. The word 'transparently' needs to be stressed here: there have been notorious cases where management teams have changed the way they report their results to achieve the opposite of transparency. Get it right and, in my experience, you achieve a higher multiple. Let's assume you increase the multiple again by two turns, taking the exit multiple from twelve to fourteen. Now you have made 4.9 times your original investment.

Back in my Nomura days I had one other trick in my magic box that other private equity firms at the time didn't understand at all: technology. One of Nomura's greatest assets was that they focused more on technical and analytical skills than sales and marketing skills. This meant they were much less likely to be impressed by an arts student from Cambridge than someone with a Ph.D. in data science. With the bank's financial support I set up what became known as the Cyber Room – a room full of extremely analytical, ludicrously intelligent, quantitative mathematicians, or 'quants', most of whom had a Ph.D. in maths or particle physics. One had that rare neurological condition known as synaesthesia, in which senses that aren't normally connected merge. In his case numbers evoked colours. He'd talk about moving a bid up or down to avoid a 'dirty brown cowpat' or to achieve a 'kingfisher vibrant aquamarine blue'. He was one of the smartest people I'd ever met, and I relied on him heavily.

With the help of the information the quants provided, I could make the most of the five ways private equity can increase value, while also leveraging the essential human element wherever I could. So, with Phoenix, for example, part of our success was down to the relationship I managed to develop with Grand Metropolitan's chairman and chief executive, Lord Sheppard. But the quant element was also crucial. Grand Metropolitan measured the company's asset value in terms of a multiple on the value of beer being sold in their pubs. Since beer consumption had been going down for some time, so had the pub chain's value. We, however, factored in what could be done with the properties, which might not have been doing well over the previous five years but had been great performers over the longer term.

When it came to Angel Trains we found that our competitors were looking at the deal as though it were a management buyout. This meant that they focused on the amount of debt a bank would give against the equity put up (normally around two times the equity check). We approached things very differently, calculating how we could reduce the cost of capital by borrowing against the cash flows of the business. People may have thought our bid was crazy, but it was based on forensic number-crunching.

Not that it was always the quant factor that gave us an edge. With William Hill, for example, which we bought in 1997, our success came down to making the betting shops less spit-and-sawdust and much more female-friendly and technologically savvy. The view of John Brown, William Hill's CEO, was that no woman would ever want to go into a betting shop. My view was that in that case we should change the betting shop. We therefore got rid of the blacked-out windows, cleaned up the inside, put in water and coffee, banned smoking and allowed people to bet on more than just horses. John Brown was also against computers and internet betting, which he worried would bring down margins by letting the punter shop around for the best odds at a time when most of his customers lived within two miles of his shops. Eventually we persuaded him to introduce internet betting, making William Hill among the first companies to do so.

John had been a runner back in the 1960s when there had been very tight legal restrictions on gambling and he had worked his way up the industry to the point where he was overseeing 1,500 licensed betting shops. During the sales process he made it quite clear that he didn't want someone from the City like me – who, he was convinced, had been born with a silver spoon in his mouth and had been privately educated – buying William Hill. Not surprisingly, therefore, rumours started to fly that the first thing I was going to do if I won the auction was to dispense with his services. And, indeed, when we met the day after the deal had been signed, his opening remark was, 'I guess you're going to fire me.' However, once I realised that it was his passion for the business that had made him so difficult during the negotiations, and he realised I was a grammar school boy just like him, we got on famously. He stayed on and even got himself a laptop that he would take to race meetings. He was one of the nicest CEOs I've ever met, and I still regret that we sold the business as soon as we did. But Nomura needed the profits that year.

Two other deals we did illustrate the two other facets of private equity. With the Unique Pub Company, we opted for expansion via a process of mergers and acquisitions. By the time we sold it we controlled 3,200 pubs and its substantial market share became a crucial factor in the premium it commanded.

With AT&T Capital we adopted a policy of repositioning. When we bought it in 1995 it had over $9.5 billion in assets held by twenty businesses operating all over the world in industries that ranged across everything from medical equipment to telecommunications to document imaging. My impression was that it had never turned down a business opportunity, whether that involved trading in taxi medallions in Hong Kong or operating a car hire venture in Wales. My analysis was that all this activity had yielded was frequent flyer miles for the company's management. We therefore sold or closed all but two businesses – AT&T's high-value leasing business and their cash-cow telephone leasing business – making the remaining company leaner and more focused, and therefore far more attractive. We went on to sell it to Newcourt, a Canadian trade buyer, in 1998.

One other all-encompassing element should be mentioned: financing. Every deal I did relied on the expertise of, and a strong relationship with, an investment bank. And in my case that investment bank was Citigroup. Here, I developed a particular regard for and a huge personal trust in David Wormsley and his boss, Michael

Klein. David was smart, Michael was highly intelligent, and with his Jewish background, somewhat of an outsider in this very corporate, very white-shoe investment bank that was so embedded in the American establishment that it even had former directors of the CIA on the board. Citi was involved in 70 per cent of the deals we did, with David providing me with the key information and Michael securing access to the highest echelons of the bank if I needed it. For a while at least, we succeeded together.

But if I was becoming ever more successful, Nomura's situation was declining. By 1997, the company's credit rating had dropped to a triple-B and its market capitalisation had shrunk to a quarter of what it had been at its peak. Nomura still had a relatively strong business in Japan but it was faltering elsewhere, and even in Japan its profits were way down. When Nomura tried to replicate the Western-style business models established by Ethan Penner and I elsewhere they failed. As Bruce Tuckman could have told them, technical skills were not enough. You needed the right group dynamics and leadership.

To make matters worse a huge scandal erupted in 1997 when the company was discovered to have made payments to *sokaiya*, organised thugs who attack Japanese corporations and disrupt shareholder meetings, either in search of bribes or at the behest of rival Japanese companies. Since most *sokaiya* are suspected of having links with the Yakuza, the Japanese mafia, they are dangerous adversaries. It emerged that on one occasion Nomura had engineered the payment of a bribe by selling one of its French impressionist paintings to an art dealer for a rock-bottom price and then repurchasing it for a much larger sum.

As the storm broke, Nomura president Hideo Sakamaki, who had always been very friendly to me, resigned. He was then arrested, convicted and given a suspended prison sentence. A slew of directors followed him out of the door.

Then, in 1998, difficulties arose with Ethan Penner's business. He had built a $16 billion balance sheet within Nomura New York from US real estate loans and had been generating huge profits via the wholly-owned subsidiary – Capital Company of America (CCA) – he'd set up in San Francisco, where he had hosted lavish investor parties, complete with music provided by such bands as the Eagles. The problem was that his deals essentially involved borrowing money in yen – with the full faith and credit of Nomura – to make loans in dollars, and these loans were highly leveraged (on average they were more than 90 per cent loan-to-value with just a sliver of equity provided by the borrower). In normal times, Ethan's team securitised the loans they made and sold them on as quickly as possible to mitigate the danger of a strong yen that left them with dollar assets worth less than the yen that had been borrowed. But the times weren't normal: 1998 saw the collapse of the hedge fund Long-Term Capital Management and a Russian debt crisis. Nomura decided that Ethan's business was too risky and needed to cut back. Ethan negotiated a multimillion-dollar exit and Nomura selected a combination of its own people and Ethan's people to manage the business. Unfortunately, the new management squabbled amongst themselves and the business started going south.

It was at this point, when Nomura had to write down around $1.5 billion, that they asked if I would look at the business for them. Their clincher was that it would be hard for the bank to spend money on further deals, including any I might want to put together, until (and unless) the CCA problem was sorted out. I felt I had no choice but to agree. I called twenty of my best staff into the office, outlined the issue and informed them that they were booked on a flight to New York that evening to audit Ethan's business just as if it was an investment we were considering. In effect, I said, we would be doing due diligence on CCA. I told them they'd be out there for a month. As it turned out, some were still out there three years later when the Twin Towers collapsed on 9/11.

I duly turned up at Nomura New York with my small team of highly trusted lieutenants. A secure room had been set aside for us, complete with computers that were not connected to the main system. We were provided with files and files of loan details, a profit and loss statement for the business, organisational charts and the employees' CVs. We were also given special electronic passes so that we could enter the building discreetly via a side entrance. At first I thought this unnecessarily cloak and dagger, but within two days I decided it was worth using. The business had 400 employees and a senior management team, all of whom realised that there was a risk that I would close down the cash cow that had been paying their bonuses. Bumping into them was not fun. Ethan was revered in New York as a huge success. His team instinctively didn't like us. Ultimately we were able to win the trust of some. But there would always be those who never saw us as anything but a threat.

Sitting in our ice-cold and windowless box, littered with empty soft drink cans, pizza boxes, used napkins and crumpled paper, we joked about whether the guys in New York would ever let us get out alive once they knew we had unearthed details of the extraordinary compensation levels they'd been paid. As my born-and-bred Brooklynite colleague, Jerry Melchionna (Melch), said in an Italian mobster accent, 'They could get a hit put on each of us for less than 6 per cent of what they're earning each day in bonuses.' The joke seemed less funny when we discovered that some of the loans had been made to distinctly questionable operations. One project in Rhode Island, for example, had involved expenditure on concrete that had been over $100 million higher than the original estimate.

After six weeks, the team, my CFO in London, Michael

Hurdelbrink – an outwardly jovial man with ice water in his veins – and I were ready to present our findings to Tokyo. The financing had been done largely off the balance sheet, we concluded. This was hardly unusual at the time and because such a swap is considered a foreign exchange transaction and is not required by law to be shown on a company's balance sheet, it still happens today. As we pointed out, though, the problem was that accounting firms and rating agencies were under pressure from governments and regulators to stop accepting off-balance-sheet structures. And Ethan's business had grown to a size that was simply too big for Nomura. Under even the most optimistic calculations, putting CCA's transactions back on to Nomura's balance sheet would push the bank below investment grade. Nomura's bonds would become junk and the bank would probably either go under or be taken over by someone else.

On the other hand, if Nomura did not admit the problem and continued to keep the business, they would end up losing several billion a year for as long as we could see, through a combination of high-risk loans, extraordinary staff costs and the likely future movement of the yen against the US dollar. The overall real estate market in the US was very stressed and it was unclear that the borrowers would repay the loans. Given the average loan to real estate value was very high (92 per cent) and in a falling market, it was clear that many borrowers would just as soon walk as pay off the loan.

Seated round a huge table in Nomura's Tokyo boardroom, we spent three hours going through our presentation to the full board and various other trusted officials. At the end of it, we went to the side room we'd been allocated and waited. Half an hour later, some sushi arrived. We were getting restless: all we had received was a thank you and lunch. What was going to happen?

Melch decided to go to the toilet – or, rather, to spy on

proceedings. We waited with bated breath for some news. Melch came back. 'The bastards have got much better sushi than we have, as well as sashimi! They're treating us like second-class citizens. Don't they know they're facing bankruptcy?' Eventually after another half hour, one of Nomura's most senior lieutenants came in to see us, with a subordinate in tow carrying all our presentations. These were plonked down on the table in front of us as though they were an infectious disease. Were we about to be fired? Then the two men – dressed almost identically in sharp dark suits and crisp shirts – drew themselves up proudly.

'Guy-san,' said the senior lieutenant, 'you have our authority to do what you need and to give the rating agencies any information you feel they should have. We are happy for you to be completely transparent with them about the situation. But please, understand that this is a very old company and a very dear company, and a lot of people are depending on you.'

It became a strangely emotional moment. They knew they needed me, but they weren't sure they could trust me. Either way, they had no choice. I was essentially their only option. I was confident that I could unwind the business in a controlled manner for them – not because I was better than Ethan (he knew the portfolio and the people and companies involved vastly better than me), but because I had absolutely no emotional attachment to the business. It was a lesson I had learnt over the years at Goldman Sachs. It's far easier to unwind from a position if you can completely emotionally detach yourself from the past and from previous decisions that have been made.

Within a month, we'd fired 90 per cent of the people in the business unit in New York and opened negotiations with a number of banks to secure the necessary liquidity to replace the yen loans with US dollar loans while we gradually sold off the assets. Eventually, Lehman Brothers, Goldman Sachs and Morgan

Stanley stepped up, and our risk position was accordingly reduced. We then spoke to the ratings agencies and agreed a stay of execution while we unwound the business. Michael Hurdelbrink and the team liquidated the $16 billion portfolio, which had been marked down to $14.5 billion. Eventually the business was completely run by PFG people parachuted in from London, with help from trusted CCA employees.

Over the next few years, all the loans were paid off, sold or securitised. Nomura didn't lose its investment-grade rating, total costs and losses were kept to under $1 billion. Nomura Tokyo could breathe again. The team that went in did an extraordinary job under very difficult conditions and they changed Nomura's fate. The bank would have been doomed without them.

All this was bittersweet for me. I'd lost some of my best people – the core of the Principal Finance Group. On the other hand, I felt I had paid back the trust Nomura had placed in me when no one else would consider my plan. They'd enabled me to start my business. I felt I owed it to them to save theirs.

I think it was bittersweet for Nomura, too. I'd helped them out, but the bank felt that in having to turn to me it had lost face. If that was so, then the next request they made must have been even more embarrassing for them, as it involved their business in Japan. The difference this time was that what they asked me to look at was not only problematic, it was also potentially very dangerous.

Nomura had found itself having to deal with huge quantities of distressed loans, many of them to people with serious underworld connections. Not surprisingly my Japanese colleagues didn't want to get involved – they'd effectively be taking on the Yakuza. I, however, was an outsider and having done my due diligence I could see that there was an opportunity there: we would be buying the loans at a huge discount to the collateral pledged against them. I was, of course, aware of the rumours that people involved in these deals had been killed. But I couldn't help wondering whether people might be pretending to have mafia connections in order to avoid having to repay their loans. Perhaps it would all prove far more straightforward than others clearly feared.

But even though I could see potential, I thought I should still check things out a little more before I signed on any dotted line. I therefore drew on my connections to speak to Walter Mondale, who had just completed a posting as the US ambassador to Japan. I asked him whether recovering these distressed loans was a good idea, or if they would prove as dangerous as some people were warning.

Walter knew the chief of police in Tokyo, had an informal chat with him and then called me back. 'Under no circumstances,' he said, 'should you get involved in this business. It's as risky as everyone's been telling you.' Getting killed by the Japanese mafia was not part of my job description, so I went to Nomura's compliance department and raised my concerns. They took me off the business. My team breathed a huge sigh of relief. My superiors, by contrast, were extremely unhappy. I think they had hoped they could use me not just to make money but to act as their trouble-shooter.

By 2000, the Principal Finance Group was almost seventy strong. With very few of the original team still in situ, it had gone from being an enthusiastic band of novices on £35,000 a year to a bunch of hired guns earning a packet. Every bonus day was a nightmare. Growing the pie had become less and less significant; splitting the pie had become more and more important. I realised we needed something big and positive to focus on.

And in London, I thought we'd found it: the Millennium Dome.

The Dome was something of a white elephant. It had taken years to get off the ground, gone way over budget and had finally topped the scales at just under £800 million, most of it covered by National Lottery funds. It was derided by the media, visitor numbers were disappointing and it would continue to ratchet up maintenance costs – long after the Dome of Discovery exhibition closed for the last time on 31 December 2000 – to the tune of £1 million per month. No surprise, then, that the government were desperate to be rid of it.

The Japanese were hugely excited at the prospect of buying the largest – if vastly overpriced and poorly received – symbol of the millennium celebrations. The UK government believed that once our interest became public we'd do everything we could not to jeopardise the deal. And my team thought that, with plans in place to turn the Dome into a leading international visitor attraction, it looked fun. On the surface, at least, it seemed a very promising deal that would make all parties happy.

The ambition we set for ourselves was to pay £105 million. We would then invest almost £1 billion in what would become 'Europe's first urban entertainment resort'. Backing was forthcoming from Hyper Entertainment, a division of Sony, which had amusement parks in Tokyo and San Francisco.

The project might have looked fun, but the research and planning that went into it was a serious business, involving more than 100 people. We looked at exhibition centres and theme parks in California, Florida, Paris, Spain, Japan and elsewhere. We weighed up the drawbacks and considered the possibilities. The risk was obvious. The potential was tantalising. Relative to the population, the UK had comparatively few grand leisure spaces and remarkably few in the London area. Yes, there were plenty of museums but many were old, tired and dusty. It seemed there was a captive market of millions of people who came to London looking for somewhere to enjoy themselves but who had very little in the way of the fun and thrills that an entertainment park could offer. If we could make our reimagining of the Dome work here in London, we could extend the concept to other parts of the globe.

The government received seventy initial approaches. By December these had been whittled down to ten serious bidders, and we were one of them. On 16 January 2000, just over two weeks after the Dome opened its doors, we were announced as one of six selected bidders and then, in May, as one of two. Legacy was the other final bidder (their proposal was for a high-tech, Silicon Valley-style industrial campus). On 27 July we were declared the winners.

That evening we were the main story on most news bulletins, and we went out to celebrate at a Chinese restaurant below the Greenwich Holiday Inn Express. I felt, though, that this was all a little premature. We might have won the competition, but that was just the start: there was still due diligence to be done and we were yet to negotiate the final terms of the deal.

I was right to be cautious because things turned sour very quickly. Our first stumbling block turned out to be the mayor of London, Ken Livingstone. His view that everyone should go to the Dome on public transport was a worthy sentiment. However, the Greater London Authority's refusal to give us the planning permission necessary for car and coach parking seemed a step too far. I never had the opportunity to discuss this face-to-face with Ken Livingstone – the view of Deputy Prime Minister John Prescott was that a dog-loving Conservative Party supporter like me would probably not get on with a newt-loving socialist like Ken (perhaps it would have helped if I had pointed out that the best man at my wedding, William Hague, also has an interest in newt conservation). But whatever bonding over newts might or might not have achieved, it was clear that without parking facilities and the revenue they would generate, the deal was starting to look a lot less attractive.

I also became increasingly worried about projected visitor numbers. Pierre-Yves (aka P. Y.) Gerbeau, the Dome's chief executive, was relentlessly upbeat, assuring us that the attraction was on course to receive six million visitors. I wasn't so sure. I admired P. Y.'s boundless energy and the fact that he was a hands-on operator. But I worried that he didn't seem strategic. I was aware that while press releases had hailed him as the 'saviour of Disneyland Paris' when he was hired, the *Guardian* had then reported that he was not even listed as a member of the team of trouble-shooters who had been given the task of saving the park. His figure of six million seemed misplaced and overly optimistic.

Next up was the shock we experienced when we tried to unpick what the situation was with the exhibits and attractions inside the Dome. The Dome was, of course, packed with them – hanging gardens, installations, Cirque du Soleil-style acrobatic performances and a huge walk-through human body sculpture that stretched 64 metres from elbow to foot and stood 27 metres high. When we first got into legal negotiations, we were told there were 1,100 contracts with suppliers relating to physical and intellectual property. It turned out there were actually 2,800 and almost every single one was different from every other. There was no such thing as a standard contract, which for a government project was a very unusual practice. To make matters worse it soon emerged that the Dome's operating company, New Millennium Experience, did not know which of the assets or rights to intellectual property involved in its exhibits it owned and which it didn't. We wanted to have an attraction that we could keep open while we added additional entertainments – our bid did not consider a scorched earth approach. Thanks to the contractual uncertainties, it was a real possibility that almost everything would be packed up and moved out at the end of the year, leaving us with only the structure itself. If we couldn't hold on to the existing content (and also the rights to the Dome's ancillary land), this would be a very bad deal indeed.

And then there was the government, which, it became increasingly apparent, wanted to get a deal done but had no real idea what that deal might look like. We needed a clear vision. There had to be a reason for the Dome to exist. Without that, and with the practicalities and the economics of the deal looking increasingly shaky, taking things forward looked risky. We all continued to work on the deal, not least because Nomura – after positive press coverage put them in the limelight – was keen to do so. But although the bank became ever more interested in their global image and ever less interested in the economics, I found I couldn't tick the same way. I experienced distinctly cold feet.

I expressed my concerns to the government. Lord Falconer, minister of state for the Cabinet Office, kept telling me not to worry. John Prescott kept telling me to sign on the dotted line and move forward like a good boy. But one attribute I have had all my life is the ability to change my mind if I receive new information, and withstand the criticism from others that invariably follows when I do so. The pain is almost always worth it and fades more quickly than people generally expect. Memories are very short. In my experience it's far better not to do something, to walk away and risk people's opprobrium than to do something that you will regret. If I pulled out of this particular deal, I risked upsetting a lot of people. But actually, when it really came down to it, the only ones I had to worry about were those at Nomura.

On Tuesday 5 September, my worst fears about the Dome were confirmed. One of my team heard on the grapevine that the New Millennium Experience Company, which had already received a substantial government bailout of £43 million in July, was begging the government for a further £40 million to prevent it going under. If that wasn't bad enough it then transpired that the independent report on the financial management of the Dome and its assets by PricewaterhouseCoopers (PwC), that the government insisted on as a condition for the bailout, wasn't going to be made available to me.

After a week of agonising, I decided to pull out of the deal and arranged to meet Lord Falconer at his suite in the Cabinet Office to let him know. At lunchtime on Monday 11 September, I told my London team what I was planning to say. My Japanese colleagues told me they would deal with Tokyo – it was 9 pm in Japan and they needed to prepare for any 'reputational damage' my decision might cause.

At 6:30 pm I arrived at the Cabinet Office. I was shown to a drab Victorian civil service meeting room with desks set out in a loose circle. Lord Falconer arrived with his entourage. The meeting was cordial. I told him that I was concerned we had not been allowed to see PwC's report, that visitor numbers had been overly optimistic and that if I couldn't have sight of a proper register of the assets I could not be confident about what I was buying. You don't buy a house without knowing whether you are getting the fittings, I pointed out. I concluded my remarks by saying that we would be announcing our withdrawal the following morning.

Lord Falconer was clearly disappointed and admitted that the government was going to be hideously embarrassed by this. We both agreed we wouldn't say anything to the press until the next day. I walked out of the gloomy office and queued at security to get my mobile phone back. By the time I got into a taxi on the Mall, Andrew Dowler – our PR man – was calling me. The news was already out there. The government was briefing against me. I instructed him to get our story out as quickly as he could. I felt we were in a race with the government to avoid reputational damage – although, in the end, the story was not covered either as dramatically or as negatively as both Lord Falconer and I had feared.

The Dome was closed for a few years and then became the O2 Arena. The eventual buyers did almost exactly what we had wanted to do, though with fewer shops and restaurants. And, as sweeteners, they received massive car parking space and were given large chunks of the Greenwich peninsula to redevelop. My belief is that they made far more money on the redevelopment of the peninsula than they spent on the Dome.

Withdrawing our bid might have been the right decision, but for Nomura it represented a tremendous loss of face. They had seen the Dome as an opportunity to be huge in the UK. They had put together a big PR plan. The head of Nomura himself had planned to fly over for the grand opening. Their disappointment was painful to observe.

Supporters in the Tokyo office tried to help me rebuild my bridges with the executive team, and I was invited to a boys' night out in Tokyo with the senior staff. It was a huge honour and a very rare experience for a *gaijin*. We had a lovely meal. Everything seemed to be going well. But then, as we left the restaurant at 11:30 pm, I was invited to go to some clubs with them in Shinjuku. I knew that while the clubs in Roppongi – where most Westerners go – are similar to the sort of gentlemen's clubs found the world over, the hostess clubs in Shinjuku are not for tourists. I had a rule, based on what I had heard about them, that I would never go to one. I told my colleagues I had to return to my hotel. One of my allies took me aside and warned me that it would not look good if I left, but I remained adamant. My Tokyo bosses lost face yet again. This time there would be no reconciliation.

In the final months of 2000, Nomura decided to list its shares in the US. There was a good rationale for this: the move would give the bank a stronger base from which to compete with European and American banks. But it had tax implications when it came to the Principal Finance Group. Under Japanese accounting rules we could effectively be held at arms' length, with our investments and debt kept off Nomura's balance sheet. Under US accounting rules that wouldn't be allowed. And if we started appearing on the books, Nomura would go from looking like one of the biggest banks in the world to something more akin to the beneficial owner of a pub conglomerate with around 100,000 additional staff working in the various portfolio businesses of which I was the ultimate boss. And because Nomura would also have to mark-to-market the valuations of each asset and business on a quarterly basis, and report the business's earnings as well, their earnings would become so volatile they would be impossible to predict. On top of all that was the fact that everyone would work out pretty quickly that it was actually the Principal Finance Group that was making all of Nomura's money.

At a stroke the ambition Nomura had once expressed to keep us until September 2020 became a desire to kick us out as quickly as possible.

I suspected I was going to have to leave, but I wasn't convinced I wanted to set up my own private equity fund. The world had changed in two years. The market had declined, the dot-com bubble had burst. And Rick Magnuson, who I hoped might run a new business with me, had departed to do his own thing. I took legal advice on what it would cost Nomura to buy me out of my contract. The number that came back was £400 million – possibly as much as £1 billion. But the picture was far from clear. My contract with Nomura, which was a business agreement rather than an employment agreement, barely ran to four pages and it didn't cover what would happen in the eventuality of my leaving. I had a choice. If Nomura wanted to terminate the agreement then we could try to find a compromise acceptable to both sides, or I could sue Nomura for loss of profits.

Neither side wanted to end up in court, but it became clear to me when Takumi Shibata, the man who had recruited me in 1994, was removed from the process that I was going to be negotiating with a company, not with friends. It threatened to be a messy divorce, not an amicable separation. I was faced with the impressive and hard-headed lawyer Tim Pryce. I found myself endlessly weighing up my options, while simultaneously trying to work out whether, once we'd settled things, I should then retire into the sunset and enjoy time with my family or start up on my own.

Ultimately it was the advice of the eminent barrister Lord Grabiner that nudged me towards my final decision. He warned me that if I were to embark on legal action against Nomura the litigation would take years and the outcome was far from certain. Ultimately it would come down to a judge's feelings about the case and how the witnesses performed on the day. I'd be putting my life on hold while I rolled the dice. I decided I had no choice but to agree to what Nomura were proposing: that I should spin out my own company from the bank, with the assets given a low value so as not to attract tax for Nomura. As I was to discover, this was a great deal for Nomura but not for me. My first tax return after the spin out in 2004 showed that my earnings had almost disappeared and it was going to take a few years before they would recover, if ever. Officials at the Inland Revenue were convinced that Nomura must have paid me a large amount of money offshore to do the deal or that the deal was much better for me than my tax returns were showing. Sadly, it wasn't so. I had simply negotiated a very bad deal.

I'd realised prior to the deal being done what a disadvantage I'd placed myself at and I decided to see whether I could renegotiate to secure some of the £400 million my financial advisers felt I had a right to. My flight was booked for 11 September 2001.

I spent that morning in a meeting with a business-to-business hotel company in which we had a stake. Towards the end of the meeting, a secretary rushed in to say that a newsflash had just appeared on one of the monitors in the reception area, announcing that a small plane had flown into a skyscraper in New York. By the time I got into the car that was taking me to the airport, flights into New York were being suspended. Halfway along the M4, I heard that one of the World Trade Center towers had collapsed. Within minutes, Nomura Tokyo had contacted me to tell me not to come.

I went back home to Sevenoaks, to Churchill Court, the home Julia had bought in 1999 and had been renovating for the past two years. Churchill Court had been given to Winston Churchill as a gift after World War II and he gave it away to the British Legion, which in turn sold it to be an insurance training institute before Julia bought it. We had moved into the house the Friday before and still hadn't unpacked. Julia was at work – attending her first board meeting at Hand Picked Hotels – and the kids were at school, so I sat alone surrounded by piles of boxes and watched the events unfolding on television. As the full horror of the situation became clear, people started talking about the possibility of co-ordinated attacks on other cities. If terrorists could bring down the Twin Towers, they could strike anywhere and do anything. The sense of uncertainty and panic was palpable.

I never flew out to Tokyo for that final meeting. There were more important things going on in the world. And although the deal hadn't actually been signed, it was still a deal. I was in the exit lounge for the second time in my business career.

On the plus side, I was gaining a great opportunity to build a business totally independent of Nomura. On the minus side was the additional stress and slog this would cause. My ninety-hour weeks were about to become 120-hour weeks. I would hardly see my children again until they had grown up.

CHAPTER 7

The Winning Team

Give yourself prudence and love your friends
Subway kid, rejoice your truth
In the religion of the insecure
I must be myself, respect my youth

LADY GAGA,
'Born This Way'

I closed the deal with Nomura on 1 April 2002. The world might have been in turmoil since 9/11, but at last I was completely in control of my fate – at least business-wise – and not reliant on anyone else. From now on, all the costs and all the responsibilities of the business were mine.

At Nomura, I had been working with a team I trusted, an investor I understood and I was backed with the equity I needed. If anything went wrong now that I had broken away from Nomura, I would have no one to blame but myself.

I had assumed that my team would stay with me after they had received their leaving bonuses from Nomura. I was wrong. Many were concerned that, were they to stay, they would not receive further bonus payments until the fund had been fully invested, or investments had been realised and investors had received at least an 8 per cent per annum return on their money. They were also unhappy about the prospect of investing their own money in the new fund if and when it was raised. They felt they had worked hard over the last eight years and understandably wanted to cash in. Two thirds of the staff left over the next two years. Since I was out on the road wooing investors for most of that time, there was little I could do to stem their resignations.

I had decided on the name Terra Firma for the new firm. It means 'firm earth' and appears to have been first used by the Venetians in the seventeenth century to describe those areas of the Italian mainland ruled by Venice. The firm's early days were stressful and dogged by uncertainty. We were still managing assets from

Nomura's Principal Finance Group while looking for capital to start deals of our own – and this proved far from easy to do.

If some staff were sceptical about what we were trying to achieve, investors were even more so. I had naively thought that the reputation I had earned from investing in pubs, trains and other assets over the last eight years would carry me through. But this was a completely new ball game and investors needed information about, and reassurance on, so many different details. What was Terra Firma's structure? Who managed it? Who did it employ? What was the pay structure? What were we going to invest in? Who were the other investors? And on, and on, and on. I could hardly be surprised: they wouldn't be investing in Guy Hands, after all. They would be investing in Terra Firma.

Most private equity firms overcome the challenge of raising capital by starting out with several partners who can share costs and risks. With Terra Firma there was only me. I felt more alone than I had since childhood. I didn't have deep pockets, so unless we raised the money soon, I would simply be left with a chunky liability, as I would need to pay off the remaining employees, the lawyers, the accountants and close everything down. I needed some people to accompany me on the road – people who understood business, could get on with investors, but who also had the kind of personality and energy that meant they were up for drinking sake and eating Chinese food with me at 11:30 pm, having just got off an evening flight for the third day in a row, while I spent the meal working out the logistics that would allow us to fit in at least six meetings the next day in up to three different cities.

Fortunately for me, both Mike Kinski and Bill Miles had those qualities. Mike had joined me at Nomura in 2000. As the former chief executive of the bus and train company Stagecoach, as well as ScottishPower, he knew how to transform ailing companies into success stories. He became one of Terra Firma's operational managing directors. I also discovered he was the ideal salesperson. Mike was very charismatic, could explain complex issues clearly and knew how to lighten the mood with his sports patter and collection of bad jokes. He became my constant travelling companion.

I brought Bill Miles on board to sharpen our fundraising efforts. I had met him twenty years earlier on a Goldman Sachs training programme. Bill knew nothing about private equity, but he had a real talent for selling the dream. Bill's view was that we needed to focus on the biggest market – North America – and he gave me invaluable advice on how to treat potential investors there. British schoolboy jokes, he said, are simply not appropriate at a dinner in the US where there's mixed company. There are also language differences to be aware of. A scheme, for instance, means a plan to the British, while to Americans it means a dodgy deal.

Some of his hints involved shrewd basic psychology. Don't focus on numbers, he said: 'If I told you my social security number you wouldn't remember it in the morning.' Do tell stories: 'If I told you my wildest night at college, you'd remember it forever,' he explained. 'People want to know about the guy, not the deal.' 'In the first meeting,' he went on, 'quit selling. If you're trying to raise black box money for ten years, that's a six-month process. Slow the bus down. You don't marry your wife on the first date. Get them to want to have a beer with you, get them to trust you and then we'll have all the time in the world to sell the maths.'

He had one other crucial insight. British business letters, he said, tend to be four-page descriptions of a deal. Americans see this as too much noise. It's much better to tell people what you're trying to do in the fewest words and with the least puff. For a dyslexic who disliked the UK school system, this was music to my ears.

We went from complex PowerPoint presentations packed full of information to bullet points printed on both sides of a rubber mouse mat which we handed out everywhere. They may have been a bit low-tech and amateurish, but they hung around on people's desks long after we had gone. During our presentations we tried to elicit three pieces of information. Did they like us? Did they trust us? Did they believe we'd make money for them? Mike would do the pitch, I would seek to close the deal and Bill would organise the army of analysts to answer any follow-up questions as the investors did their due diligence.

At the end of the first year, we had raised £140 million – a pittance in private equity terms. Our lives had become perpetual motion routines. We would jet off for several days and nights at a time, sleeping in the air, showering at the airport, going to meetings, then back on another plane to snatch a meal, getting our clothes pressed as we went. I piled on weight, became ever less fit and was constantly sleep-deprived. I went up two shirt sizes and gained six inches around my waist. Within a year, I was diagnosed with type 2 diabetes and had to embark on a programme of lifestyle changes and medicines that would treat the symptoms but never cure the disease. It was a horrible period. I longed for home and to see Julia and the children but whenever I was there, I just fell asleep.

It was ultimately a meeting in Toronto that proved pivotal. I was running out of money, time and energy, but had managed to secure a meeting with Canada Pension Plan (CPP), a huge public investor with a global mandate to invest in private equity. Their head of private equity, Mark Weisdorf, had slotted us in on a Friday afternoon between 4 pm and 4:30 pm just before he was aiming to leave to meet his wife for an early dinner. We had been delayed by a storm and were feeling stressed – Mike because of the storm, me because I was worried about being late.

We sped from Toronto Airport to CPP's office, arriving just before 6 pm to find Weisdorf with his coat on about to leave. He agreed to give us ten minutes, and we set to work. He listened intently at first, but soon stopped listening and began firing questions at us. He was keen to understand what motivated me and wanted to know how I would cope with the transition from having one boss to simultaneously having lots of bosses and no boss at all.

'I do not doubt that you are a good investor or that Terra Firma has a good strategy and that you have the people to execute it,' he said. 'But are you the right personality to run an institutional fund in private equity or are you really an entrepreneur who has worked well within the discipline of a big organisation?'

It was the same question I had been asking myself over and over. I assume I gave the 'right' answer, but even today I'm not sure what the right answer is. At the time I said I enjoyed investing, I wanted to build a private equity firm and then an alternative asset management firm. But was this enough to make me the right personality to run institutional money – or, in reality, was I an entrepreneur? Today, I know that I am at heart an entrepreneur. I'm still not sure what exactly I lack to make me an institutional investor – I'm only sure that I'm not one.

Finally, Weisdorf asked his killer question, one that I'd never had to worry about in my Nomura days: 'Are you willing to take as much risk as I am?' he enquired. 'I am willing to take a bet on you. Are you willing to risk everything on that bet?'

Within the space of two hours, we had agreed a deal. CPP would put in €150 million if Terra Firma committed half as much. To get our new cornerstone investor on board, I agreed personally to put in €65 million, which was most of the free cash I had retained from my time at Nomura and far more than I had originally intended to invest. The rest of the team would contribute €10 million. We also had to trim our fee structure to 1.5 per cent, when most private equity firms were being paid 2 per cent per annum. No matter – Mike and I left the meeting feeling elated.

CPP unlocked the door for us. Soon another €100 million came from the state of North Carolina. Now we moved on to Abu Dhabi, where we gave a number of presentations to the Abu Dhabi Investment Authority (ADIA), a sovereign wealth fund. At our meeting in an old building in the Arab quarter, they told us we were competing with two blue-chip private equity firms for investment. As we left in the blazing heat, Mike and I talked about how we had done. We decided we had probably not quite made it. Half an hour after we got back to our hotel I received a call from ADIA. They agreed to commit €100 million.

Securing money from one would-be investor in Japan came with a culinary challenge. He insisted we join him for dinner at a restaurant that served the potentially lethal *fugu*, or blowfish. Halfway through dinner the speciality of the house arrived: deep-fried *fugu* testicles. Mike managed three of these delicacies, each about the size of a golf ball, without disgracing himself. Out of respect for me as the leader of Terra Firma, the largest one was reserved for me. Somehow, I managed to close my mouth, bite down and avoid gagging as the warm, salty liquid flowed down my throat.

Our experience at the Buddhist monastery we visited near Osaka could not have been more different. While individual monasteries in Japan do not have the same level of endowments as the Church of England, the Vatican, or the evangelical mega-churches in the US, some have quite considerable reserves which they use to provide social support for the poor members of their community. Given the sheer size of a city like Osaka, such support is contingent on a canny investment strategy.

When we arrived, we were taken to a beautiful modern room with light wood panelling and a huge electric organ against the far wall, where we were told we should spend some time in quiet contemplation. Slightly incongruously, Bach was being piped in through the speakers. The Japanese people I knew were very talented classical musicians. What I hadn't appreciated until I travelled there regularly was how deeply ingrained Western classical music had become in their culture.

As a sign of respect, before entering the monastery we had to remove our shoes and place them in the cubbyholes provided. I was horrified to glance down and see a large hole in my sock. In a desperate bid to avoid a display of naked skin to my hosts I took to shuffling along awkwardly, dragging my right foot behind. We gave our presentation to the head monk and he seemed impressed. In fact, he went on to pledge €25 million to our fund, called Terra Firma Fund II (the money I'd managed at Nomura we named, after the event, Terra Firma Fund I). At a later visit from one of my Japanese colleagues, he sang our praises. 'We were very pleased to invest, especially because Mr Hands is physically disadvantaged.' I felt I had no option but to revert to the limp at subsequent meetings.

As well as setting up our own meetings we also used placement agents, who function a bit like matchmakers and put private equity firms that raise capital in touch with the potential investors, who provide capital to private equity buyout funds. In this case, we used Merrill Lynch and Citigroup, and both address books proved invaluable in this respect. The two firms also helped us to fine-tune our pitch to institutional investors and high-net-worth individuals. For any money raised, they earned a 1.5 per cent fee.

Ultimately, I realised, it was our simple pitch that carried the day with potential investors. Whether people liked us, trusted us and believed we would deliver was key. Whether they detected passion in what we were pitching was the clincher. If they didn't sense passion, they wouldn't conclude a deal with us.

By the time Terra Firma Fund II closed in February 2004 we had travelled to seventy countries and seen 400 potential investors, most of them many times. Some eighty-seven backers had contributed a combined €1.9 billion to Terra Firma Fund II, setting a new record for a debut independent fund. Now we had to go out and invest it.

The first thing was to go on a hiring spree. I still had around twenty people from when I had left Nomura, but I was aiming for a team of around 100. One successful recruit was, ironically, Tim Pryce, who had negotiated on Nomura's behalf during the spin out. As I told him during an interview I conducted on the way to Gatwick Airport, he had been a pain, but I liked how he negotiated. He became Terra Firma's general counsel.

The rest of the team I recruited came from a variety of nationalities, backgrounds and careers. I had noted that those who had worked hardest for me at Goldman Sachs hadn't been British or privately educated. I wanted true diversity among my colleagues to make sure that we had a true diversity of opinion. I didn't want us to be yet another classic City of London institution.

Diversity is certainly what we achieved. Yes, there was the occasional former public school boy but he was the exception rather than the rule. So, for example, we had an Old Etonian who used to regale us with stories of his schooldays – in particular, how on his seventeenth birthday he and his friends got very drunk, climbed up onto the roof of his house at Eton and hurled bottles into the quad below. When they came down, they were marched to the housemaster's study where they received what he described as 'a well-deserved caning' – with the housemaster wishing him a happy birthday at the end of it.

At Terra Firma, however, my Etonian found himself rubbing shoulders with people who ranged from comprehensive school kids, whose first language was often Bengali, to one of our managing directors, Mayamiko Kachingwe, who as a child had to make a 10-kilometre round-trip bicycle ride to school as one of the first cohort of Black students in a previously all-white government school in newly independent Zimbabwe. The two things that my Etonian and Mayamiko had in common were the caning they both received for infractions of school rules and the broad outline of their subsequent path in education. Mayamiko won an undergraduate place at Oxford University and proceeded to win a Rhodes Scholarship and earn a doctorate in economics.

Such a diverse pool of talent resulted in an extraordinarily creative and dynamic environment, and also a very competitive one. Everyone felt part of Terra Firma, but everyone wanted to excel. One of my senior team members, Julie Williamson, told me that her husband had informed her that she hadn't eaten a single meal at home for sixty-three days straight, instead eating all three meals a day (including on Saturdays and Sundays) at the office. We took working long hours to a whole new level.

Having raised the money, we began buying businesses and transforming them – applying the simple strategy we had outlined to all those sceptical investors. It paid off. In those early years, there was a strong correlation between the improvements we made to a business and its ultimate valuation, and a similarly clear correlation between the amount of hard work we put in and the profits that we and our investors made.

Our first success came with our purchase of the German motorway services group Tank & Rast (German for 'Fill-up and Rest'). The company had a virtual monopoly along the

German autobahn system and served around 500 million visitors every year. It was run like a real estate business, with thirty- or forty-year concessions from the German government, rents from 276 tenants and commissions from oil companies to sell fuel. In some cases, a petrol forecourt, restaurant and shop sitting on either side of one particular stretch of autobahn could all well be run by completely different people.

It all looked financially pretty healthy – until you benchmarked the business against its international peers. Only 6 per cent of Tank & Rast's potential customers were actually stopping at their outlets, as compared with twice that proportion in the UK, France or Italy. Of those who stopped, only half did so to spend money – as compared to 75 per cent of visitors in the UK. The reason the company made a profit was because it charged so much for fuel, but the fuel was not a popular brand. Motorists, we discovered, would sooner leave the autobahn and go to what was described as an autohof – a service station close to a junction off the autobahn – than go to a Tank & Rast station. The money they saved outweighed the small amount of inconvenience involved.

Once we had acquired the business, we consolidated the operation of 400 sites under 150 of Tank & Rast's most effective tenants, renegotiating their agreements and implementing initiatives that would help improve performance. But the most important change we made was to the toilets. Terra Firma's Julie Williamson pointed out that while we were trying to find ways to attract more custom by overhauling fuel and food, we were ignoring the main reason why people stop at motorway service stations. She also pointed out that Tank & Rast's toilets were in a terrible condition. Generally constructed out of prefabricated concrete blocks and stuck in the middle of the car park, they looked and smelled atrocious. Invariably, there would be a little old lady from

Eastern Europe standing outside holding a toilet roll in one hand and a begging bowl in the other.

As we considered a solution to the toilet problem, we came across a proposal buried in the company archives to spend €100 million on a bathroom upgrade. It had been met with an unenthusiastic response from their tenants, who questioned how the economic model for it would operate, and it had been rejected by the previous shareholders. But for us it was a very useful starting point. First, we cut the cost of the programme to €60 million by standardising the type of toilet we were going to install: self-flushing, self-cleaning, all the same size and all the same colour. Then we negotiated with each German state to introduce a voucher system – if you spent fifty cents on a trip to the toilet, you got fifty cents to spend in the restaurant. The revenue generated in this way would help to cover the cost of the upgrade while simultaneously not costing customers anything as long as they used the restaurant too.

When we bought the business, customer satisfaction with the toilets was languishing around 35 per cent. By the time we'd finished it had reached 97 per cent. The success of Tank & Rast's bathroom upgrade prompted us to develop Sanifair, a subsidiary of Tank & Rast that licensed clean toilets and the voucher system to railway stations and shopping centres.

Having solved the toilet problem, we then centralised procurement and standardised signage. We also introduced branded food outlets, such as Burger King. This was a controversial move. Some tenants argued that we should continue promoting the traditional German food currently available: bratwurst, pork knuckle and beer. But as we pondered whether to be a cultural fitter or a cultural breaker, it struck us that if German motorists were driving 400 miles on an autobahn, pork knuckle and beer might not be what they wanted or needed. We risked the fast food option. And we were proved right.

We did get one thing completely wrong. Tank & Rast had a chain of hotels that were very tired and very cheap. Remarkably, though, they also had a very high occupancy rate, often turning rooms more than once a day. We looked at the locations, did the numbers and decided we should upgrade them and turn them into conference hotels. We took on a partner who had done something similar in France with great success, then we refurbished a number of hotels and waited for bookings to increase.

What actually happened was that bookings went way down. We were bewildered. The penny finally dropped when a local explained that the hotels' biggest customers had been couples seeking a quick illicit liaison or prostitutes serving lorry drivers. They didn't want or need shiny, well-lit atriums. Quite the reverse, in fact. Now that the hotels had been spruced up, clients were worried that they might bump into a boss or colleague attending a conference. Add to that our higher room prices and a policy of no longer letting a room for four hours at a time, and it should have come as no surprise to us that lorry drivers had now decided that their cabs were big enough for a 'quickie'. It was a classic instance of failing to understand our customers.

The hotels were eventually successful, but it took quite a few years and by that time, the Anglo-French alliance had been disbanded and the hotels were being run by Germans again. Even so, the venture overall was successful. Earnings grew to €180 million in 2007 and to €236 million in 2014. We were able to distribute more than five times the original investment to Terra Firma Fund II and other investors in roughly three years. And when we finally sold, in 2015, to a consortium of Allianz Capital Partners and several other infrastructure funds, we had achieved a total return of seven and a half times on the original investment.

Another deal we did in the early days of Terra Firma in a way represented a return to my Angel Trains days – but this time with aircraft. In March 2006 we purchased aircraft leasing company Ansett Worldwide Aviation Services (AWAS) from Morgan Stanley for $2.5 billion. Mayamiko Kachingwe and his colleague Riaz Punja had pointed out that the number of commercial aircraft in service was expected to double to 30,000 by 2030 and that this represented an extraordinary opportunity to grow businesses that leased aircraft to airlines. In 2006, they explained, approximately a third of aeroplanes were being leased to commercial airlines and the proportion was rising.

AWAS had been set up by Rupert Murdoch's News Corporation and a Belgian leasing company in 1985. It had started life with an order with Boeing for twelve 737–300s. Over time, it became a major player, finally attracting the attention of Morgan Stanley, which bought the business in 2000. Then came 9/11. The aviation market plunged, and Morgan Stanley's interest cooled even though the valuations eventually ticked back up.

By the time we bought the company the average age of the aeroplanes it owned was twelve years. That made them unattractive to the premier airlines, which meant that they were rented out to airlines with lower credit ratings, with all the risks that those ratings entailed. Our aim was to take out as much cash from the older aircraft as we could while bringing down the average age of the portfolio by buying new aircraft. But since the waiting list to buy new aircraft was between three and six years, we opted for Plan B and bought another leasing company – Pegasus Aviation Finance Company – with a younger fleet that we could bolt onto AWAS. As the average age of our aircraft dropped to seven and a half years we put ourselves back in a zone where the big airlines would deal with us. At the same time, we went from being a bit player to being number three in the market, with forward orders with Boeing for thirty-five new aircraft in the pipeline. Our fleet now had an independently appraised asset value of over

$8 billion. And to achieve longer-term growth, we put in an order at heavily discounted prices on seventy-five Airbus 320s and thirty-eight Boeing 737s worth $4.5 billion.

Most aircraft last for twenty-five years, which means you can budget for three lease changes in each lifespan. We made our money from the spread between the rent we charged airlines and the financing costs we paid to acquire our aircraft. If you lease a brand new plane to the likes of Singapore Airlines, you will make up to a 9 per cent gross return in terms of rental to aircraft value. If that plane is then leased to a riskier mid-market airline when it's eight or nine years old, which is the usual pattern, then rents increase and returns can go up to 13 per cent. By the time it is seventeen years old, returns could be as much as 20 per cent.

Even in good times, of course, airlines go bust. Such airlines tend to be start-ups, and so our policy was to lease them our oldest aircraft, factoring the risk we were taking into our financial calculations. Even then, there's a risk because when an airline starts running into trouble, it often cannibalises its fleet for spares. AWAS had leased five Airbus A320–200s to Indian entrepreneur Vijay Mallya's low-cost carrier Kingfisher Airlines. The company was perpetually suffering losses so we stationed someone at Kingfisher's main hub in Bangalore to keep an eye on the aircraft and make sure nobody was taking them apart. Kingfisher finally ceased trading in 2013 when the Indian aviation authorities scrapped its domestic slots and international flying rights. It cost us $35 million to repossess those aircraft and re-lease them, but Kingfisher continued to pay us the full market rental and maintenance throughout. We had made a sufficient profit on the deal to cover the repossession costs.

Kingfisher wasn't our only challenge. Some of the planes we bought got caught up in a coup in Fiji. Some were impounded in Iran, and had their seats torn out to transport lambs during Eid. I was constantly and acutely aware that we had to diversify our portfolio if we were ever to create a business someone would want to buy from us. Otherwise, all we would have done was invest in a declining cash cow whose leasing model involved constant risk. The downside was the cash that the existing planes would absorb before they were scrapped. The upside would be apparent if we could grow the company, diversify its credit mix, extend the expected remaining life of the planes and refinance it more cheaply.

Hence the risk we took with Hawaiian Airlines. At the time there were two airlines serving the Hawaiian Islands – Aloha Airlines being the other – and it was clear that only one independent local carrier could survive in the long term alongside the international carriers that flew there. When looking to diversify I always sought to keep the credit of individual businesses at under 5 per cent of the portfolio – in fact, ideally 2 per cent – and here was Hawaiian Airlines at over 10 per cent and facing potential bankruptcy. Cold logic dictated that we should walk away, but over several meetings and a couple of dinners I formed the view that the management team was good and decided to stay with them. It proved the right call. In the end, it was Aloha that went out of business and Hawaiian, having become effectively the only large inter-island airline, started to make reasonable profits.

GOL Aerolineas in Brazil posed a still greater challenge. It had completely run out of money, and we had fifteen to twenty planes with them that were being pillaged for parts. I decided to send in my Three Musketeers: Mayamiko; Georg Kulenkampff, our German operating managing director and along with Mayamiko, one of the two senior people responsible for AWAS; and Lorenzo Levi, a very bright Italian analyst with a tendency to debate everything and anything until anyone who disagreed simply gave up (I had often found myself closing the door on him while he continued to argue on the other side – only to hear him still arguing when the door was shut). The team's mission was very simple. Go down to Brazil, locate the planes, recover the stolen parts, have them replaced, persuade a judge to hand the planes over to us and find pilots to fly them out. And do this without getting killed.

The combination of legal expertise, a handful of pilots and the determination and courage of the Three Musketeers resulted in us getting all our planes returned in flying condition, if missing a few bits (what on earth someone used the luggage bins from one of our planes for we never worked out). We'd lost money, but at least we still had planes (not all leasing companies were so lucky).

This was nail-biting stuff, but I don't think I appreciated how frightening aircraft leasing could be until the day I got a phone call from a mate in the airline industry. He informed me that he'd heard on the grapevine that a certain Russian was so angry with AWAS that he was threatening to kill me, my family or someone close to me in Terra Firma. (I was no stranger to what angry Russians are capable of – I remembered all too clearly the 1995 oil offtake deal that brought me to a bloodstained and bullet-sprayed concrete bunker 50 miles outside of Moscow, trying to reason with a man named Big Peter.) I immediately sought the advice of Kroll – a world-class private intelligence and security service – who had sometimes helped us in the past. Their advice was chilling: we had to solve his problem. I was told that this particular individual tended to carry out his threats, and that there was no guaranteed way to ensure our protection. We had to negotiate a deal.

The issue was that he wanted a Boeing Dreamliner for his own personal use and one of our South American salesmen had, without our knowledge and certainly without our authorisation, already taken a $20 million payment for agreeing to supply one – but we didn't have one to hand. The Russian oligarch wasn't prepared to accept either repayment of the $20 million or repayment plus another $20 million in compensation. If anything, our offer just seemed to make him angrier.

In the end I asked Stephen Alexander, an operating managing director who had taken over responsibility of AWAS from Georg, to do the only thing we could – speak to Boeing and explain the problem. I was convinced they must have seen this happen before. They had. A plane on lease to a third-party Southeast Asian airline made its way to the Russian, who had it stripped out and fitted to his personal specifications. He was apparently very happy with his purchase, and I was told that I had been invited to have a look around and perhaps even take a flight in it. I was not tempted.

One way or another, AWAS was a challenge. But our hands-on and down-to-earth approach paid dividends. We made huge operational changes, cut some massive expense accounts and improved corporate governance and best practice. A large number of managers and employees left in the first few months and during our ownership we changed many more. By the time we sold the business, it had gone from being a gun-slinging, entrepreneurial, seat-of-the-pants operation to a professional, well-run, risk-evaluating corporate finance business, which just happened to have aircraft as collateral. In 2015, we sold a portfolio of eighty-four aircraft for $4 billion to the Macquarie Group. In April 2017, we sold the remaining portfolio and the business to Dubai Aerospace Enterprise for more than $7.5 billion, making 1.6 times the cash-on-cash return for our investors. It wasn't the result we had hoped for but bearing in mind just how tough the credit crash in 2008 had made things, and in comparison with the record of other aircraft-leasing companies, it was an extraordinary achievement. We had created a diverse customer base of eighty-seven airlines in more than forty-five countries and gone from being a company that leased 15 per cent of its fleet to the tiny Hawaiian Airlines to one whose largest customer was the Russian flag carrier Aeroflot. AWAS's operating profit before tax went from $35 million to $273 million at its peak.

Our success went further than AWAS and Tank & Rast. In twelve great years, Terra Firma – and the Principal Finance Group before it – had acquired and sold fourteen companies and delivered a world-beating 41 per cent compound-annualised rate of return for our investors. For our investors in Terra Firma Fund II, we had already made a net profit of €400 million and returned all their money within two years (normally it takes five to seven years to return all an investor's money). We'd also made a lot of Terra Firma employees very wealthy. As one of my senior lieutenants said to me at the 2006 Christmas party: 'Guy, the twenty of us who've stuck with you have earned nearly half a billion euros in thirty months. I wonder what those bastards who left the sinking ship are thinking now.'

Terra Firma nevertheless faced real challenges. We had achieved financial success far beyond anyone's expectations. But investors had concerns. What was Terra Firma about other than Guy? What was the succession plan? Was there a succession plan? Where were the checks and balances? Why does Guy never have time to see us? Why are his staff so tired? And why are the teams working on particular deals constantly changing?

I realised that while Terra Firma might have gone from nothing to the hottest European private equity company in just four years, it had to become more institutionalised. If we were to grow, if we were to do an initial public offering (IPO) as investment banks were trying to get me to do, I needed to hire people to fill boxes on organisational charts, with the right skills and CVs – people I would never get to know and who might never fully appreciate our original culture.

Me, aged fifteen months, with the family dog, Shawn.

In Judd school uniform, aged twelve.

Me, aged seventeen.

Julia (in one of her hand-knitted jumpers) and me on her eighteenth birthday – she was not quite sure what she had landed, but she knew my jumper wasn't as smart as hers.

Honing my photography skills in the bluebells with Julia, who has just turned eighteen.

The Oxford University Conservative Association hustings, 1979. The Tory Reform Group, at whom I am gesticulating, won all four officer roles but Richard Old (second from left) switched sides after the election to me and the Magdalen faction, and became unbeatable.

Me in one of Julia's jumpers. I was speaking to an empty chamber at the Oxford Union. In order to run for office one had to make two qualifying speeches each term. By the time I had built up enough courage to speak, attendees had left for the bar.

Trying to sell a picture of Fowey, Cornwall, to a bemused Oxford resident.

Goldman Sachs trader, 1982. No computer, no electronic trading, just row on row of direct push-button phone lines.

With my best man, William Hague, on my wedding day.

Further honing my photography skills with Julia on our honeymoon in Rome.

My first significant public securitisation, Pearl Street.

Forming PFG at Nomura.

PFG at Nomura, 1996. Desktop computers w
well named, as they dominated the desk.

Contract chaos over the Millennium Dome was
the public reason for killing the deal, but the truth
was the deal was already dead when the Mayor of
London insisted that people arrive only by public
transport.

News

Japanese bank realised that it didn't know exactly what it was paying £105m for, reports **David Millward**

Troubled zone: figures estimating the number of visitors to the Millennium Dome at Greenwich were shown to be 'wildly optimistic' and caused alarm at Nomura

Contract chaos kills Dome deal

Four ministers will decide its future

Angel Trains – the deal that mad
my reputation and provided suffi
financial support for life, or so I
thought.

The Terra Firma offices, London 2004. With computer screens having advanced so much in the previous ten years it was possible to design a truly open-plan office.

mping ship and going solo. I might be iling but the arm bands weren't going to e me from the sharks.

At the Terra Firma offices,
London 2005.

Two of the Three Musketeers, Mayamiko Kachingwe (far left) and Lorenzo Levi (far right), having arrived safely back from outh America; pictured with colleagues at the AWAS head office in Dublin.

On my way to the EMI staff meeting at the Kensington Odeon in London, January 2008.

Over 50 per cent of EMI staff were let go; almost all senior-level staff were released from their contracts. Meanwhile, market share increased and cashflow moved from £100 million a year negative to £250 million a year positive.

STILL KEITH, I DO HAVE SYMPATHY FOR THE DEVIL

TERRA FIRMA

UBS ACTION

STONES QUIT EMI

BAKER TILLY LAWSUIT

STONES

ROBERT THOMPSON

The Rolling Stones leave EMI after sixteen years.

THE TIMES
Obama flies in to fortress London

I leave the UK for Guernsey after 47 years, 1 April 2009.

Arriving at court with Julia and David Boies in New York, November 2010.

Terra Firma's twenty-first anniversary party at the Old Royal Naval College, Greenwich, 2016.

EverPower windmill. Trump put paid to ~~re~~ being a pot of gold at the end of the bow.

Deals, deals and yet more deals.

The proud owners of 435 McDonald's restaurants in the Nordics where, together with approximately 200 direct employees, 75 franchisees and 20,000 restaurant managers and crew members, we serve approximately 150 million meals a year. My favourite job, even if I paid over £400 million to get it.

Supporting CPC's initiative to raise awarene[ss] for mental health issues, 2021. The shirt is designed to get people talking. Lots of sma[ll] conversations amongst lots of people will solve the big problems of today, not direct[ly] from the top.

In a traditionally male-dominated industry, [it] employs approximately fifty jackaroos and [ ] jillaroos. They look after 250,000 cattle loc[ated] across more than 6.5 million acres, largely s[ ] in the Australian Northern Territories. The [ ] of climate change on the Australian outbac[k is] front and centre every day.

Giving back: the Hands Building, Mansfiel[d] College, Oxford. Since Julia and I started to support Mansfield in 1999, the ratio of stat[e] school entrants there has risen to 96 per ce[nt] – the highest of any Oxbridge undergradua[te] college. Being able to support Mansfield an[d] witness its success at promoting the advant[age] of diversity and inclusion over the past twe[nty] years is what I am most proud of.

THE
HANDS
BUILDING

Meanwhile, the banks, and particularly Citigroup and my closest business confidant Michael Klein, who was aiming to be Citi's CEO, were pointing out just how much Terra Firma could be worth if I raised another fund and took Terra Firma public. With that thought echoing in my brain, I set out on another money-raising odyssey. The previous experience had been quite extraordinarily tough and draining. This time it seemed easy. Within six months we had raised €5.4 billion, which was €400 million over the amount I had agreed to as our initial cap, and €3 billion less than what we could have brought in from other investors impressed by our track record and strategy. Had we maximised what was on offer, that would have made it the second biggest private equity fund ever raised. As it was, it was already the largest second-time fund. Terra Firma Fund III was raised from 160 worldwide blue-chip investors, giving us a total of 220 investors.

The success was dizzying, if a little frightening, but there were dissenting voices. While most of my investors at the time wanted me to raise more money, Canada Pension Plan (CPP), which had proved so critical to getting Terra Firma Fund II off the ground, wanted me to raise less. Mark Weisdorf, who had quizzed me five years earlier about whether I was best suited to running a big organisation, had moved on and his successors were worried I didn't have the correct leadership structure in place. Goldman Sachs – so often right – similarly declined to invest. One former colleague said to me: 'Guy, I'm saying this to you as a friend: things are bound to go wrong. You need to pause.'

I thought I had the business under control, but the swelling workforce and the short period of time they'd been with me should have set off alarm bells – and certainly would have done if I had been a potential purchaser rather than the actual owner. Of the 128 people we had working for us in 2006, more than 100 had been hired in just the previous two years. Moreover, although I didn't realise it at the time, we had lost our mojo. We were no longer a bunch of outcasts who saw things in technicolour. We had become a corporation whose sole reason for existing was to generously feed more and more mouths.

In my desperation to find a partner, I ended up hiring twenty-three managing directors, all reporting directly to me, all wanting to be 'The One' and all resenting anyone who looked as though they might stand between them and me. I had developed the business from something I could just about manage on my own into something that needed a traditional organisational structure and good management. And as with so many entrepreneurs, organisation and management are not skills at which I excel. I know what both look like and I can structure the rules. I'm just not very good at following them. I might have been forty-seven, but I was still running my business in the same way that I'd run my art business back when I was eighteen. It was effectively all about me, 'The Guy'.

While I was grappling with the institutional and structural challenges that Terra Firma now faced, I was also becoming increasingly uneasy about the broader economic picture. In a number of speeches at the time I said that I worried that private equity prices were too high, that the market might well collapse, that there might be a banking crisis. In such circumstances, I argued, the best strategy might well be to sit on one's hands and do nothing. I even went so far as to get one of our advisers on political and economic matters, Lord Birt, former head of the BBC and Tony Blair's strategy adviser, to arrange for me to see the Cabinet secretary, Gus O'Donnell. Over lunch with him at the Savoy Grill, I talked of my fears about the strength of the banks and my sense that their balance sheets were too stretched. Gus persuaded me that my concerns were misjudged.

As we went into 2007, we got everyone at Terra Firma to vote on what we should do with the enormous pot of new money we had raised. Three paths were open to us. We could go out and invest it right away. We could start to invest but do so cautiously and slowly. Or we could put everything on hold for a few months, and then look at things in the autumn again. Bill Miles and I voted for option three. Option one received overwhelming support.

So bullish was the market about us that investment bankers saw Terra Firma as a prime candidate for an IPO. After all, Blackstone was about to list its shares on Wall Street with a valuation of over $30 billion (the offering would value the personal wealth of Blackstone's chairman and chief executive Stephen A. Schwarzman in excess of $10 billion). Bankers – including my friend Michael Klein at Citi – told me that the implied value of our management company, based on between 20 and 30 per cent of the assets under management for private equity firms, was around $2.5 billion. They tried to persuade me to sell 20 per cent of the firm for a minimum of $500 million, with more to follow over time. They suggested a US listing because they felt it would help me get US investors into Terra Firma funds in the future.

In the end, the banks couldn't persuade me to do an IPO. My fear that the markets were overvalued led me to worry that while I could sell 20 per cent of the business in the IPO and get $500 million, that would still leave me with 80 per cent of the business and therefore in a situation where I would have public investors who would be upset when the share price went down, as I believed it inevitably would. I either wanted to sell 100 per cent or keep control of 100 per cent. I didn't want, on the one hand, to receive a lot of money but, on the other hand, not actually exit our portfolio businesses. And the thought of having to report to a public board, endure quarterly earnings calls and speak to analysts about how the business was going, all filled me with dread.

It's possible that if I'd had the right management structure in place I might have gone for it. Given how those firms that went public at the time did, perhaps I should have done it. But I didn't.

In April 2007 I ventured on the last deal that I was to run personally at Terra Firma. Stefano Pessina, executive deputy chairman of the Alliance Boots group (which ran Britain's iconic high street pharmacy chain), had teamed up with buyout group Kohlberg Kravis Roberts (KKR) to take the business private. If he was successful, it would be another feather in the cap for a man who had transformed his family's ailing drug wholesaler business in Naples into Alliance UniChem through a string of deals, and then led the £8 billion merger with Boots in 2006 – a transaction that left him with a 15 per cent stake. The merged company had around 3,000 retail outlets, including more than 2,500 health and beauty stores, pharmacies and optician practices in the UK as well as operating 380 drug distribution depots across Europe.

The Alliance Boots board had rejected a £10-a-share takeover bid from Pessina's consortium but an increased offer of £10.40, valuing the company at £10.2 billion, persuaded directors to open the books. We for our part joined forces with the Wellcome Trust, the UK's largest medical charity but also a large institutional shareholder, to explore a bid. I intended to attack the deal in the same way we had when we were buying pubs – by forensically examining the business on a more or less store-by-store basis. We sent people out to hundreds of Boots branches to count customers and watch what they were doing. I spent an afternoon in a Boots, clicker in hand, observing what people spent their money on and how they circulated around the shop.

What we discovered very quickly was that most of the space in the stores wasn't being used well. Having rung several retail bosses to seek their wisdom and, maybe, their partnership in the deal, I concluded that the logical move would be to sell off or rent out all the space that was making no money – which was most of the space devoted to anything that wasn't related to health or beauty. Such a move would, on its own, enable me to recover 50 per cent of the purchase price. The deal was a steal.

Other opportunities suggested themselves. Boots' food and drink offering struck me as dreadful. No one could have been worse at sandwiches, sushi, coffee and soft drinks; only people already there to pick up a prescription could possibly ever consider buying lunch as well. I made a round of calls and found that we'd have to join a bidding war to gain concession space.

Then there was health and beauty. My interest in Boots had originally been piqued by a conversation with the owner of a small independent chemist chain in which he said that he was sure his profitability on medicine was greater than what Boots reported as a percentage of turnover. That Boots, the market leader, could be making a smaller margin selling drugs than a far smaller chain seemed extraordinary to me. What became clear as we did our due diligence was that Boots was losing a lot of money on its retail business, and that was dragging down its pharmacy business. There was an opportunity here to make a lot of money if the retail business could be sorted out or shrunk. The pharmacy business was very stable and highly profitable. About 85 per cent of its custom was repeat prescriptions, which made it an astonishing cash cow. And 85 per cent of those repeat prescriptions were paid for by the government. It was an incredibly monopolistic, profitable business and it was not going to change.

One way or another, I concluded that the business was worth vastly more than its market valuation – at least double the £10 billion that was being touted. For our bid to be successful, however, it would be essential to keep my partners positive. Terra Firma on its own certainly didn't have the money to bid for the whole of Boots. As we entered the bidding war with KKR, we were relying on the continuing support of the Wellcome Trust and the Bank of Scotland. Other commitments and distractions meant that perhaps I didn't give our partners the attention they needed.

On 17 April 2007, we tabled an indicative cash offer of £10.85 a share and asked for additional due diligence. Three days later, KKR went to £10.90 so we responded with an indicative £11.15 offer that valued Alliance Boots at £10.8 billion. Our offer was higher than Pessina and KKR's. Nigel Rudd, the chairman of Alliance Boots, agreed to allow our consortium access to senior management and the company's books to give us a chance to make our more attractive offer firm. However, following talks with KKR and Pessina that went on through the night the Alliance Boots board recommended an increased KKR bid of £11.39, or a total of £11.1 billion, which is what they ultimately paid. KKR started buying shares in the market, and we knew it was all over. We had got the shareholders £2 billion more out of Pessina and KKR. But we had lost the deal.

Over the years, I've occasionally fished off Kona in Hawaii for marlin and tuna. My younger son once caught a bluefin tuna out at sea with a value at the quayside of over $1,000. The rule is that the captain of the boat gets the fish. Our captain would have had the tuna flash-frozen and flown overnight to the Tsukiji fish market in Tokyo, where the world record for a single bluefin was $1.76 million in 2013 (it weighed 489 lb, whereas my son's was a mere 240 lb).

When fishing for marlin and tuna, you try to avoid the barracudas because they can rip your gear apart. I always release them if I happen to hook one. If you land one, you have to be very careful how you handle it, particularly if you don't have metal gloves on. It can take a bite out of your leg or arm.

Pessina got my tuna. The next bite on Terra Firma's line was a barracuda – EMI.

CHAPTER 8

Buying the Dog

Well it's a dog eat dog
Eat cat too
The French eat frog
And I eat you
Businessman, when you make a deal
Do you know who you can trust
Do you sign your life away
Do you write your name in dust

AC/DC,
'Dog Eat Dog'

I've always admired David Bowie's quirkiness, intelligence and willingness to be different. I liked the fact, when I was young, that he came from a part of the country near where I was living – Bromley, on the border of Kent. I liked him even more after the 1986 film *Absolute Beginners* in which he featured on the soundtrack alongside Sade and the Style Council. The film also allowed me to claim a link with him, however tenuous: the property in Pimlico that was the main character's house in the film was actually one Julia and I had recently bought.

David Bowie and I had one other thing in common: we both embraced financial securitisation. In 1997 he struck a licensing deal with EMI for his back catalogue, as well as unreleased studio and live recordings, whereby he securitised his rights and turned them into $55 million of Bowie bonds, offering a 7.9 per cent annual coupon. Moody's blessed the deal with an investment-grade credit rating. The following year, he founded the technology company Ultrastar and his own internet service provider-cum-fan club, Bowienet. His website sold promising art students' work without the high commissions of bricks and mortar galleries. Why did he do this? Because he could see the way the music industry was heading.

In 2002 he gave an interview to the *New York Times* in which he warned that 'the absolute transformation of everything that we ever thought about music will take place within ten years . . . Music itself is going to become like running water or electricity.

You'd better be prepared for doing a lot of touring because that's really the only unique situation that's going to be left.'

David Bowie wasn't the only person with a crystal ball. After his original deal was handled by Manhattan investment bank Fahnestock & Co and the bonds sold to Prudential Insurance, Nomura's Ethan Penner established a $1 billion fund to invest in the fledgling entertainment bonds market. With Ethan's departure, his department came under my control, but my brief at that time did not include building on what he had done. Others, though, reckoned they saw potential in this kind of venture. Between 1997 and 2007 several banks sought to get in on the securitisation of royalty streams.

Intellectually it made huge sense. Operationally, however, it proved impossible to do at scale. Getting a large group of artists together and agreeing a securitisation of their assets was tricky, unless, of course, you owned the assets. You needed skill and credibility to structure and execute the securitisation, to get the rating agencies to agree a rating, to service the assets, to distribute the bonds and finally to use the excess cash that came back after interest charges to build the catalogue of assets.

Even so, I became convinced that the music industry offered potential and that technology was improving to the point where many of the challenges others had faced in securitising it could be tackled. By 2004 EMI was on my radar. It fitted a model that had served me so well: it sat in a sector that was struggling with change and that I felt many misunderstood. If we approached it creatively, I could see ways in which we could transform it and increase its value.

The 1980s and 1990s had been boom times for the record industry as it switched from records to CDs, and the profits earned had served to convince the industry that it was superhuman. My analysis suggested otherwise. CD sales were a one-off success. There was no guarantee that a future technological revolution would reap similar rewards for the industry. It might, indeed, undermine it, just as DVDs wiped out the VHS industry and digitalisation later pretty well wiped out DVDs. In the meantime, the success of CDs had served to mask the very real challenges that the big players faced. The cost of discovering acts and developing them had become prohibitively expensive. An ever-increasing number of artists were simply not profitable. And the industry was shrinking. To assume, as so many record executives did, that everything could be solved by trying to push new albums down consumers' throats was dangerous in the extreme.

And that's even before the seismic technological changes coming down the road were factored in. The record companies assumed they had all the power. They didn't fully grasp that, thanks to such innovations as file sharing, the power was shifting to the consumer. Or that the compilation Christmas albums (our favourite was *Christmas with the Chipmunks*) and greatest hits collections that had proved such a brilliant way of making new money from old songs would give way to playlists that any bright four-year-old could put together.

Connected with this – and arguably worst of all – music executives hadn't yet realised they now worked in a business-to-business environment rather than a business-to-consumer environment. The music industry had lost control of the end customer. Now they were selling to retailers, TV companies, moviemakers, restaurants, advertising executives – any commercial business that used music. It was businesses, not consumers, that were willing to pay for music and they were the ones who would ultimately distribute the product for the labels, and the ones who would ensure fans would continue to listen to music and continue to fall in love with it.

By the early 2000s there were four major music groups.

Warner and EMI were independently owned. Universal and Sony were bound up in a broader conglomerate. Arguably, EMI's independence made it easier to acquire. From our point of view it also helped that, unlike the other companies, the firm was headquartered in the UK, where most of our deals were struck and where we knew the regulators and potential investors well.

EMI had nurtured so many household names. The Beatles, Rolling Stones, Pink Floyd, Iron Maiden and Radiohead ran like a spine through the history of Britain's global music success. It had also suffered a torrid time. Precisely because it wasn't part of a larger media company, it could not rely on income from cable television or Hollywood movies to offset the falling sales of an industry in flux.

While other labels were holding their heads above water, EMI had been losing market share. It had tried to merge with its closest rival, Warner, on numerous occasions, each time unsuccessfully. Leaving aside the fact that regulators in Brussels might well have deemed such a merger anti-competitive, there had been disagreements over the price at which a merger could take place and this had caused bad blood between the two companies. There was clearly an opportunity for us to throw our hats in the ring.

The problem was that we didn't have sufficient capital. Terra Firma Fund II was too small. So was Terra Firma Fund III, which we were busy raising in late 2006 with the help of Citigroup and Merrill Lynch, the two organisations that had helped us raise Terra Firma Fund II. It was possible, though, that if we combined both Terra Firma funds it might just be enough.

It was David Wormsley at Citigroup who alerted me to the fact that EMI was now a potential target. Since his days at Schroders, the two of us had numerous conversations about potential targets for Terra Firma. Sometimes we discussed business over a quick phone call, sometimes over coffee and occasionally with our wives at social events. We'd done so much business together – seventeen transactions totalling £27 billion in value and representing about 70 per cent of all the business I gave to investment banks – that I regarded him as *my* investment banker. His employers hadn't done too badly either. Through his efforts, by April 2007 Citigroup had earned more than £136 million in fees from Terra Firma. In an email to me sent the same month his boss, Michael Klein, wrote: 'As you know, Citi and David and I personally would like to work with you on every major event that is important and adds value to you.'

Things had kicked off in 2006 with abortive discussions between EMI and Permira, a large UK-based private equity firm. The market was led to believe that EMI had rejected Permira's bid because it was not high enough. In reality, it was Permira's concern that the earnings were likely to be lower than they had anticipated that caused them to back down. By mid-December, EMI was back in play and preparing itself for sale. Its executives knew they needed to find a new owner or risk being broken up and sold piecemeal, or, even worse, be taken over by a competitor who would then doubtless shed a slew of senior jobs. To get top dollar they needed to give the impression that the company was healthy and that there was more than one buyer interested.

In fact, all the signs indicated the opposite. Days into the first month of 2007, EMI had to issue a profit warning, disclosing that revenues for the financial year for its recorded music division would be down between 6 and 10 per cent. In the same statement to the stock exchange, the company announced that Eric Nicoli would move to the more conventional role of chief executive and that John Gildersleeve, a gritty Tesco veteran, would step up to become chairman. On the morning of the Brit Awards in February, the UK industry's showpiece event, a second profit warning predicted that sales would be down by around 15 per cent.

Late in April 2007 David Wormsley informed me that an auction for EMI had kicked off. He also said that the leading indicative price was £2.62 a share and that Citigroup could help with advice, financing and arranging a meeting with Nicoli to find out more. Wormsley had an inside view of the auction as Citigroup was EMI's main adviser. This was not an unusual state of affairs. Since my time at Goldman Sachs, investment banks had morphed from being advisers to institutions and traders in securities to being institutions themselves, playing on all sides of a deal. Indeed, at Citigroup, providing the financing, buy-side advice and the sell-side advice on a deal was called a 'triple play', and it was hugely profitable.

I'd already made up my mind that while from the outside EMI looked like the worst business in a terrible sector, there was potential there. Now I was confident that the transformative change it needed was practicable. Getting organisations to alter the way they operate can be extraordinarily difficult. However, if people can see that *unless* their organisation evolves the consequences will be terrible, they are more likely to accept change, particularly if change offers the possibility of rewards for those prepared to embrace it. By mid-2007 it must have been apparent to everyone at EMI that not changing would mean bankruptcy, that the status quo for vested interests simply wasn't going to hold. At the same time, they should have been able to see that a private equity route offered a substantial upside for those willing to embrace it.

Rumours swirled that everyone from Sir Philip Green through to Simon Cowell and Rupert Murdoch were entertaining the idea of making a bid. An offer had come in from Warner within a week of EMI's second profit warning. It was quickly repelled in early March. EMI disclosed the price – £2.60 a share – which looked like an attempt to set a minimum bid as a new sales process geared up. Then, a stock market statement on 18 April announced the dividend was being suspended, but at least confirmed that trading had not declined further since February. All the while a Terra Firma team was working on a deal, which they code-named Tumbling Dice after the Rolling Stones song.

Spring 2007 was a hectic time for the City. A lot of money was chasing a handful of opportunities, and prices in many industries were spiralling higher. We for our part were scheduled to close our third fund in May, having raised €5.4 billion in one year from 160 investors in twenty-six countries. It was an extraordinary achievement by any measure. In just five years Terra Firma had grown from nothing to being in the top ten alternative investment funds in the world. Nobody doubted that with this vote of confidence in our strategy we would be able to raise a €10 billion fund by 2010, which would make the business worth at least €5 billion and produce cash in excess of €250 million per year. As the sole owner of the business, I was expected to become rich beyond not just the wildest dreams I had entertained in my Goldman Sachs days but beyond anything I would have considered possible even a year before.

We were looking at various new deals around this time. There was the Alliance Boots opportunity that ultimately and frustratingly we lost out on. Earlier, we had been the underbidder for Thames Water. EMI was obviously large and risky. Thanks to our third fund, we had plenty in the kitty to pursue larger transactions – but the music giant was still, on the face of it, too large a business for us unless we could put in place a sizeable debt package and invest from more than just one fund. Whether we could create a large debt package would depend on the banks we dealt with. Whether we could use both funds would depend on whether we could get the advisory boards – the representatives of the fund investors – to vote in favour of the deal.

If nothing else, though, as David Wormsley said, it would be worth my while to meet Eric Nicoli. Interestingly, from my point of view, it had been announced in the press that EMI was exploring a securitisation of its back catalogue. If they pulled that off, it would represent a new pinnacle for securitisation and provide the music industry with a new and cheaper funding model. What was not to like? Maybe losing out on Boots and being the underbidder for Thames – both relatively safe deals but not on the face of it particularly exciting ones – was not so bad.

Nicoli and I needed to find somewhere discreet to get together if we were to avoid press attention so I chose one of our hotels, Woodlands Park, in Cobham in Surrey. We met on Sunday 6 May. Nicoli turned up in tight blue jeans, looking just like the music industry figure one would expect to encounter. He was as cool as a cucumber. He gave no hint of a suggestion that he was the CEO of a company in crisis.

Today I know that intelligent, experienced CEOs can give Oscar-winning performances if there's enough at stake. Trying to winkle genuinely useful information out of them is therefore largely a waste of time. Back in 2007, I was more naive. We talked about his family, the band he played with in his spare time and the protective view he took of his EMI team. He managed to tick all the boxes that would make me feel good about someone.

The plan he outlined for the future of the company made sense. But he said he couldn't attempt it while EMI was listed on the stock market, because it would cost a lot of money and, in the short term, earnings would be more volatile. He also gave me a good summary of the industry trends affecting the business and how these might shape EMI's performance over time. I came away from the meeting thinking Nicoli was a man I could work with. That same evening, I reignited all the work we had begun on EMI the previous November.

On the evening of Tuesday 8 May, we submitted an indicative bid of £2.65 a share to EMI's lead adviser, the boutique investment bank Greenhill. We didn't sign the requisite non-disclosure agreement until 10 May, so we had less than two weeks to conduct all our due diligence, interview EMI's senior management team, agree terms with the pension trustees and secure financing. This was because the EMI board had set a bid deadline date of Wednesday 23 May (later brought forward to Monday 21 May). Sellers often insist on short bidding deadlines to increase competitive tension and to minimise the risk of bidders dropping out, and other bidders finding out that the competition has reduced. I was used to pushing my team hard but I knew this could be too tight.

Judging from David Wormsley's view of the price at which we would need to pitch our offer, it was clear that if we were successful the transaction would be over three times the size of the average deal we had done in the previous twelve years. As the largest investor in the fund, I would be putting in up to €200 million of my own money. Back in my trading days such considerations would have immediately had me delving into the potential downsides. At places like Goldman, you quickly learn that you're only as good as your last trade. I'd seen traders who had been successful for years banished or fired for making just one mistake. Indeed, the reason I ended up running the Eurobond desk was because my boss had made a mistake when he was learning the London business. There was no forgiveness despite his thirteen years as a star trader for Goldman. In the heat and excitement of the moment, I neglected these essential lessons.

If you're a private equity company looking to buy a private company, insisting on a period of exclusivity is what enables you to understand the business before you buy it and minimises the risk of relying on information that may not be accurate. It gives you time and opportunity to extract all the information you need to make an informed decision. If, however, you are involved in an auction for a public company that leverage disappears. The seller will try to disclose as little as possible, hurry things along and rely on competitive tension for a good result. The Panel on Takeovers and Mergers – the main regulator responsible for public takeovers – is obviously there to protect the shareholders of the company being taken over, not the buyer, and will put in place timetables that tend to make it difficult for the buyer to extract as much information as they would like.

When we had bought private companies in the past we became known for being very picky, very difficult and very good at chipping away on price. Now that we were trying to buy a public company, those tactics weren't available to us and, according to the rules of the takeover code, we ran a real danger of running out of time. Due diligence would only get us so far. We had to rely on third parties who already knew the company. Provided, we thought, those third parties believed in EMI and had skin in the game, we should be all right.

Although Citigroup brought us the deal and were aggressively pitching to be the funder, we initially talked to other banks if only to benchmark what Citi were proposing to charge. Citi made it clear that they would be able to get there quicker because they knew the company well and had confidence in the credit. But other banks were very interested, too. The fees for arranging a bridge loan on a complex securitisation like this would be far higher than those on a traditional corporate loan. And, of course, EMI, with its extraordinary roster of talent – from Pink Floyd to Kylie Minogue – would not only offer a securitisation deal on which they could dine out for years but would afford them the ultimate calling card for other ventures.

But there were catches there, too. Any bank that came in on

the deal would have to provide Terra Firma and me with a loan that was probably beyond their traditional limits. Furthermore – in my eyes – this was not the usual short-term bridge loan to a securitisation, but a loan that we would have to rely on if, for any reason, the securitisation couldn't be done. To give us time to implement a turnaround at EMI, we would also need that loan to be in place for seven years – far longer than the maximum two years a bridge loan tended to run for. It's this kind of scenario that helps to explain why in most banks there were strict divisions between credit lending and structured finance – the loan teams and the securitisation teams – to ensure that those in charge of the loan book did not have undue pressure put on them by bankers trying to earn a healthy bonus.

We found ourselves in a double bind: to do the securitisation we first needed the company but to buy the company we needed a good corporate loan in which the covenants, term and pricing would be stretched to their limits. Ultimately it was the time factor that proved conclusive. The other banks we spoke to felt uncomfortable about the speed at which they would have to move. Only Citi said they were able to deliver the funding needed in the time frame available.

Even with Citi, the set-up was far from ideal. Like us, they would be taking a considerable risk. And while they would be lending because they had confidence in us, we understood that – not wishing to hold a $5 billion exposure to a UK music company – they would want to sell their position down very quickly. We needed a collaborative relationship where both sides would make money, but where Terra Firma would have the time – seven years if the securitisation couldn't be done – to execute our business plan. What we were going to face was a relationship with a bank who, if things went badly, would be desperate to get out.

On Tuesday 15 May, Terra Firma's Investment Advisory

Committee (IAC) met to consider whether to keep working towards a bid for EMI, and recommended that we continue. Afterwards, Tim Pryce – Terra Firma's general counsel – asked whether it would be possible to get the bid completed in time. He also expressed a concern that we'd face the same challenges we had when bidding for Alliance Boots – where we did not have support from Citi. I assured him that the bid was worth prioritising because – as I understood it – David Wormsley was keeping us informed about other bidders and would help arrange the necessary financing.

The following day, as I was taking part in Terra Firma's annual staff conference at the Old Government House Hotel in St Peter Port, Guernsey, I received worrying news. We had not obtained approval from Citigroup's credit committee for the £2.5 billion loan that was vital for financing the deal. I rang David to establish whether Citigroup was concerned about EMI's credit. He assured me it was a technical issue that he could smooth over. The next day – only a couple of days before the bid deadline – David called me on my mobile. I passed it to a worried Tim Pryce. David told him that, although final terms remained to be agreed, Citi's credit committee had approved the financing.

According to one scenario we ran, all we needed to do to make the deal work was to sort out recorded music – the division that signs acts, manages bands and releases new albums. We'd established that about 85 per cent of EMI releases never made a profit, so the business had to become a lot more selective. At the same time, we needed to maximise the value of the back catalogue and publishing. Our aim was to pay off all the debt and return most of the equity to investors within eighteen months by borrowing against EMI's back catalogue while still owning and operating the business. In the long term, we believed we could make a fortune from selling the music copyrights that EMI had put together

over decades. I thought it was one of the most undervalued assets
we'd ever seen. Quite apart from the collected works of the many
major artists the company boasted, it also owned the publishing
copyrights to 1.3 million songs, including 'Somewhere Over the
Rainbow', 'Santa Claus Is Coming to Town' and 'Smells Like
Teen Spirit'. Every time one of these songs was played on TV,
radio, video games, advertisements or mobile phone ringtones,
EMI received a small payment. Were we to do the deal, not only
could we bolt on smaller music catalogues but we could securitise
the earnings from those catalogues alongside EMI's existing catalogue. The two things we needed were a bank that could ensure
the securitisation and a stable market.

A continent away, however, something was happening that
would have rung alarm bells had any of us realised what it
presaged. In April, New Century – a US real estate investment
trust specialising in securitisation – had filed for Chapter 11
bankruptcy protection. It was the first collapse in what would
become the subprime mortgage crisis and would eventually lead
to the great credit crash of 2008.

As the deadline for the bid approached, I decided to seek
advice from Michael Klein. I had some concerns about the profit
warnings issued by EMI in early 2007 and wanted to know
whether Citi still believed EMI to be a good investment. His
response was unequivocal: Citi was very supportive of our bid
and believed it was an exciting investment opportunity. Moreover, he added that the bank would itself have wanted to make an
equity investment in the business had it not been acting as an
adviser to EMI.

On the evening of Friday 18 May, Greenhill piled the pressure on us, saying that the bids needed to be in by Monday

morning – two days earlier than we had expected. At that point, we believed (and I still believe that David Wormsley believed) that there was one other bidder: Cerberus Capital Management. Cerberus, the American buyout fund, was small in Europe at that time but very close to Citigroup in the US. My assumption was that David would know all about its bid and would be able to give us guidance.

That same evening Julia and I went for dinner at the home of some close friends. I had to constantly excuse myself from the dinner table to answer endless phone calls. What compounded the drama was that Terra Firma was weighing two other bids at that time: InterContinental Hotels Group, an attractive proposition given the growth in their Holiday Inn brand and the sell-on value of their trophy hotels, and the hedge fund manager Man Group, whose purchase would have given Terra Firma a global platform in alternative investments (their chief executive happened to be at the dinner that night). Any one of these three deals in play could be done, but we could only choose one of them.

There followed a frantic weekend. The irony was that Citigroup, through David, was hurrying us to make a bid by Monday, while at the same time their financing team was running behind. We had received approval for our financing from the bank's credit committee, but the term sheet was still the subject of negotiation. We were going to have to trust that Citigroup would not try to re-trade the transaction after the signing of the deal.

On Saturday I went to the FA Cup Final with my younger son where we hoped to see Manchester United beat Chelsea (things went against us when Didier Drogba poked home a goal in extra time). My son, who had drawn Chelsea to win 1–0 in a sweepstake, begrudgingly accepted his winnings as blood money. I kept half an eye on the match but was more focused on putting the financing in place for EMI. I knew I didn't have enough money to do the deal unless Citigroup or another bank got there by Monday morning.

With us at the match were some Bank of Scotland financiers who worked for Peter Cummings, the banker who had backed Sir Philip Green's failed attempt to buy Marks & Spencer three years earlier. His team had helped us on the Boots project, and I had been discussing EMI with them, along with some other banks. But, as with the match, the outcome of our conversation was disappointing. They might be able to get there, they said, but not on this timescale. The deal was now dependent on debt from one of three banks and equity from both funds. We were being pushed to the limits of what we could do under the terms of our agreements with our limited partners (LPs). While the advisory boards had been consulted and had indicated their support for us going ahead, I knew that if anything went wrong, they would be unforgiving.

On Sunday I flew to Guernsey to attend board meetings with the directors of Terra Firma's second and third funds. We spent a couple of hours in an aircraft hangar at the airport conducting a strange, impromptu boardroom discussion, complete with a collection of private planes as backdrop. Having missed several meals, I found myself scoffing a plate of chocolate biscuits throughout, which wasn't the best way to calm my nerves. In the end, the board agreed to the EMI deal – subject to financing becoming available, a pension issue being resolved and no material changes being involved.

I flew back to Biggin Hill Airport in London and returned home to my attic office, where I tended to work during evenings and weekends. I was angry. Every time we thought we were close to finalising the financing package, Citigroup attempted to tweak the terms in their favour. Finally, a few minutes before midnight, we received word that Citigroup had agreed to the latest proposal.

David told me in a midnight call that Cerberus were going to bid the following morning and we needed to get our bid in by 9 am. He then informed me by email 'not to play games on price'. All along he had said they were there at £2.62 and made plain we needed to offer at least £2.65 to win the day.

At 7:30 am on Monday 21 May, the committee of the two Terra Firma boards agreed that the bid should be submitted. The lawyer preparing the final versions – who had worked non-stop through the night – struggled to scan all the documents. I lost it completely. All this work, all this time, all this pressure, all this heartache and we were going to lose the deal because someone couldn't work a fax machine. I wasn't exactly the calmest person in the room; indeed, some of our advisers who witnessed my behaviour were quite shocked. At 9:01 am, my business assistant confirmed she had emailed the bid and by 9:03 am we were in a very competitive auction – or so I believed.

There then ensued a deafening silence. I kept ringing David to find out what had happened but couldn't track him down. The lack of news was more stressful than the frantic activity that had preceded it. I became convinced that we had been beaten by Cerberus.

I now know that what happened that morning was that EMI held a series of meetings, at which Wormsley was present, that culminated in a board meeting where the two offers were supposed to be considered. In the event, however, there was just the one offer – ours. When the board realised this, they decided that they wanted it accepted and announced publicly as soon as possible. Once the announcement was public, it would be virtually impossible for Terra Firma to back out.

Suddenly, it all changed. Radio silence was replaced by action stations. Speed was imperative. 'We want you to get a press release out,' Wormsley told me when we finally spoke at around 3 pm.

By 4:30 pm, as the stock market closed, the terms of our £3.2 billion recommended cash offer had been published.

A little later that day, I attended the opening evening of the annual Chelsea Flower Show. The custom is that once the Queen has inspected the displays, the place is largely handed over to City firms, who host clients and customers at a charity gala that has become a must-attend event for the UK's public limited companies. After drinks in hospitality chalets, bankers and chief executives accompanied by their partners spill out onto the main avenue. They wander about ostensibly to view the gardens but actually to gossip.

That night Terra Firma was one of the main topics of conversation. People recognised that our takeover was a bold move and wanted to hear about my plans for the business. At the dinner we threw for clients at Kent House in Knightsbridge, some said they regarded EMI as such a terrific business for us to transform that they wanted to co-invest with us. Within a few weeks we had notched £4.9 billion of informal interest. We had followed Citi's advice and bid £2.65 a share. Once that became public the stock rose immediately to £2.71 on hopes that Warner would counterbid. In the press some investors grumbled that we had lowballed our offer and were trying to get the company on the cheap.

When you buy a private company, you reach an agreement with the seller and leave the lawyers and accountants to thrash out the details. When you buy a public company you also need to get the support of 90 per cent of the shareholders within a sixty-day window from when your offer is submitted. EMI had thousands of shareholders, all of whom needed to be contacted and persuaded to accept our offer. Shareholders are traditionally slow in coming forward to accept an offer: they want to see whether something better might be around the corner and they know that the bidder's ability to back out is legally very limited.

As I was to find out, they were right: even if everything changed, it was unlikely that we'd be able to back out of this transaction.

The weather on 21 May 2007 was wet and windy. While Gus O'Donnell's colleagues in the UK Treasury hadn't spotted anything untoward, in the US financial storm clouds were beginning to form. As June wore on it started to become apparent that US credit markets were drying up and the willingness of banks to make loans was plummeting. Bear Stearns put up $3.2 billion to bail out two hedge funds it had created to invest in subprime mortgages. Then in July 2007, they had to inform their clients that the two hedge funds contained very little or effectively no value for investors. In August, both funds filed for bankruptcy. Together, at their peak, the funds had controlled over $20 billion of assets and had been sold to a broad investor base.

So concerned was I by the early chapters of this unfolding story of disaster that on 27 June I emailed the team to ask them to check that Citigroup were still comfortable with lending us the money for EMI. Obviously the £2.5 billion loan would benefit Citigroup to the tune of more than £100 million in fees. But we also knew that they only intended the loan to be a temporary measure and that they planned to slice and dice it and then securitise part or all of it, transferring all but £40 million of the lending risk elsewhere within two years. In the process, of course, they would also earn more fees. But for all this to happen smoothly the financial weather needed to remain calm.

The skies, however, continued to darken, and with them, my mood. I started to sense that the bankers who had previously wanted to finance my every deal – including Man Group and Intercontinental – were backing off. Despite our best efforts, Deutsche Bank and Barclays, which had been competing with Citigroup to lend us money, decided not to participate in the financing. I worried that Citigroup were cooling on the deal too, and probably wanted a way out of the loan, even though we were joined at the hip on this transaction whether we liked it or not. I hoped and believed, though, that since our relationship with Citigroup was so close, the bank would support me.

Terra Firma's plan was not dissimilar to Citigroup's. We too expected to sell down our position to other institutions. Allocating 30 per cent of our second and third funds to a single takeover was a big bite. My plan was to sell down to less than 20 per cent as soon as possible. But if you are selling down equity you need to do it quickly, while people are still excited about the initial takeover. Summer was coming, but very soon it would be winter. We needed the long-term borrowing in place if we were to attract other investors.

On 12 July I was in transit in Houston on my way to a family break in the Galápagos Islands when I heard a rumour from my PR adviser that Citigroup were looking to back out of the EMI financing. When I eventually got through to Klein, he maintained that the bank remained fully committed to the transaction and any reluctance to agree terms stemmed from the shift in financial markets and from Citi's need to bring in other banks.

As July wore on, two things became clear that made the deal far less attractive. First, EMI's trading was getting weaker. Second, Citigroup were dragging their feet over fixing the facilities agreement – essentially the specifics of the debt package that had only been outlined in a commitment letter when we bid for EMI in May. Because no other banks were willing to participate, Citigroup tweaked the interest rates and debt covenants to protect themselves, making our projected returns worse in the process.

Our proposal was still to split the business into two – the recorded music and the music publishing businesses. These would have separate debt packages, which would make both the equity and debt easier to syndicate. A number of investors had expressed

strong interest in the publishing assets. Once those were separated from the recorded music assets, a sale of recorded music to
Warner looked very doable, not least because such a deal was
unlikely to raise many competition issues.

This strategy seemed to me an elegant solution to the challenges facing Citigroup and Terra Firma. It would ensure that
some of the money Citigroup had lent to Terra Firma to buy EMI
would be repaid. It would also ensure that Terra Firma could continue to own the publishing part of EMI. Unfortunately, the
relationship between the two firms was coming under huge strain
as Citigroup – one of the biggest subprime lenders in the US –
started to suffer from the developing credit crunch. The news
coming out of the financial markets was grim. Mortgage-related
issues were threatening funds at Bear Stearns, the German bank
WestLB, BNP Paribas and even Goldman's Global Equity
Opportunities Fund. It was starting to look less and less likely
that we would be able to securitise the reliable future earnings
that came from the publishing arm. All in all, it was not the deal
we hoped it would be.

I have never worked out whether Citigroup were nervous
about this deal specifically or the market in general. Either way,
the market jitters were showing up in Citigroup's overall performance. Shares in the bank slid that summer and would fall further
in 2008. Yet Chuck Prince, the group's chairman and chief executive, appeared bullish on the liquidity of the financial markets as
late as July 2007: 'As long as the music is playing, you've got to get
up and dance,' he told one newspaper. 'We're still dancing.' It was
a statement that would come back to haunt him.

The legal advice we received was that we had to let the maximum sixty-day offer timetable run its course. Acceptances had
trickled in and we had extended the deadline as far as we could.
Once keen, I was now deeply concerned. Could we issue a

statement to the stock market along the lines of: 'We have with-drawn our offer as our financing partner does not have the sufficient strength to do this,' or: 'We've withdrawn our bid because our financing partner no longer feels supportive of the deal'? Such a statement would have done the trick. At the same time, it was apparent that we – like Citigroup – could not back out without causing ourselves reputational damage. Indeed, Citi-group were warned by Simon Borrows from Greenhill that if they let Terra Firma and EMI down at the same time, they could 'ruin [their] corporate reputation in the UK, as well as put the nail in the coffin of the large integrated investment banks.'

EMI acted by forcing Warner to declare itself in or out as a bidder. On 17 July Warner declared that it had no interest in com-peting with us. Shareholders began to fall into line behind our offer. Our options narrowed. With a week to go until the end of the offer period, acceptances were at 76 per cent. Citigroup appeared no keener than us. It is common practice that the finan-cing bank waives the 90 per cent condition once a 75 per cent threshold has been passed, but Citigroup were showing little inter-est in doing so, clearly hoping the deal would flounder on its own.

Two days before the sixty-day maximum, with acceptances at only 84 per cent it looked as though it was all over. Citigroup and Terra Firma could walk away from the deal, reputations intact. But then EMI went to the Takeover Panel and requested an extension to the final deadline beyond the sixty-day maximum, arguing that a recent postal strike might have held up some acceptances. The panel agreed, leaving us in an invidious pos-ition: either we could go along with the ruling, or we could challenge both the company and the watchdog.

I had just been in Tokyo and was due to arrive in Sydney early on the morning of Saturday 28 July, so Terra Firma convened a conference call for late UK time on 27 July – two days before our offer was due to lapse – to run through the options. I landed in Sydney, went straight from the airport to the hotel and lay in bed at the Park Hyatt looking out at the Sydney Opera House feeling dazed – both by jet lag and recent events.

Just before I left Tokyo I had told my colleague Quentin Stewart, the deal-doer I was closest to, that I was erring on the side of getting out. Tim Pryce, who had spoken to our takeover lawyers, advised that this would be too difficult to do. The legal situation was complicated, the reputational issues would be impossible to deal with and there was a strong moral reason for going forward with the transaction. I dialled in to Terra Firma's General Partners meeting and listened to a long conversation in which people involved in the deal gave reasons why we had no choice but to let it go through. In the end I consented and drifted off to sleep. Several hours later, I woke up with a start, convinced I had done the wrong thing. I rang Tim to tell him that I had changed my mind. It was too late. We'd extended.

On 1 August, ten weeks after we had submitted our £3.2 billion offer for EMI, I was finally informed that it had gone unconditional – that it had been finally accepted by sufficient shareholders, and it was going to be ours. At that point we had effectively taken ownership of the company, though the precise details of the financing that Citigroup were offering us were still up in the air. By now, the passion I had felt for the music industry and how we were going to transform it had evaporated. Instead, I felt incredibly low.

When I had finished my meetings in Sydney, I took a flight to Hawaii to join Julia and the children. Before embarking I typed a rather clumsy text message: 'We've got the EMI.' The predictive text feature corrected my message to 'We've got the dog.'

CHAPTER 9

Facing the Music

When I was younger, so much younger
    than today
I never needed anybody's help in any way
But now these days are gone, I'm not
    so self-assured
Now I find I've changed my mind and
    opened up the doors

THE BEATLES,
'Help!'

We had bought the dog, the bankers were applauding the most audacious deal of the year and my team were celebrating the end of an extremely difficult process. I knew, though, that such celebrations were premature. Experience had taught me that the really hard work actually starts when the ink is dry. After all, now it's your money on the line. Furthermore, I was acutely aware that with 30 per cent of our two flagship funds now invested in the EMI deal we'd broken in a single stroke the two cardinal rules of private equity: keep your investment in any one company below 10 per cent and avoid cross-fund investments, so that one bad investment doesn't infect the results of other funds. What I hoped and assumed was that we would be able to sell enough of the company down to bring our holdings below 10 per cent.

When we started looking at EMI the market was as hot as it had been just before the dot-com crash in 2000. By the time we closed, things had cooled down enormously. The flow of cheap money that had been hiding all faults had largely disappeared. As Warren Buffett had said back in 2004 in one of his investors' letters: 'It's only when the tide goes out that you discover who's been swimming naked.' I was about to feel very exposed.

Closing the deal in August 2007 in the teeth of the financial crisis meant the chances of selling the deal down were becoming less likely by the day. I had no idea that as early as June 2006, Richard M. Bowen, the chief underwriter at Citigroup's Consumer Lending Group, had begun warning the board that they had a problem. Like most other financial conglomerates,

Citigroup held massive portfolios of collateralised debt obligations (CDOs) and mortgage-backed securities (MBSs) – the majority of which were subprime. The company had used elaborate mathematical risk models that looked at mortgages in particular geographical areas but did not allow for the possibility of a national housing downturn, or the possibility that millions of mortgage holders might default on their mortgages. For a group that bought and sold $90 billion worth of residential mortgages annually, this lack of risk assessment seems surprising.

At the time Bowen warned the board that at least 60 per cent of Citigroup's mortgages were defective in some way. Within a year that initial figure had been revised upwards to 80 per cent. He was ignored. Even after Bear Stearns nearly went under in summer 2007, Citigroup believed that the likelihood of trouble with its CDOs was so tiny that it excluded them from its risk analysis.

The Terra Firma team as a whole remained very confident that we would be able to sell down at least two thirds of our investment in EMI. I was becoming less sure by the day. Unlike most people in private equity, I had once sat at a trading desk and could still vividly remember the market crash of 1989. In any case, we couldn't even begin to sell down until we had finalised the financing with Citigroup.

And yet, when I walked into the chairman's office at EMI in August 2007, I was less immediately concerned about what the future might bring than about EMI's obsessive need to live in the past. There were photographs on the wall of everyone from Maria Callas to the Beatles and Robbie Williams. To me they were an unquestionable sign that this was a company transfixed by its own former glory; the glory of vinyl records and the profits of compact discs. Even the office ambience – black leather couches, dim lighting and garden furniture on the adjacent patio – seemed more suitable to entertaining artists than conducting serious business.

The building itself was very conventional. The only thing I remember standing out was a listening room with settees and very high-quality hi-fi. On the surface, this didn't seem an unreasonable thing to have – it was clearly people's job to listen to music after all. However, the rumours of what really happened on those settees quickly made the set-up seem less reasonable.

A conversation with Doug Morris, the chairman and chief executive of Universal Music Group, was revealing. He had been in the industry for years and knew where the bodies were buried. 'The US music industry was very dirty, but we cleaned it up in the 1990s,' he said. 'It needed doing. We made too much money, the industry had flown too high in the sky, and we did things that were politically and socially unacceptable. What I never understood is why EMI did not follow our lead. I thought you Brits were straight and square.' He hoped the new owners of EMI would prove him right.

The word was that EMI was spending £20 million a year on 'fruit and flowers', the music industry code for cocaine and prostitutes. Whatever the truth of that, there's little question that the Mayfair flat we discovered on the company books and later sold for £5.6 million was clearly there to fund staff perks and entertain journalists rather than serve the immediate accommodation needs of the talent. When I insisted on itemised receipts for all spending, I found myself receiving unwanted attention from the drug gangs of London. 'Be careful out there, I hear you're angering people,' said an acquaintance with a connection to the Metropolitan Police one afternoon, having arranged to meet me well away from the office. I started to feel that I was living in a B movie.

Soon I was having to take steps I never thought I would need to. I employed private security. My driver went on a defensive driving course. He then proceeded to demonstrate his new skills by driving through the Dartford Tunnel at high speed to shake off a motorcyclist who had been following us for some time. I hid in the footwell and tried not to throw up. On another occasion, the police had to be called when a petty drug dealer tried to enter the EMI building to see me to discuss 'the harm Guy has done to my business'.

If the drug fraternity were unhappy about Terra Firma's arrival on the scene, so was the music industry. Many were hostile behind our backs. A few, such as Robbie Williams' manager, who hurled a violent insult at me, had the decency to criticise us to our faces (he also had the decency to apologise). Among the staff at EMI views were split, but it was unquestionably the case that those at a senior level – who invariably wanted to preserve the status quo – were mostly against us. With a nod to a real-life Serbian terrorist group, they formed the Black Hands Gang with the intention to undermine me, if not get rid of me altogether.

Criticism was something I was used to and could take. Some of the deals I had done were, after all, controversial to one degree or another. As an employee of a Japanese company (Nomura) I had acquired housing from the Ministry of Defence. I had bought rolling stock from British Rail, until recently a nationalised industry. Inevitably such deals didn't play well with everyone. But whatever adverse reactions I had experienced then were nothing to what I found myself subjected to now.

At first, I tried to bring the Terra Firma tribe – which EMI wags dubbed the Terra-ists – and the Black Hands Gang together. It proved virtually impossible. Both groups believed passionately that they were right. They believed equally passionately that the other side was immoral. The Terra-ists were concerned about EMI's bad old ways. The Black Hands Gang assumed that we didn't like creative people and so we didn't like them. This simply was not true. If we'd found a creative, thriving business we would have been delighted. The problem was that the company we had taken on and so desperately wanted to turn around was living off past glories and finding little new success. One of its chief income streams – royalties from the Beatles' back catalogue – had started to flow roughly when most of the senior executives had been born.

It was profligate, too, particularly in the artists and repertoire – or A&R – department. One complaint I heard from artists early on was that each year they found that their royalty account had been charged for parties they never attended and that their earnings had decreased accordingly. Some of the money that seeped away wasn't even blown on entertainment. One senior EMI member of staff funded his wife's personal training regime as well as dinner parties, groceries and who knows what else from the company budget. It really was a case, for some people, of taking anything that they could get away with.

There was another fundamental problem. EMI's books made it appear that their record sales were higher than they actually were because they tended to report albums shipped rather than albums sold. Robbie Williams' *Rudebox* album, for example, might have looked like a huge hit on paper because so many copies were produced, but the number meant nothing until you knew what quantity had actually made their way into people's collections. In some cases, only around 5 per cent of the stock shipped ended up being sold. The balance would sit in warehouses awaiting shredding and then export to China where it would be used in road construction. In an attempt to hit quarterly targets, managers distributed what they needed to, booked the profits and worried about stock levels later. It was a classic retail trick.

The brutal truth was that EMI had not made money from recorded music for a decade. It was spending a fortune trying to find tomorrow's hits, but, effectively, it was just throwing jelly at the wall and hoping some would stick. Ultimately, it was a handful of artists on both sides of the Atlantic who were generating the lion's share of income. On top of that was the fact that EMI was late to capitalise on the growing market for digital music. In an attempt to get sales going as CDs waned, it had then struck hundreds of digital relationships with the result that 90 per cent of its digital income came from Apple (that figure rose to 99 per cent if you included the company's top ten digital partners). All in all, it was very far from being a rosy picture.

I had initially thought that we might keep the CEO, Eric Nicoli, and his team in place. Away from the glare of the public markets, perhaps they could make the big changes needed. It wasn't to be. First Martin Steward, the finance director, announced that he intended to leave. Then I came to the conclusion that Eric would have to follow him out of the door. He left in August 2007.

Ever one to speak my mind, and not always thinking what the consequences might be, I couldn't resist sharing my findings when I appeared on a panel at a Royal Television Society conference in Cambridge on 13 September 2007. The event had been programmed by BSkyB chief executive James Murdoch, who was keen to extend the media debate beyond the usual narrow confines of television. I was appearing alongside Nikesh Arora of Google to talk about my early impressions of the music industry. 'We look for the worst businesses we can find in the most challenged sectors,' I told the room of TV makers. 'We get really happy when things are really, really bad. EMI, our most recent investment, is a classic case.' I likened the challenge to what I found at Odeon when we bought the cinema chain in 2004. That company had its fair share of managers who would jet off to attend Hollywood film premieres for no obvious reason. My attitude was: 'They thought they were in the movie business, but actually they were in the popcorn business.' That line and others reported out of context were sufficient to persuade previously neutral staff, artists and managers to join the Black Hands Gang.

The farewell dinner for Eric Nicoli offered me my first opportunity to see the whole management team together. I was shocked. The table was completely dominated by middle-aged white men dressed like slightly overweight interior designers in black jeans and black shirts. There were no women, not one person of colour, and, most likely, no one under the age of fifty. The lack of diversity would have been depressing enough in any industry. The lack of diversity in an industry whose customers were not, for the most part, middle-aged white men was terrifying. As I recall, the conversation that night revolved around record deals, advances and trying to do more of the same. But as I looked round the table, I realised that these senior A&R men had no hope of spotting the next money-spinner. They had, after all, rejected Justin Bieber because they decided they 'didn't need another male teen idol'. Their assumption was that hanging out with artists made them creative. Some even tried to act like rock stars, frequenting after-parties at concerts and living a life of sex, drugs and rock 'n' roll. But they were nothing like EMI's artists or its customers. It came as no surprise to me to find out later that one new music executive, who was getting paid $20 million a year to find the next superstar, simply wasn't finding them. His taste for music was that of his generation and while I would have listened to his playlist, I wasn't the customer we needed.

So much for identifying the problems. Now we had to come up with solutions, and fast. And the first thing we needed to do in the wake of Nicoli's departure was to pick a temporary leader. The names of various Terra Firma managing directors were put forward, but none passed muster with Terra Firma's second most senior figure, Quentin Stewart. He worried that the team as a whole were too much in love with EMI to make the tough decisions that were required. He suggested that I should do the job.

I can't say the prospect filled me with enthusiasm. In fact, it was the last thing I wanted to do. I was an investor, not an operator. Taking direct day-to-day control of a company with 6,000 staff was alien to me. Besides I could recall David Farrant, head of HR at Nomura, once explaining that the Japanese do not believe that the leader should be the person running in to the centre of the battle holding the flag. One should always protect the shogun, he said. That way, rather than charge into combat, they continue to lead.

I should have observed that insight. Instead, I ultimately came to the conclusion that if someone was going to grasp the nettle it might as well be me. We needed to act quickly and decisively, hence the reason I had installed thirty-three Terra Firma people in the business when in the past I had made do with a handful. I knew that half the staff would have to go if we were to achieve the turnaround we planned. And 80 per cent of the artists would have to follow them out of the door. The sooner we began, the better. And perhaps this was one occasion when it was time for me to lead from the front.

Quentin was convinced I would need to be in charge for only a few months. Then we'd find someone else and I'd be back in my office overlooking the Tower of London and Tower Bridge. In the meantime, though, I had to wade through a quagmire of challenges. On occasion these were accompanied by miscalculations and missteps of my own making. I made it clear, for example, that EMI needed experts in areas such as consumer marketing and digitalisation. I was right, but perhaps I was insufficiently sensitive to the implicit message to people that they were yesterday's heroes and that it was the nerds who would win today. At a meeting with EMI management, I said that we all worked hard, but that the difference between Terra Firma and EMI staff was that Terra Firma people were up early and in bed before midnight, whereas the music industry typically started late and finished even later. They thought I was implying they were lazy. Having established my family's love of karaoke, a TV interviewer tried to coax a performance out of me. 'Would you sing us your favourite karaoke song?' he asked innocently. 'I heard you're really good at 'My Way'. Just give us a few bars, Guy.' The thought of my terrible singing voice being broadcast was too much for me, and I completely froze on live TV. After that I stopped doing interviews for a while and tried unavailingly to lower my profile.

My unpopularity within the building increased further when I let the UK music chief Tony Wadsworth go. He had once had a Midas touch for talent, but I calculated that in recent years his division had cost EMI £1 billion by placing bets on the wrong artists. To be fair to him, CDs were not selling at the level they once had and he was doing his best to find fresh talent. Our original plan had been to shift him into a role where he would maintain all his vital artist relationships but relinquish control of the budget. Unfortunately, he wasn't having it. 'Tony, you're a lovely guy,' I said to him, 'and you probably have a better heart than almost anyone I have met, and you know music better than just about anyone I have met. But your area has cost EMI a billion.' 'Guy, I'm having a bad run,' he responded.

Attempts to freshen up the talent pool proved problematic. Those among the younger people in the organisation who showed promise didn't have the experience. And when I brought people in from outside, some went native quicker than anything I've ever seen. Within a matter of days or weeks they would be singing a cappella competitively in the Thursday talent shows held in the atrium, when I was working in my office and longing for them to be poring over numbers.

A general atmosphere of unreality continued to hang around the place – along with a wholly misplaced confidence about actual achievement. When presented with the following year's projections, for example, I realised straightaway that they were hopelessly over-optimistic. Indeed if you added up sales predictions on an album-by-album basis you arrived at a number greater than the combined sales of the other three major labels the year before. Bearing in mind that this was at a time when the industry as a whole was shrinking, not growing, this struck me as bullishness gone mad. It was forecasting that made no attempt to engage with reality.

Rather than focus on this pretty fundamental problem, though, or address the challenge of how to improve their hit rate, EMI showed real commitment only in one area of their operations: the war against the file sharers. They were convinced that it was the illegal downloading of music that was destroying their business and, along with the other major labels, were spending an enormous amount of money, time and effort bringing legal actions all over the world. And yet even here – in the one area where the company showed genuine unity and enthusiasm – I thought their strategy was wrong. They hadn't made an effort to understand digitalisation. They didn't appreciate that it could be an opportunity as well as a threat. Our analysis showed that the file sharers were not only the biggest consumers of music, they also spent the most on it. As one young file sharer explained to me: 'I download hundreds of records each week, and I go out to buy the two or three that I like the most. I'm one of the best clients of the record labels, and yet they're trying to destroy me. Why don't you all get together and offer us a subscription model to allow us to sample music? I would happily pay a subscription for access. But I'm not laying out money for hundreds of crappy albums, when I know within the first few bars, that I'm not going to want to listen to them.'

For a while, we tried to put together a label-based digital sub-scription, but we never managed to get traction with the other labels and we didn't believe that EMI by itself could be successful. At least, though, EMI ended up with a small stake in Spotify.

In business, you need to be tribal. If you are McDonald's, you're McDonald's, not Burger King, and you have to want to beat Burger King. It's what drives you each day. It's what creates team cohesion. It's how Shaka Zulu built his empire. Ultimately, the problem that Terra Firma and EMI faced in trying to work together was that we were two different tribes with different objectives. Paradoxically, my attempt to be collegiate amid the divisions and to find a way forward arguably lessened my effectiveness as a leader. I found myself constantly listening to others, striving to see both sides of the argument and trying not to get angry or frustrated. But in so doing, I left behind the tribal mind that had worked so well for me in the past – the tribal mind that had given Shaka his success. Some historians argue that Shaka's decline began when he started to consider other points of view. Ultimately, he was poisoned. Management gurus sometimes argue for what they regard as a creatively disparate culture. I suspect they've never run a business. Ultimately, you cannot create a great tribe from a mix of people who will work till four in the morning and give their grannies for a successful deal, and those who occupied the higher echelons of EMI. If, at the same time, the leader is doing a job out of their comfort zone, while simultaneously seeking to implement a complete transformation of the music industry, the prognosis is unlikely to be good.

When I initially went into EMI, I intended to make a series of radical changes, changes that I thought would signal both that a new tribe was in charge and ensure obedience. These would have included a commitment to stop producing CDs by the end of 2012, to introduce drug testing by the end of the year and to provide each artist with complete transparency as to what was being charged to their account, and so on. Together these strategies would have constituted a manifesto for what we as a tribe believed in. However, once I was persuaded – or persuaded myself – to attempt to bring at least some of the EMI tribe along with us, the focus, speed and momentum we needed was lost. The ambitious turnaround slowed. Had we been given seven years, it would have been fine. But in private equity, you rarely have seven years. If things can't be achieved in three years, you're unlikely to be granted the chance to achieve them at all, particularly when a storm is raging in the financial markets.

Among the casualties in what followed were several key relationships. Radiohead, one of EMI's best-performing artists, quit, describing the new regime as being like 'a confused bull in a china shop'. Their main vocalist and songwriter Thom Yorke explained that what they wanted was 'some control over our work and how it was used in the future by them – that seemed reasonable to us, as we cared about it a great deal. Mr Hands was not interested. So neither were we.' As with so many tumultuous break-ups, both sides can believe they are in the right, and from where they are coming from, indeed can be. To me, the real debate with Radiohead was over the size of advance we were willing to pay them. My bean counters had come up with £1 million, pointing out that even that would be difficult to earn back given the perilous state of the album industry. Radiohead wanted many multiples of that sum. Eventually they decided to release their brilliant album *In Rainbows* on their own website, allowing music lovers to pay what they wanted. Over 60 per cent of the people who downloaded the album paid Radiohead nothing. Whether this was a good decision or a bad decision for Radiohead, and whether it was good or bad for the record industry, has been debated ever since.

In those difficult early months every critical utterance made by an artist was reported in minute detail. The singer Lily Allen, who I admired and whose music I loved, told the media: 'I hate Terra Firma.' Looking back years later I'll admit I found Lily Allen difficult, though I do admire her outspokenness and willingness to stand up for her beliefs, and I have sympathy for her when she's attacked in the press or through social media. But it's easier to be a fan of her music than be a business partner.

Not all meetings with artists and their managers were hostile. Indeed most – including my initial meeting with Lily Allen's team – were civil and cordial. There was, for example, the lunch I had with Sir Mick Jagger to discuss the Rolling Stones' new contract. We had an enormous number of people working on the Stones and we weren't making much money – they are a catalogue band. The new albums didn't sell, and the income from old CDs was small. What really worked for the Stones was touring. The bid we had in mind for their new contract – the bid we thought made economic sense – was unlikely to be what they were hoping to achieve. The only way we could boost the number and pay them more was if they did some TV work for us, put their name on a computer game and gave us a share of their concert revenues – none of which was going to happen.

It was a very pleasant lunch. We each had a glass of white burgundy and Jagger talked about his antique collection and what it was like to be a grandfather. We'd both grown up in Kent and gone to local grammar schools, so we had a few things in common. But when, with the small talk out of the way, we turned to the contract discussion, it immediately became clear that we were not going to be able to reach an agreement. We were very blunt with each other: 'Look, this isn't making much sense for us economically, but we would love you to stay because you're such an iconic band,' I said. 'But if we're going to pay you the sort of sum you want, you're going to have to do a lot of other stuff. And I'm not sure you really want to do that.' The gist of Jagger's response was just as straightforward. 'Relative to what I earn from my concerts – and I'm not sure how many more tours I'm going to do – what you're proposing is not economically interesting.' I got it. The activities we were suggesting were suitable for people seeking to build their career, not for an act that was already one of the biggest in the world.

Having cleared the air, we talked about EMI. Jagger's view was that the business was incredibly inefficient, particularly when it came to staffing levels. He was blunt. 'Every time we do a concert, EMI turns up with at least eight beautiful young women to hold the water bottles for the four of us. When I was a lot younger, a couple of really attractive women holding my water bottle would have been a real positive. But frankly, I'm a grandfather now and I can hold my own water bottle. You're spending money on a whole lot of people who are not relevant to our music.' I left the lunch thinking Jagger would have made a better CEO than me, but then he had his day job and I had mine.

A few weeks later, we put in our bid to retain the Stones and of course we lost. The split received enormous press coverage. I was on a business trip to China that week and was on a treadmill in a hotel gym when I saw the TV screens fill with pictures of me, and the newsreader announce the Stones were leaving EMI after sixteen years. I'm sure everybody else in the gym wasn't actually looking at me but it felt as though they were. Once I was back in my room, I received a phone call from my mother who had rung to check I was OK. She'd seen the story on the BBC and was really worried about me. I tried to explain that it was just a commercial decision and that the Rolling Stones didn't actually hate me.

Janet Jackson was another act where the numbers did not add up. She had a contract that befitted a megastar from the 1990s but that made no sense in 2007. Not only did we have to pay her a lot, we were also contracted to spend a fortune promoting her work. The 'wardrobe malfunction' that occurred during the half-time show at Super Bowl XXXVIII in 2004 hadn't done much for sales and Jackson had taken most of the heat for the incident, both professionally and personally. Her ambition now appeared to involve producing music that was pretty raunchy and included some S&M-inspired lyrics. We could see ourselves losing an absolute fortune on the projected album, so we paid her a large sum to go. *Discipline* was released on Island Records in 2008 and proved to be the least successful album of her career.

And then there was Joss Stone. Prior to my joining, EMI had signed her on a generous contract, which, given where the music industry was, I thought was never going to deliver financially. She came to my office to discuss her contract going forward. It was an emotional conversation. Joss was accompanied by her poodle, named Dusty Springfield, who understood that I'd rejected her owner's proposal. Dusty's reaction was to poo on the carpet.

One band that I was desperate not to lose was the Beatles. Not only did their back catalogue provide a vast percentage of the company's profits, if not all of them, but it also constituted, in prestige terms, the crown jewels of the music industry. Crown jewels, though, with a difference – not stuck behind glass but alive and constantly being reborn in different forms.

At the time all the Beatles' tracks were being remastered by Sir George Martin, who had produced the original recordings at the Abbey Road Studios, the historic recording facility that we acquired as part of the EMI takeover. The Beatles were concerned that the re-releases were being put out too frequently and were not of a sufficiently high artistic standard to help their long-term legacy. There were also significant artistic disagreements between the Beatles and Cirque du Soleil, whose 2006 show, *Love*, was based on their music.

I held various meetings with the group and their inner circle, sometimes together, sometimes separately. Yoko Ono made a huge impression on me: she had great presence and a single-minded focus on protecting John's legacy. The money seemed less important to her. Pattie Harrison, similarly, was passionate about her husband's music and about protecting him. Paul McCartney was the most commercial of them all and the least emotional about the Beatles' relationship with EMI. For him it was a very straightforward economic arrangement – he had done the numbers and realised that without the Beatles EMI wouldn't have stayed afloat. He almost never came to the meetings, choosing instead to send a representative. It was one of the reasons why he was so effective. He never placed himself in the position of personally having to make a decision in a meeting.

Ringo Starr was very friendly and very positive. At one point, when discussions were going particularly badly, he popped up to the CEO's office to see me, found I wasn't there, grabbed a bit of paper and wrote a little note to me along the lines of 'Don't let the buggers get you down. Love, Ringo.' People could be a little bit wary of Yoko and Paul, but I never met anyone in the organisation who didn't have only lovely things to say about Ringo.

Paul wanted to renegotiate the Beatles' contract, giving us some of what we wanted but also wresting other things away. When I bumped into him on a plane back from New York he was surprisingly and aggressively business like. Not at all a soft, mild-spoken creative, he was in full negotiating mode. He was sat in seat 1A, of course, and carried a couple of guitars with him. I was in 2A, directly behind. By now, EMI was starting to look shaky and rumours were spreading that we were going to be taken over. I think his view was that the Beatles had the power to starve us out, or feed us and keep us going.

The line he took would have been tough even coming from a

hardened Goldman Sachs banker. 'Look,' he said in essence, 'this is our music. You guys have it because of an accident of history. We should have it back.' Once I'd got over the fact that this was coming from a musician who had his guitar with him, I had to accept that all he was doing was laying out very firmly what his commercial view was.

The compromise we eventually struck, like so many compromises, left no one particularly happy. If we had been financially healthier as a company, we could probably have got a better result. If Paul had been negotiating alone without the pressure to agree a deal from the other three Beatles representatives, my guess is he would have pushed aggressively for an outcome more favourable to the band. He might well have secured it, given how weak our negotiating position was.

Then there was Kylie Minogue – one of my favourite artists to work with. It was extraordinary how energetic and fit she was and how hard she practised in pursuit of perfection. Her work rate was something you would expect from a sportsperson. At the same time, she was also incredibly friendly and gracious, as my daughters found when they came with Julia and me to Manchester to watch Kylie in concert.

We'd done some market research on Kylie and discovered from our panel of 20,000 listeners that there appeared to be something of a mismatch between her intended and her actual audience. At Manchester that night, her concert was aimed squarely at young girls and women. Our testing, however, suggested that she should focus on dance music and that if she wanted to build her presence in the States, she needed to cater more for the gay scene – I don't think she realised just how many of her fans were young American men. We didn't want to dictate the artistic direction she took, but we did think she and her manager might find it helpful to have sight of the information we had gathered. After all, there is something to be said for listening to an audience's views rather than the gut reaction of an A&R person.

The next time I saw Kylie perform, in Dublin, there was no doubt in my mind that the show had changed a little. Both performance and music had been tweaked. Now Kylie was accompanied by far more male dancers on stage and there was an element of the homoerotic in the spectacle. A splash zone had been introduced, too, where men could throw water around and take their T-shirts off next to the stage. It looked to me as though Kylie had found an audience she really loved and that adored her.

The fact that I was turning to market research as I examined the business led people to assume that I thought I could tell artists how to produce records. Nothing could have been further from the truth. What I was focusing on was how artists could best share their music with their fans in what was becoming increasingly a digital world. In fact I can recall only two conversations about how to actually produce music in my whole time at EMI. The first was at the Grammys where a wise old A&R guy told me: 'Guy, if the music doesn't have rhythm, it doesn't move you. If it doesn't make your feet dance, then it has nothing.' I had always listened to music in a very academic way. Thanks to the A&R man I now went on to discover bossa nova and a whole new way of thinking about emotion in music. I liken the experience to when I started considering 'mouthfeel' when drinking wine – not just what a good wine tastes like, but how it feels in your mouth before you swallow it. It is about discovering a new dimension of pleasure.

The second conversation was a consequence of the first. I had been given the new Coldplay album to listen to. Coldplay were one of the biggest bands in the world at the time and the perceived relative success or failure of their albums could move the company's share price in the days when it was still listed. There was therefore considerable pressure within EMI to release their latest album to boost that quarter's earnings. I listened to the first cut of *Viva la Vida or Death and All His Friends* and, to be honest, thought it wasn't that great – it didn't have enough rhythm and it didn't move me. The guy running A&R for Coldplay was surprised when I said, 'I think this could be tighter. It doesn't make me stamp my feet. Would you like some more time?' He responded slowly, 'OK, but I thought you needed it now.' The album, when released, was a smashing success. My sole contribution had been keeping Citigroup away from the door for a few more months, so that the creators had time to finish their work.

There's no doubt in my mind that the need to produce work by specific dates was part of the problem at EMI. Artists were under pressure to meet deadlines and when they didn't, the share price suffered. Two years earlier, in 2005, EMI's stock had tumbled when the company had revealed that a Coldplay album and another from Blur frontman Damon Albarn's Gorillaz project would be delayed. But look what happened when things got rushed. Robbie Williams delivered his album *Rudebox* on time, but from a sales point of view it was a complete flop. Everyone I spoke to in A&R at EMI told me that it would have been so much better if Robbie had been given more time.

The irony, of course, was that the image people had of me was of someone who believed exactly the opposite. They didn't appreciate that my view was that greater creativity chimed with better financial returns. EMI didn't make money on that many new releases because the amount spent promoting an album and manufacturing the CDs in those days was huge and often outweighed earnings. The company derived its income from the tail, after the music had gone into EMI's catalogue. What I wanted to do was slow down the drive to get as many CDs as possible out to the record shops. Instead, I wanted fewer, better records released. It made far more commercial sense to have thirty records that people would buy for the next fifty years and produce long-term revenue than 1,000 records that people would buy today and forget in twelve months' time. We'd bought the best catalogue in the world and my dream – commercially and emotionally – was to build upon the historic legacy of this music industry giant that had lost its way.

For the best acts I would have liked to strike some straightforward profit-sharing deals that would have meant – apart from anything else – that they would have expended less on their management entourage. For the unprofitable acts, I floated the idea of paying them a day rate while they worked on new material: a tougher deal than what they had been used to, I accepted, but a reasonable way to run a company.

Such steps, I believe, would have reaped dividends, but they wouldn't have helped with the problem created by having me as head of EMI. One of the earliest and most contrarian rules I established in private equity was my insistence that in determining the strategy for selling a business the CEO should not have a vote in the decision. Likewise, in determining the financing strategy for the business the CFO should not have a vote in the decision. The information they can provide to the shareholder is useful, but it's the shareholders who need to make the final decision – and they need to make it calmly, coolly and in a considered fashion without concern for the day-to-day noise that exists in any business. By becoming CEO I had put myself in a position where I had broken one of my own cardinal rules. I had immersed myself in the noisiest of businesses when I should have been intellectually detached. On top of all that I was leading only half the tribe – and I had abandoned my tribe back at Terra Firma to do so.

CHAPTER 10

Going Down with the Ship

When I was young
I never needed anyone
And making love was just for fun
Those days are gone

ERIC CARMEN,
'All By Myself'

Warren Buffett's famous advice to investors during the crash was to 'be fearful when others are greedy, and greedy when others are fearful'. As the credit crunch hit, most private equity companies were fearful, withdrawing into storm shelters and weathering the chaos as best they could.

Regardless, all private equity companies suffered. Blackstone Group – the largest fund in the world now – had a successful IPO a few months ahead of the crash, suffered a $502 million loss in its third quarter in 2008, wrote down about a third of its portfolio companies and for a while focused on consultancy and took the opportunity to profit by buying up distressed mortgages. Kohlberg Kravis Roberts pulled out of a proposed $8 billion takeover of audio electronics firm Harman and delayed their proposed 2007 IPO for three years. The Carlyle Group let some of their port-folio companies go to the wall – Hawaiian Telecom, the German auto parts manufacturer Edscha and the energy company Sem-Group all went bankrupt in 2008. Oaktree Capital took Buffett's advice, putting more than $6 billion into distressed debt. Leon Black's Apollo saw their home furnishings retailer Linens 'n Things go bust and ended up in a flurry of lawsuits as they pulled their investments from other firms.

To get through the crisis Terra Firma's private equity rivals used a combination of letting their portfolio companies go bank-rupt, buying up bundles of mortgages for peanuts and stopping doing deals. The largest of them prospered, though even a decade later there had still been no full recovery and the volume of private equity backed deals had struggled back to only half the size of the market it had represented in 2006 and 2007.

I did the opposite. Rather than accept that the shit had hit the fan and that the best thing to do was just to move on, I decided to fight for every penny. If the ship was going to sink, I would be the captain on the bridge not the person manning the lifeboat. It was no doubt a gallant and romantic notion, but it wasn't one that has any real place in business. If I'd followed the pack, Terra Firma today would probably still be in the top ten and the market would have forgiven us for the EMI fiasco. Smart money picks no fights, follows no principles and certainly doesn't throw itself personally into saving portfolio companies.

Instead I continued to break my personal cardinal rule, allowing emotion rather than objectivity to rule me. EMI should have been a commodity to manage. Instead it became a child to mend. And as I embarked on a new career as nursemaid, my problems multiplied. My closest business relationships collapsed around me. Citigroup became more and more nervous, and more and more distant. Many there had voted to make the EMI loan only because they saw me as a friend of the firm and believed I could turn the record giant around. Others had been sceptical and less supportive. Now that the credit markets were worsening and the debt markets starting to close down, Citi were looking for a way out of funding the transaction. The friendship was being tested to breaking point.

It slowly became obvious to us that EMI's loan was sitting in Citi's Institutional Recovery Management unit (IRM), which had been set up to deal with creditors Citi believed presented a high risk of defaulting. The people who ran Citi's IRM unit did exactly what it says on the tin – they recovered money for Citi. That might not have involved sending the boys round, but then they didn't need to. They had lawyers and accountants who could achieve the same result quite legally while breaking no bones. They certainly weren't my friends.

As for me, the discovery that would change my view of my friendship with Citigroup and eventually destroy it came in October 2007. By now I had been the chairman of EMI for several months, and we had developed a shortlist of potential CEOs for the recorded music division. One logical candidate for the position was Roger Ames, the former head of Warner Music and EMI's North American executive. I arranged a meeting with Roger to discuss the possibility of elevating him to the role of CEO.

During the course of that meeting, we discussed the EMI auction, and something Roger said left me feeling uncomfortable. He had a unique perspective on the deal as he had worked with Cerberus on a competing bid, and he gave me the distinct impression that ultimately Terra Firma had been the only bidder at the May auction for EMI. This was not consistent with what I felt I had been led to believe by Citigroup at the time. The only reason that Terra Firma bid the price we did, on the day we did, was because I had believed that we needed to beat off a simultaneous rival offer from Cerberus. Roger's suggestion made me wonder whether Citigroup had used the Cerberus bid simply as a stalking horse. I relayed the conversation to Terra Firma's general counsel Tim Pryce, who launched an investigation.

In November 2007, when it was finally confirmed that our EMI debt was in IRM, we were also told that, in Citi's view, there had been a material deterioration in the condition of EMI.

While my preference was to reach some sort of compromise with Citi to allow the company to continue to operate under our control, I could only conclude that the IRM's ambition was to take EMI from me as soon as it could. Meanwhile, Citi were faring badly. Chuck Prince left in November as the bank announced

$18 billion in write-downs – one of the biggest casualties of the subprime mortgage crisis. There was every indication that 2008 would be worse. By now banks that had gone under included Lehman Brothers and Washington Mutual. Citi would require the biggest bailout of any American bank as it teetered on the brink. US taxpayers pumped $45 billion into the business, most of which converted into a 34 per cent stake.

Citi alleged on a number of occasions that we were in breach of various provisions of the loan agreements. Exchanges of lawyers' letters followed. After a standstill there was a partial, challenging and at times infuriating renegotiation of the financing. Citi, it became clear, were reluctant to budge. They clearly didn't want to go through with the restructuring.

While all this was going on, we continued our search for a CEO to replace me at EMI. And in Allan Leighton we thought we had found one. Allan, along with Archie Norman, had transformed Asda from an also-ran in the supermarket sector into an asset that retailers fought to acquire, energising both Asda's people and its investors in the process. He had understandably acquired a great reputation as a fixer of businesses. So advanced were our conversations that the press release to announce his appointment was ready for distribution.

In early December, we organised a two-day off-site meeting for EMI's investor board at the Buxted Park Hotel in East Sussex, one of Julia's Hand Picked Hotels. It was an opportunity for Leighton to get to know everyone. Over dinner, he made a wonderful speech to rally the troops. 'Look for the jewel in the toad's head,' he said, which wrinkled foreheads in the room. And then . . . I can only say that he must have balked. He got up, left early the next day and called me a few hours later. 'I've changed my mind,' he said. 'This is just too difficult.'

As we reached the end of 2007, we were gearing up to make

deep cuts in staff numbers, a key part of our strategy to get EMI into better financial shape. Other parts of our plan, however, were running into the sand. Because credit was in such short supply it seemed increasingly unlikely that we would be able to undertake many of the transactions we believed would have added value to EMI. Project Blackjack, for example, which involved acquiring the recorded music division of Warner, EMI's closest rival, was looking less hopeful by the day. And even if, by some stroke of luck, we were able to pull it off, I had little confidence that Citi would agree to allow us to finance it through Project Poker – a plan to establish new music (the 'problem child') as a separate entity from the rest of the business (which, despite the difficulties of the time, was very successful and profitable). By my calculation Project Poker would make it far easier for Citigroup eventually to syndicate the £2.5 billion of EMI debt it was still carrying. I spoke to Michael Klein about all this and ended the call downcast. EMI would drag me down unless I could win Citi over to work with us, but the support clearly wasn't there. Even so, I still wasn't willing to jettison the company.

At 7 am on 15 January 2008, I gathered with my advisers at EMI's headquarters on Wrights Lane in Kensington in preparation for a meeting with EMI staff at the nearby Odeon cinema, where I would explain my plans for the company. It was a day I had been dreading. If I was going to share my vision of how I planned to revive EMI's fortunes I would have to say how many jobs I intended to cut. My speech had been drafted and then redrafted, but it still didn't capture what I wanted to say.

As we geared up to make our way to the cinema a question arose: given that there would be quite a crowd outside, should I walk in through the front door or go round the back? The view of

Pat O'Driscoll, who was leading the human resources effort for me at EMI, was that I should enter via the front door – to use any other route would appear cowardly. Pat was the former chief executive of Northern Foods, producer of Fox's Biscuits and Goodfella's pizzas, who had risen to the top levels of business in male-dominated boardrooms. When she spoke, I listened. I did as she advised.

I wish I hadn't. I set off down Kensington High Street on foot, flanked by one of my public relations advisers, Andrew Dowler, on one side and EMI's chief security officer on the other. As I rounded the corner and the cinema came into view, I actually gasped out loud. What was meant to be a private event for staff, artists and their managers had snowballed into a much larger spectacle. To any passer-by, it must have seemed that the army of TV camera operators and reporters milling about by the entrance were awaiting A-list stars attending a movie premiere. It was a mêlée of fluffy microphone booms, tangled cables, waving notebooks and people in anoraks shouting into their mobile phones. On this murky Tuesday morning, however, there was no chance of a celebrity sighting. Instead, with tousled hair and rimless glasses, dressed in a grey suit with a lilac shirt and tie, I was the unlikely leading man – and I was not about to be afforded the red-carpet treatment.

As we closed in on the cinema, pandemonium broke out. Cameras were waved in my face to try to provoke a reaction. We couldn't move. Andrew and the security officer tried to propel me forwards. Video equipment clattered into us. In the end, Andrew linked arms with me, and we shouldered our way through the scrum. No wonder he was mistaken for my bodyguard. The walk to the cinema, which should have taken a few minutes, took nearly half an hour. I was bruised and battered, both physically and emotionally.

People tried to persuade me to take some time to recover my composure, to gather my thoughts, to calm down, to take a breath. Today, I do yoga. If something stressful arises I pause and do a few pranayama breathing exercises. Back then I didn't.

I charged into the event, apologised for being late, discarded my prepared words and with the adrenaline flowing, proceeded to be blunt and unfailingly honest. Afterwards, many EMI staff said they knew what I was going to say. If they did, I certainly didn't. The words that emerged from my mouth were not carefully considered but a passionate stream of consciousness. Their company was haemorrhaging money, I said. Their salaries were too high. Their expenses were out of control. Of their 1,400 artists on their books, a third had never released a record. 'EMI needs a new business model; we need to be much closer to the consumer – and this will require a smaller company with fewer artists, and we know how to do this.'

Eventually I let up. I was breathless and my mouth was dry. I grabbed a bottle of water I had been handed and sucked the contents down. Only then did it hit me – the speech I had given, one that I hoped would bring everyone together, had simply sown further division. I had created a 'them' and an 'us'. 'They' were the problem and it was down to 'us' to sort it out. It was a disaster.

I felt utterly dejected. So, too, did the EMI staff drifting out of the cinema afterwards. Given my torrent of words, they suspected that things would be even worse than I'd said they would be. Even so, a few came up to me and thanked me for being straight with them. One went so far as to say: 'I'm sure I'm on the list of those to be fired. But I'm pleased you're doing it. EMI's survival as the British music label is more important than me. I just hope you can save it.' I choked up, left through a side door, went back to my CEO office at EMI and waited for the press reports. They were brutal; focusing on redundancies, they reported that a third of the workforce – 2,000 jobs – would be gone within six months.

ITV, BBC, Sky, Channel 4 – the story was covered in every major bulletin. My address had even made it on to the Press Association's photo schedule, which is designed to alert the media outlets that receive its pictures of the most newsworthy events it would be covering that day. In a spectacular piece of miserable timing, my speech ran in the same editions of newspapers as reports that Citi had stunned Wall Street by reporting a $10 billion quarterly loss – the worst in its history – alongside a write-down of $18.1 billion related to soured mortgage investments. Despite a $12.5 billion bailout from investors in Kuwait, Singapore, the state of New Jersey and $25 billion from the US government in Troubled Asset Relief Program funds, job losses would eventually top 100,000.

By this point, the personnel we were dealing with at Citi had completely changed. In the course of the previous three months, our business had been moved from Wormsley and Klein to Chad Leat and Lesley Lynn. Chad's job was to shrink Citi's balance sheet as quickly as possible. He was the man who would – by getting rid of Citigroup's bad loans – determine how long it would take Citi to be free of the US government. Lesley's job was to make sure that the liquidation of those loans within the UK cost Citi as little as possible and was done as quickly as possible. The future of the borrower was not their worry. Their only concern was closing down the loans and getting the money back as fast as they could. Not only was Citi no longer a partner and a friend, it was now the enemy. What was seen as good for me and EMI was seen as bad for Citigroup. I wanted to build EMI over seven years. They wanted the business liquidated and their money back as quickly as possible. My business plan and their objectives were completely at odds.

I tried to see Vikram Pandit, who had succeeded Chuck Prince as Citi's chief executive. As luck would have it, and though I had not previously had financial exposure to India, I was one of the first investors in Pandit's Indian fund and had put in $3 million. It turned out to be a disastrous investment. Whatever bond I hoped that transaction might have formed, he was in no mood for discussing EMI and refused to meet me.

There was one bright spot on the horizon. In July 2008 I was at last able to announce the appointment of a chief executive of recorded music. Elio Leoni Sceti had spent many years at Reckitt Benckiser, the grocery group behind brands including Cillit Bang stain remover and Air Wick air freshener. Elio might have seemed a strange choice but he understood marketing and business discipline. I didn't need him to make music, I needed him to distribute it. After all, we already had the best music catalogue in the world. We just needed to ensure we had the best distribution system in the world.

Elio's appointment aside, disappointments and challenges continued to mount. While we knew that the costs of recorded music needed to be driven down, one of our ambitions had been to invest in music publishing and scale it up. The platform was being digitised. It needed as much music as possible fed into it so that corporate customers looking for material for movie soundtracks and advertising campaigns wouldn't need to go anywhere else. That's why we were so keen to acquire Chrysalis, another famous name in the music industry. In fact, we had been tracking it even before we bought EMI. If we could add a small publisher with £70 million of revenues and £50 million of cost to EMI's platform, the cost would evaporate and those extra revenues would fall to the bottom line. We weren't the only ones trying to do that of course, but we had a head start on the smaller players. Sadly, in the end, we just didn't have enough money to buy Chrysalis. It all came down to relying on support from Citi – and that support was not forthcoming.

Then there was the continuing saga of our deteriorating relationship with Citigroup. Tim Pryce's investigation in the first half of 2008 indicated that Citigroup might have lied to us during the EMI auction. If this was to be the case, then we would probably have a legal claim against them. However, since our principal goal was to reach a settlement of the debt package and we did not want to make the relationship any worse by accusing them of lying, we did not ask Citigroup to explain if and why they had misled us during the auction process. We continued to try to find some accommodation with them. But now that we believed they had grossly misstated the status of the auction, our trust in them wholly evaporated and the negotiations became harder as a result. In any case, most of the people I had been friends with had gone and the bank's priorities had changed dramatically, as became even clearer in November 2008, when the US government effectively nationalised Citigroup, investing $20 billion and underwriting a further $306 billion in loans and securities.

As 2008 neared its end, I appeared on the outside to be my usual resilient, wind-tossed, punchbag self. But the stuffing was starting to come out. I couldn't go to restaurants without people coming up to me and asking about EMI. Discussion of the company dominated every dinner party I went to. Overnight it appeared that I had fired everybody's favourite artist. Problems were crowding in on me from so many different directions. People within EMI were willing me to fail. The British media, having built me up, were looking for any excuse they could find to knock me down. Citi, it seemed to me, were undermining what I was trying to do, even though the numbers were good. I found the collapse of my relationship with them almost impossible to bear. And while plenty of banks wanted to talk to me, they were like vultures circling a carcass – a carcass that happened to be me.

I faced an additional problem. When Terra Firma had been set up in 2002, Nomura had wanted us to move offshore and had transferred its private equity assets to Terra Firma for management in Guernsey. The British Inland Revenue finally accepted that the assets didn't actually belong to me. But, they said, even though the income from managing them was being paid to a Guernsey company, it should be treated as income I received as a UK resident and taxed as such. Every tax lawyer I spoke to said this was nonsense. But clearly the Inland Revenue had chosen us as the private equity fund to try this argument out on, with the result that I had not been able to close my personal tax files or corporate accounts for several years. No claim had been made against me by the Inland Revenue – nor was ever made – but I had been inundated with queries from them and spent millions on providing answers. Such lengths did they go to that one of their number even travelled to New Zealand to check that there was physical evidence of an investment in trees I had made there with the large US insurance company John Hancock.

I realised that if the Inland Revenue were ever to bring an action against Terra Firma and win, we could be stuck with having earnings in one company and costs in another. This could bankrupt the company, and me and indeed our investors, who would then have to find another organisation to manage the businesses. My only option was to leave the UK. I'd been constantly shuttling between home and Guernsey for company board meetings. Now, I decided, I would become a Guernsey resident. In practical terms it was the right thing to do. Within a year of my moving to Guernsey, the Inland Revenue had accepted that Terra Firma was based there and that my tax affairs – and those of the company – could be closed. In emotional terms, it was very tough.

From 1 April 2009 I was living on an island, separated from my family and my friends.

Personally, it couldn't have been a worse time to leave the UK. If I had moved to Guernsey when I set Terra Firma up, Julia and the family would have come with me and the children would have regarded Guernsey as their home. I would have been with them through most of their childhood; even if working extraordinarily long hours, at least their home would have been my home. Economically, with hindsight, it also made no sense – the earnings I was concerned about were the fund earnings, not my personal earnings. Post-EMI, Terra Firma was never going to raise another blind pool fund. So the issue that the Inland Revenue had decided to attack us on was going to be a moot point anyway. But my ship had sailed, and returning to the UK would be difficult as I was going to build a new life for myself in Guernsey.

Over the course of 2009 EMI made considerable progress. In the year leading up to March 2010, the business reported underlying earnings of £334 million compared with the £68 million it had made in the twelve months before our acquisition. Put another way, the business had been consuming £100 million in cash each year and now it was generating £250 million in cash each year. Those higher returns came despite flat sales, demonstrating the benefits of the efficiencies we had introduced.

But that wasn't enough for Citi and they kept pushing us to do more. The last straw was a disastrous meeting in August 2009 in New York. I had asked for – and Lesley Lynn had offered me – one last chance to repair the relationship. She had therefore arranged a meeting for me with John Havens. Two years older than me, John had worked with Vikram Pandit at Morgan Stanley, risen through the ranks with him, and, when the two were passed over for promotion, had left with him to form Old Lane, a private equity business focused on India. When Citigroup bought Old Lane for $800 million in 2007, he and Vikram joined Citigroup, and although Old Lane proved to be a disaster, not only for investors like myself, but also for Citigroup, the two men continued to flourish (in June 2008 Citigroup announced that they would be closing the fund). When Vikram became CEO of Citigroup in December 2007, John was his right-hand man.

Vikram had come to the United States at the age of sixteen. John, by contrast, was white American establishment writ large. He came from wealth, had married an heiress and attended Harvard. Even though he was as different from me as chalk is from cheese, I felt that if we could meet, I might be able to persuade him to give us more time to turn EMI around.

The meeting did not go well. I wasn't taken to John's deep-carpeted 'corner' office but to a conference room that he used as a side office. Once seated, we tried to make small talk. When he asked where I was going after my New York trip, and I said the Mauna Kea resort in Hawaii there was a brief moment of connection. The Mauna Kea Beach Hotel – perhaps my favourite hotel in the world – is located on a very beautiful bay, with a stunning sandy beach, and spotlights that shine through the clear blue waters at night, attracting sea turtles and manta rays, illuminating the myriad of tropical fish and the rocks below. Julia and I loved the area so much that years before we'd bought a piece of land next to the Mauna Kea Beach Hotel where Julia had proceeded to build her dream vacation home from scratch. It turned out that John Havens, fifty years earlier, had taken his childhood summer holidays there with his family. I had to admire his family's taste.

But once we had both enthused about Mauna Kea, the meeting turned frosty. I failed to change his mind. He told me he was leaving all the negotiating to Lesley. At the end he politely wished me luck. I took it that he was wishing me luck in another life, not luck in conjunction with EMI. As I walked away I realised that there was, quite simply, no deal to be done with Citigroup. Their sole aim now was to take control of EMI and liquidate their position. Ironically, we'd improved the value of EMI so much over the previous two years that they would probably be able to liquidate the business without taking a loss, or only a small one.

If Citigroup were keen to wash their hands of EMI, so were a lot of people in my camp. I discovered later that one of our advisers at the meeting made contact with Citigroup on his way to Kennedy Airport to tell them that, in his view, I was being completely unrealistic. Many of our investors felt the same way. They wanted us to stop wasting our time with EMI and start looking for new opportunities. Many of my colleagues were of the opinion that all this effort was helping Citigroup, not us, and that I should give the keys back to the bank, wish them the best and hope they made a large loss. Their whole loyalty was to Terra Firma. They felt mine should be, too.

CHAPTER 11

Pounding the Table

I fought the law and the law won

THE CLASH,
'*I Fought the Law*'

Citi's chance to seize control of EMI from Terra Firma eventually came in early 2011, by which time, ironically, both the market and EMI's prospects were on the up. Effectively there were only really two ways in which they could trigger a recall of the loan. One was if we failed to abide by the monthly payment schedule – and Terra Firma had always met every repayment commitment. The other was if the business became 'balance sheet insolvent' – that is, if the debt became greater than the value of the company. The value of a company, however, varies from day to day and is highly subjective. Fluctuations in currency rates, for example, are sufficient to vary it.

It is extremely unusual for a bank to take control of a company on the basis of balance sheet insolvency, particularly in a turnaround deal where significant investment and restructuring may be required. But that is ultimately what Citibank opted to do. And by exploiting this financial technicality, with no notice given to Terra Firma, they were able to wrap up the business in less than a day, walking into Terra Firma's offices in the early afternoon in what was clearly a tightly orchestrated operation and announcing that the business was now theirs. These days such 'pre-pack' administrations are more tightly regulated. A decade or so ago they were relatively easy to effect. Citi were able to sell EMI to themselves for £20.

It took eight months for Citi to complete a search for new owners. In the end, EMI was broken up and sold to Sony and Universal, two of the three remaining mega-international labels.

The recorded music business was sold to Universal and the publishing business to Sony. The sale raised a little more than £2.5 billion, covering the loan to Terra Firma.

Ironically, by 2012 the market had completely turned around and the true value of the publishing and catalogues business was duly appreciated by the market. Warner, which Len Blavatnik purchased in 2011 for $3.3 billion, went public in 2020 for $12.8 billion. Len, always a canny operator, earned $1.9 billion when Warner floated and kept a majority stake in the company. Meanwhile, Vivendi, the owners of Universal, which we'd always seen as our biggest competitor in the publishing game, sold 10 per cent of the company to Chinese tech company Tencent in 2021, suggesting a total value for the company of $36.5 billion. My conservative view is that if EMI had still been a single empire, it would have been worth $25 billion. My reputation, rather than being destroyed, would have been confirmed. But then as I had discovered when I was young, playing poker in the Bullfinch pub, it doesn't matter how good your cards are if you don't have the money to stay in the game. It's to my eternal regret that I didn't apply that basic rule to EMI. I still think I was holding good cards but I didn't have the bank I needed to stay in the game. I was on my own. And I felt bitter. Citi, I was convinced, had not played fair with me. I wanted redress.

I didn't welcome the prospect of a lawsuit but in 2009, after the disastrous meeting with John Havens, I started to seriously consider it. It would be distracting. It might go on for years. Its outcome was unpredictable. And it would involve taking on what had been the world's biggest bank. Besides, as Tim Pryce warned me, we might struggle to find top lawyers to represent us. The Magic Circle firms – the most powerful and prestigious firms in the City – didn't like to act against the banks, because the banks were their biggest paymaster.

But this wouldn't be a normal piece of company litigation. This would be personal. Citigroup would want to distance themselves from it as much as possible, leaving Wormsley to take the fall – if there was one. In our camp, it would be me rather than Terra Firma who would be seen as the claimant. To that extent, this would be a 'he says/he says' trial.

An Italian lawyer once said to me: 'Litigation always favours the bad and harms the good. The bad don't mind lying, it's just about money. The good won't lie and it's not the money that matters to them, it's the principle. I'd have a far better chance of winning representing the bad than the good, which explains why I like Mafia clients.'

Meanwhile, my brother Philip – a litigation lawyer – warned me that the legal professional's approach to winning a case would be that if they could win on the law, they would win on the law; if they could win on the facts, they would win on the facts; if they couldn't do either, they would be pounding the table. Citigroup, he suggested, would be pounding the table. I had better be prepared.

The first thing we needed to do was determine how strong our case was, what damages we might be awarded and how much it would cost. Tim arranged a series of meetings with Clyde & Co in the UK and Boies Schiller in the US. Both sets of lawyers came to Guernsey towards the end of summer 2009 to give presentations on the relative merits of fighting the case under English and New York law.

Boies Schiller proved more bullish than Clyde & Co. And once they told me and my fellow members of the General Partner board – which represents our investors – that we had a case against Citi I felt that if there was any chance of getting some of my investors' money back, I had to give it a go. As someone frequently bullied at school, I recognised and cherished an opportunity to fight back. My instincts were taking over. As they did so, they deadened me to what a personal sacrifice this battle would be.

Initially I thought we could secure a result without going to court. We could send Citi the court materials we had assembled to see if these were sufficient to shock the bank into having a proper discussion with us, in the hope that they would agree to a standstill on the debt so that we would have time to weather the credit storm and implement our business plan. Effectively, we would be offering a quid pro quo: we would call off the litigation if Citigroup would stop trying to seize the company. I strongly believed that the music industry would come back even more profitable than it had been in the past. All we needed was the opportunity time would give us to prove the truth of that.

Boies Schiller argued that if we opted to fight our case in New York, we should arrange for a hearing to take place as soon as possible. They felt that the longer we left it the more difficult we would find it to win. Memories would be less reliable. A judge or jury might question why, if our case was so strong, we hadn't brought it earlier.

We put the matter to the Terra Firma General Partner board. Each of Terra Firma's funds is managed by a General Partner, and the board of each General Partner comprises a small group of non-executive directors and me, the executive director. The General Partner must vote on all issues and decisions have to be unanimous, meaning that I or any other member of the General Partner board can always block a decision. As we debated the wisdom of going ahead with a court case, the consensus view favoured the Boies Schiller approach over the quid pro quo one: 'Look, it makes sense to file,' people said. 'We're getting advice that we're going to win this. We should do it.' I decided to go along with the consensus view.

And so, we filed the lawsuit without giving it to Citi in advance. In retrospect, I wish I'd had a mentor at that moment, someone who could sit down with me to discuss the full implications of what I was agreeing to and what would follow. True, I had low-key support from my peers in other institutions who felt that, in the post-financial crash world, 'someone has to take on the banks'. But they weren't there to offer considered advice: they were simply curious to see what would happen. I also regret not taking the advice of my family. I had three lawyers to listen to – my brother was cynical about the process; my father, a contract lawyer, hated litigation; and Julia felt that proving a case like this would be extremely difficult regardless of what had actually happened and was concerned we wouldn't have sufficient proof. All three wanted me to drop it.

By the end of December 2009, we had spent €2.6 million on determining whether we should file, drop the case or send draft statements of claims to Citigroup so we could discuss our grievances. By the time everything was over in July 2016, our total legal costs, including those we paid for Citigroup, exceeded €78.2 million. I can understand why people say that the only winners in a legal fight are the lawyers. The United States spends more money on litigation after deducting damages than they spend on research and development for the entire country – including both state and private.

As we prepared our case, we asked ourselves three questions. How cast-iron was our argument? What would the likely damages be? How much would it all cost? But those were the wrong questions. What we should have been considering was the legal truism that between your case being filed and the summing up speeches being delivered, your chances of winning will become ever less certain, the damages that can be gained will become ever smaller, the costs will become ever more and the responsibility for the result will move from the lawyers to you – and how good a witness you are. The last factor is impossible to predict.

We began the formal legal process in spring 2010 with the taking of depositions, transcripts of which were then made available to Citi's lawyers. These are obviously a crucial element of any case: anything you say in a deposition can be brought up subsequently in court and can prove deeply damaging if, under cross-examination, you say something slightly different. But although our team and Citigroup's team were both preparing for a trial that would start in ten months' time, I was still hoping that we could strike a deal with Citi and settle. Citi, I have been told, felt the same way. The case, however, was assigned to Judge Jed Rakoff, who has a reputation for putting cases on a fast track and getting them off his docket. We didn't have much time to talk things through.

In the complaint we asked the court to find that Citigroup lied to us (either knowingly or recklessly) and that we had relied on the information they had given us to the detriment of our investors. Our legal team spent the first half of 2010 conducting discovery and wading through mountains of documents from Terra Firma, Citigroup, EMI, other parties involved in the auction process and various advisers to the various parties, as well as hundreds of hours of depositions and endless internal Citigroup emails. Context is everything with certain types of information, and in hindsight it seems to me that many of the emails could have been interpreted almost any way you liked. But the view of our lawyers was that they demonstrated the validity of our position and confirmed that we were doing right by our investors. Presumably Citigroup's lawyers were reading the same emails and telling Citigroup the exact opposite.

Where internal Citigroup emails did prove valuable was in showing how banks evaluate credit (especially troubled credit), how they view their relationships with their clients and how they handle their competing and conflicting roles. The picture that emerged may not have been a welcome one to me, but it was an education. I came to have a much fuller understanding of the basic truth that while the large global banks may come across as single, coherent entities, they're actually a mass of competing interests. Individual business units vie with one another to provide advisory services and financing to any and all parties. And while the advisory role is key, it can be all too easily distorted by the eye-watering incentive and bonus schemes so many banks offer their staff. Citigroup claimed we knew that the bank was on both sides of the transaction and had 'waived' any conflicts, but the truth is, Terra Firma had no idea how deep the conflicts went.

Despite the looming trial date in mid-October 2010 and the mounting stacks of documentary evidence, we continued to negotiate with Citigroup, hoping for a resolution that would include a restructure of debt. We tried every possible approach to resolve our differences right up to and into the trial itself: one-on-one sessions, mediation with a neutral former judge, even discussions via third parties that were designed to ameliorate any built-up resentment Citigroup's side might feel as a consequence of having dealt directly with us. But all attempts ultimately broke down because we could not reach an agreement on the appropriate value of EMI – either as a single entity or as two separate ones (music publishing and recorded music). Citigroup were also unwilling to allow another lender to buy the debt at a big discount. Their concern was that this would cause them reputational harm. I believe we were close on some occasions, but an agreement that would make sense for all constituencies eluded us.

With ten days to go before the start of the trial, it seemed as though a breakthrough might have been achieved as Chad Leat and I, neither of whom wanted a trial, agreed to make one final push for an agreement. I felt that I might be able to work with the deal that was now on the table. A restructuring of the debt at this time would have allowed us to keep control of the business and in as little as a year later, this sum would have been at least £1 billion – and by 2012, at least £3 billion. We didn't know it, but the market started to come back almost as fast as it had gone down at almost the exact time the trial started. With hindsight, just as May 2007 was the worst time to buy EMI, October 2010 would have been the best time to have bought it. A restructuring in 2011 would have allowed us to restart the clock but with the benefit of three years of business transformation already under our belt.

Unfortunately, I was by now probably the only believer in the future of EMI. On the Terra Firma side, most people didn't want to see a music company ever again. They just wanted vengeance. As for Citigroup, they passionately believed the lawsuit was wrong and wanted to prove themselves in court. The people who were most strongly against the deal were the lawyers on both sides, who had tens of millions to earn from the trial going ahead, regardless of the outcome.

Our team busied themselves trying to formalise the proposal in a very short space of time. It was a huge undertaking. The document rewriting the debt packages and resetting our relationship with Citi ran to 15,000 pages. Three law firms were involved. Much of the risk rested on our side – for example, if governmental competition clearance was not granted when EMI was sold on in whole or part to one of the other music majors. We also had to agree unilaterally to abandon litigation as the price for striking the deal.

Terra Firma ploughed on with good intentions, even to the extent of block-booking rooms at the Hilton hotel on 48 Church Street in New York, near the courtroom, and converting them into an office, so that no one needed to waste time travelling to and from home during those vital days. I have a suspicion, though, that while everyone in our team looked keen when I was there, some clearly didn't trust Citi and wanted us to have our day in court. I also strongly suspect that the Citi team working on the compromise weren't that committed. I heard stories that their 'deal team' were often out and rarely available – they would be at church, walking their dogs, collecting the kids from school, seeing their parents, and, on one occasion, spending time at the beach when we called; one particular person chose to go on holiday just as things were hotting up. We weren't getting the answers to our queries we needed.

The people running the litigation had 'banned' me from being involved with negotiating the settlement. There was just too much for me to read and try to take in before the trial started, they argued, particularly for someone who was dyslexic. They weren't wrong – I needed masses of time to prepare and had already left myself too little. Initially I ignored the ban, but by the Wednesday before the trial start date, I had no choice.

This, in retrospect, was a mistake. Without my involvement and with my team split on the wisdom or otherwise of pursuing a deal with Citi, we were left with no one on our side to communicate positively with Chad Leat. Little things that needed to be sorted out weren't dealt with and the stakes were constantly being raised by both sides, who were sending increasingly demanding emails without talking through what exactly they were asking for.

When I finally had time to read the last few days' exchanges, it was clear to me that there was no way either side could agree to what the other was asking. The deal Chad and I had put together relied on both sides acting in good faith and trusting each other. But both good faith and trust were sadly lacking. Negotiation had moved from trying to find a solution to trying to score points. As is so often the case in important negotiations, when opposing teams feel hugely emotional and have lost trust in the other, it needs representatives from both sides to stand above the fray, provide leadership and press for a deal that might not leave everyone happy but will almost certainly be better than the alternative. This, unfortunately, was an occasion where my leadership was insufficiently forceful to achieve the outcome desired.

At the last moment, on the Sunday afternoon before the opening day of the trial, Chad led what was meant to be a joint conference call. I was told not to attend by my legal team. They didn't want me to become distracted from the trial itself – and they didn't want me to settle. Chad was therefore left with no one from my side to bounce potential solutions off. I am told he was hugely frustrated. It was clear to him that agreement was not going to be reached in time.

Had both sides asked for a delay to the start of the trial, it would have been granted. However, while the two sets of lawyers agreed that postponement made sense, they disagreed over who should make the request. Boies Schiller felt that were we to take the initiative it would suggest weakness on our side. Citigroup's lawyers felt the same for their client. The logical solution – that they both make the request – somehow was deemed to be impossible. I was told that someone's name has to go first and neither legal team could agree which name that should be. It all smacked to me of the playground rather than the courts.

On 18 October 2010, we trooped into the Manhattan courtroom, where I would be based for the next three weeks, in order to hear the judge's opening remarks. I noted with grim irony that it was located on Pearl Street, the name of one of my first big securitisations at Goldman Sachs. That deal helped to build my reputation, I reflected. Would this lawsuit damage it irreparably?

Leading our case was David Boies, a renowned and revered US trial lawyer with a long history of success in complex civil litigation. He puts his cases together brick by brick and builds his wall without a lot of glitz and glamour. He doesn't rattle on, has little use for small talk and more patience than most, certainly more than I could muster. He painstakingly assembled all the individual components of our claims, moving forensically from witness to witness, expert to expert and document to document.

Citigroup's lead counsel was Ted Wells of Paul, Weiss, Rifkind, Wharton & Garrison, who had made his name defending some of the most notorious and high-profile cases, from Eliot Spitzer to Lewis 'Scooter' Libby. Sitting through the entire trial at the front table next to David Boies and his colleagues, I could observe Wells up close and I noted his uncanny ability to get at the emotional centre of a case, and thus connect with the common-sense approach of the average juror.

As everyone knows from the cut and thrust of courtroom scenes in US films and on TV, the American approach to justice is very different from that of other countries, the UK included. The lawyers effectively speak on behalf of the witness to the jury, so their influence is huge. Wells struck up a rapport with the jury, promising to take them to 'detective school' when they examined my Guernsey phone records. Then there's the whole jury selection business, which both sides enter with a keen understanding of the profile of their 'perfect juror', as defined by professional background, gender, race and socio-economic position. By the time the selection process had been completed for our case, we had an eclectic group drawn from a variety of races and socio-economic backgrounds. Because so many reporters had assembled, the judge arranged for the courtroom across the hall to broadcast the selection process. This was a case that would be avidly followed by legal and business professionals, and a fair number of members of the public.

As we began to present our evidence, I became convinced not only that we were right, but that we would win. That was unwise.

A famous curse that lawyers bestow upon their clients or colleagues they dislike is: 'May you have a lawsuit in which you know you are right.' The fact that I passionately believed that I had been led to understand there was another bidder at a critical moment in the auction process, and that it was that knowledge that had caused us to take our bid forward, was not what was important. For my view to carry weight, the jury would have to believe me, would have to disbelieve Citigroup and would have to believe that it was the information about Cerberus bidding that propelled us to make our bid.

Our lawyers put all types of documents into evidence: they were trying to lay out the intricacies and nuances of public to private transactions. They had to explain the inevitable emotions and frustrations of a transaction conducted at the peak of the credit boom and the depths of the credit bust and they had to introduce the jury to the world of banking with its myriad of conflicts. In less than three weeks, we were asking the jury to absorb mountains of information and sift through and assess conflicting viewpoints and analyses.

In the end, for all of the documents analysed and emails examined, the case as put forward by both sides' counsels boiled down to a battle of two witnesses – David Wormsley and me. We had documents that showed Cerberus had made the decision to drop out of the race on the Friday before the Monday deadline. EMI knew that, and we assumed Wormsley had known as well. There was an email from Wormsley to Eric Nicoli around midnight on the night before the bids were due saying he had just spoken to me and told me not to play games on price. The problem was, we had no documents actually proving that Wormsley knew Cerberus had dropped out and that he'd told us otherwise. All we had was my recollection of three conversations with Wormsley, and his version of those same three calls. The burden of proof was on us so the cross-examinations would be crucial. While my team was convinced that I would be far better on the stand than Wormsley, all I could remember was how bad I'd been at answering questions in class. There is a huge difference between sitting down with your own lawyers and being questioned by people whose job it is to destroy you.

Wells' skill impressed me. When the jury wasn't in the room he adopted an erudite tone as he parried with our counsel. But when the jury reappeared, he changed from highbrow to street-smart in an instant. He was a brilliant showman and he worked hard at it, coming in every morning at 7 am to practise in front of the jury's seating area. Citi loved him because two years earlier he had successfully defended the bank against allegations that it was involved in the fraud at Parmalat, the Italian dairy company. Not only did Wells win that case, but he also turned a $2 billion claim against Citi into a $364 million award. That's a good day at the office.

When I faced him on the stand, I stressed the conflicting roles played by Citigroup and its employees and the lies that were told by people that I trusted. I was not alleging that Citigroup had duped us into bidding for EMI: we wanted to bid for EMI. My argument was that we would not have bid at that point in time and at that price if we had known that we were the only bidder. We would have waited and paid less, and that would have allowed us to approach the deal with far more information. Just having a little more time would have reduced the price we needed to pay as the market started to collapse so soon after our bid.

David Wormsley took the stand the day after me. He could not recall the details of our Sunday night conversation hours before we submitted our bid for EMI. Nor could he recall when he found out that Cerberus was not going to bid – whether it was in the EMI board meeting he attended that Monday afternoon when the bids (or should I say bid) were debated, or later.

Towards the end of the trial, which ran for fourteen days, the last Citigroup witness took the stand and explained that when Citigroup funded the loan for the purchase of EMI, they had immediately put the loan into their 'Class 2' category, where bad debts are placed. Effectively, they admitted that when they loaned us the money, they knew there was a good chance the company would go bankrupt unless we managed to do the securitisation and the refinancing. Bizarrely, one of their reasons for making the loan – besides the huge fees that they would earn and having their existing loan paid off – was a belief that I could apply my magic to the business. This would make it easier for Citi to securitise the debt, producing yet more fees.

If the securitisation market hadn't died back in the summer of 2007, they would have been correct. The cash flow the business was achieving would easily have produced a securitisation that could have paid off all their debt and provided us a substantial return on our equity. However, trying to explain to a jury the motivation of people over three years before, when those people themselves couldn't agree, was extremely difficult. Our lawyers focused instead on internal emails within Citigroup that showed the bankers viewed EMI as a 'pig' and a 'terminally ill cancer patient'. Observing Citigroup witnesses having to read the emails out provided a great courtroom spectacle. Unfortunately, it didn't actually move our case forward. Whatever evidence was intro-duced, whichever witnesses were questioned, it all came down to two interconnected questions: did we rely on what David Worms-ley had said, and did he know it wasn't true?

Four days before the verdict was delivered, Citigroup started the day's proceedings with a bombshell. Wells suggested that the one juror with a degree – and the only one who had made copious notes – was biased against Citigroup. He then played in open court for all but the jurors to see, a snippet of the Michael Moore movie *Capitalism: A Love Story*. In the movie, Moore heavily criticises US banks, and Citigroup specifically. It was surreal to hear 'The Internationale', the famous left-wing anthem, play in the courtroom as the credits of Moore's movie rolled while Wells dramatically and emotionally explained the attenuated connection that the identified juror had to the movie (they had merely been thanked along with thousands of others in the credits). Wells exclaimed that his 'foreign client' was entitled to a jury free of bias against it.

I sat and listened in shock, wondering how in the world this supposedly 'new' piece of information got into Wells' hands. Nearly three weeks into the trial, and this was only now being raised. Wells was putting labels on this juror that he had no way to back up. But the judge agreed, and the juror was dismissed.

The night before the verdict felt very strange. Boies wasn't there, he had flown to California for another case starting that afternoon. Without our chief counsel, I took it upon myself to take the team out and thank them for their hard work. Heads were down. We sensed we had lost. I tried to rally people's spirits by reading out Rudyard Kipling's poem 'If': 'If you can keep your head when all about you are losing theirs and blaming it on you,' and so on.

The following day we assembled in the courtroom canteen at lunchtime. Every day, that room had been an extension of the court. Battle lines had been drawn even over food – Citi's huge team had cordoned off an area where their own lunch would be delivered. It was a sumptuous spread. Our much smaller team mingled with everyone who worked in the court and ate whatever was on the canteen menu.

The verdict was delivered quickly. In relation to our claim of fraudulent misrepresentation, the jury unanimously found Citi not liable. With my lead counsel in California, I was standing alone as the judge left and the courtroom emptied. Bizarrely, the first words of comfort I received as I stood in my private misery were from Ted Wells. He moved towards me, cutting through the throng of delighted Citigroup supporters flocking to congratulate him, put a hand on my shoulder and wished me good luck. 'I hope things work out,' he said softly.

After the verdict was read out and the jury dismissed, some of the jurors spoke to the press and to the legal teams as they left the building. They explained that while they had been 'leaning towards Hands' they were convinced by Wells' closing arguments. At the trial Wells was given the last word. This is not the traditional way trials operate in the US, or indeed the UK. The reason for this is that the plaintiff has the burden of proof and does not know what the defendant is going to say in their closing comments, while the defendant does know everything the plaintiff is going to say. Consequently, the plaintiff is allowed almost always to give their response to the defendant's arguments. I believe that not having the ability to rebuff Wells' closing arguments was a significant disadvantage for us. Had Boies been able to blunt Wells' closing argument, I believe we might have won.

As I left the building, I found myself face to face with one of the jurors. It was a very tense moment, and rather embarrassing. I don't think it was supposed to happen, but it did. All he could do was mouth 'sorry'. All I could do in response was avert my eyes and stare at the ground.

I could not get out of there fast enough. On the way back to the hotel I darted into a fancy-dress shop. It was approaching Halloween and the following night Julia and I had a party to attend in Guernsey. I went as a 1960s hippy and she was Wonder Woman. It was a welcome antidote to the grave disappointment I was feeling.

*

However, my lawyers had not given up. They pointed out that although the case had been tried in New York, the rules of English law had been deemed to apply. To win our case under New York state law, we had to prove that it was more likely than not that we relied on Citi's false information to price our bid. To win it under English law, we had to prove that Citi lied, at which point it would be assumed that we'd relied on Citi's information unless Citi could prove otherwise. It was a small difference and it seemed a technicality to me, but, according to the lawyers, because the New York state judge instructed the jury to use the New York state rather than English approach they had answered the wrong question. Since an appeal wouldn't cost us anything – our law firm would handle it automatically as part of the original provision for the case – it seemed to make sense to let it go ahead, even though I was told that the verdicts of jury trials are rarely reversed.

On 3 October 2012, the appeal was heard in New York. I flew in circuitously from Guernsey via Paris (although the Inland Revenue had a general rule that you could spend ninety days a year in the UK without being deemed a tax resident, I always worried that it might not follow its own guidelines, for which reason I hadn't set foot on the mainland since leaving on 1 April 2009). Tim flew in from London. Terra Firma's litigation lawyer, Denelle Dixon, flew in from San Francisco. And the other lawyers flew in from all over the US. The day before the appeal we all met at Boies Schiller's offices with David Boies and his legal team. We assumed we had no chance, but we also thought that he was the best appellate lawyer in the US and if anyone could win it, he would. David didn't disagree.

Besides being an extraordinary lawyer, David personally appealed to all three of us – though for different reasons. For me, he was a fellow dyslexic who had been unable to read until he was nine, but who had nevertheless made it. Denelle respected him for representing Al Gore, albeit unsuccessfully, against George W. Bush in the contested 2000 presidential election. Tim admired him for helping to overturn California's Proposition 8, which banned gay marriage in the state – a legal move that opened the way to the legalisation of gay marriage in the US. That being said, all three of us knew that away from these landmark cases he'd had a controversial career, and we didn't approve of all his current clients or some of his firm's past activities.

The Terra Firma trio had dinner that evening at Aquavit, a Swedish restaurant just a brisk ten-minute walk from the Marriott Essex House hotel. It was an ideal place to prepare for the next day. I ordered the tasting platter – three types of herring, cured, poached and smoked salmon, chilled octopus and prawns along with boiled potatoes, Västerbotten cheese and black bread. We washed it down with a selection of twelve of their aquavits, starting with aniseed, caraway and fennel. We kept going until we reached mango and chilli pepper.

The next morning, we arrived at the ninth floor Ceremonial Courtroom of the Daniel Patrick Moynihan US Courthouse, at 500 Pearl Street in Manhattan to find our hearing was listed for 10 am. It was held by a panel of three appellate judges who were hearing a few different cases back-to-back. The judges began by saying they were loath to overturn jury verdicts. I relaxed: another trial was looking highly unlikely.

That was the last thing I understood. For the rest of the session, I sat there as the two sides argued the exact meanings of words from English court cases going back over 100 years and precedents based on previous trials where the participants had been pushing up daisies for many decades. The whole thing was surreal. Eventually the babbling stopped, and the lawyers picked up their binders and belongings from the counsel tables. Terra Firma's people and Citigroup's people stood up, and stood out from everyone else there – dressed as we all were in expensive suits, shirts and ties. All was noise and bustle as the next case started sidling in and we, en masse, tried to exit the courtroom.

The presiding judge – alarmingly named Judge Lynch – welcomed the newly arriving attorneys. 'We'll just give the one per cent a chance to make their way out of the courtroom now,' he said to a smattering of laughter. I don't remember joining in.

The hearing had taken almost an hour and a half – thirty minutes longer than expected. As Denelle rushed to catch her afternoon flight, she told Tim and me that she thought David had done a spectacular job. We headed for Kennedy Airport, both desperate to get out of New York. I flew back to Paris to meet friends and family for a long weekend. Thanks to the Eurostar, Paris had become the place I most frequently spent time with those I'd left behind in England. It was, I thought, the end of the saga.

Several months later – on Friday 31 May 2013 – I was in Spain, joining a board meeting from holiday. We'd allowed no more than an hour for it since there didn't seem to be anything significant to discuss. But, as it turned out, Tim Pryce had news. He, too, had taken the week off and was in Nice, but he'd just heard that we'd won the appeal and been granted a full retrial. We were all taken aback. By Sunday I was flying via Paris to New York where Tim joined me at David Boies' offices. The proverbial gift that wouldn't stop giving was handing yet more money to the lawyers.

We decided we wanted to understand what had gone wrong the first time, so we employed some jury consultants who put together a group of prospective jurors and then conducted some mock trials to see how these jurors would react to what their predecessors had seen. It quickly transpired that Citigroup had used their objections during jury selection very effectively. Those who had not finished high school almost universally found against us. They needed physical proof of fraud – a letter or a recorded phone call. Of course, this didn't exist. By contrast, those who had doctorates looked at the case completely differently and took into account all the circumstantial evidence, deciding on the balance of probabilities which story was most likely. They had little interest in what was said by the witnesses, as they assumed both sides would say whatever it took to further their own cause. What we needed, I realised, was a jury of university professors who were willing to sit in a New York court for two weeks in return for $30 and three good meals a day.

We held an all-hands meeting with our UK lawyers, our US lawyers, Tim, other members of the Terra Firma team and our jury consultants. Everybody had a vested interest. The US lawyers were trying to convince us that they would win the case in the US. The UK lawyers were trying to convince us that we would have been better off had we brought the case to the UK. It was becoming a predictable and rather boring meeting.

Then I asked the youngest member of the jury consultant's team for her view. She was the person who'd done most of the hard work and actually sat down and debriefed the 'jurors' after the mock trials. As she spoke, it soon became obvious why she had that job. She was engaging, empathetic, humble and above all gave the impression of being someone who was honest and reliable. She went through what we already knew but in more detail. Then I threw at her the open question, a question I hadn't asked the others, but which was of course the obvious question: 'If it was you, would you do a jury trial on this case in New York, or would you rather do a trial in front of a judge, either in New York or elsewhere?'

Her answer was like an electric shock to the room. She explained that in her view, we had no chance of winning in front of a New York jury. All evidence from previous mock trials suggested that we could not possibly win unless the majority of jurors were university graduates, and that, she said, was something she had never seen in her career as a jury selection adviser. She believed that we were more likely to get jurors from similar backgrounds to last time. Even if we did secure a jury made up mostly of university graduates, she added, we should be aware that in New York, everybody who had a degree would have friends who worked at Citigroup.

The New York lawyers and the jury consultant's bosses could see we were shocked. They tried to get her to back down. But she held her ground: she was going to speak the truth, the whole truth and nothing but the truth, even though, as she said to me privately later that day, she could have lost her job for doing so. As the day finished, Tim and I caught up over a drink in the Essex House hotel bar. We had both come to the same conclusion: regardless of what the lawyers were telling us, the second trial in New York would just be a re-run of the first, and we were almost certain to lose again. It seemed as though, with three weeks to go before the new trial, we were sleep-walking towards the edge of a cliff.

About a week later something happened that I was assured was extremely unusual. Judge Rakoff, who would be rehearing the trial, was presiding over another jury trial – the US government suing Bank of America for fraud. Our US lawyers had sent people to watch proceedings to get a sense of his mood and attitude towards big banks, as in 2010 he had seemed very supportive of them. We wanted to know if what had emerged about them in the last few years had changed his mind. It became increasingly apparent to our people, though, that whatever Judge Rakoff's views might be in the autumn of 2013, the Bank of America case looked set to run and run for a long time. There was no way it was going to finish by 7 October, the date scheduled for the beginning of our trial. Sure enough, on 25 September, Rakoff convened all parties by telephone and said he would have to move the trial date back. The earliest available date was 7 July 2014. Given that both sets of lawyers had other trials lined up, the earliest practical date was at least a year away.

This enforced breathing space gave Tim and me the opportunity to consider moving the trial to England. Of course, that would mean further delay, as yet more lawyers would require briefing and more documents would need to be prepared. We'd also be even further away from the time the events we were disputing had occurred, with all the added potential for confused memories that would entail. But there was something to be said for a UK-based trial. Citigroup favoured London, too. In their case, I suspect they were anxious to avoid further publicity in an America that, in the time that had elapsed since the previous trial, had become ever more hostile to the banks.

We asked David Boies his view. It was clear and unambiguous: we had nearly won the first trial; we now knew what to do in the second trial; Citigroup had given the first trial its best shot; we hadn't; this time we would win in New York. Besides, he said, if Citigroup wanted to move the trial to London, surely we should do the opposite. Our UK lawyers were equally clear and unambiguous. 'David would say that, wouldn't he?' they pointed out. Look at what he stands to earn if the case stays in New York. Tim also felt we should move the case to London. A jury is never going to understand the case, he argued, but a judge will focus on facts and not emotions.

What everyone on my side had missed was the psychological disadvantage that a trial run according to British rules would involve for me. In the US a witness is presented by their own lawyer and then cross-examined by the other side. The witness is therefore able to use the spell of friendly questioning to acclimatise to the courtroom. Only then are they subjected to a barrage of hostile fire. In the UK, the process typically occurs the other way round, leaving the witness no initial breathing space and no opportunity to get their bearings. Since the plan was for me to be the first witness, I would be placed straight in the firing line. Citigroup's lawyers would be able to rip straight into me with no holds barred. UK judges, unlike US juries, are not squeamish when it comes to watching a skilful lawyer tear someone apart through clever questioning. As it happens, our legal team was offered the opportunity for me to give 'evidence in chief', whereby I would be allowed to present my evidence and then have it questioned, but the adversarial nature of the courtroom proved too great a temptation for both sides. We opted for an approach not suited to someone of my temperament.

In hindsight, I should have dropped the case there and then. It was time for me to move on. After all, by now EMI had been sold, and the damages we could win in the UK were likely to be far less than we might gain in the US – possibly as low as a couple of hundred million. But then running through my mind were all the reasons to keep going . . .

There were the investors that I felt I had let down. There was the frustration of losing the UK its major music company when I knew we had been well on the way to turning it around. There were the friends and business colleagues I had lost because of EMI. There was having to leave my home in the UK and move into exile in Guernsey. There was not being with Julia, not seeing my daughters' teenage years, not seeing my sons through university and into their early twenties, not seeing my parents and my siblings. I couldn't bear the thought of all this having been for nothing. In deciding not to cut my losses, I had only one person to blame: myself. It had been my decision to bring the case back to the UK and roll the dice one more time. It was my life and I had chosen to waste seven years of it on a lawsuit.

But the 'Under Toad' hadn't finished with me yet. My mother-in-law, Betty, had been suffering from stomach pain for some time. Like Julia, she was a stoic, and both mother and daughter initially assumed she would be fine. In March we flew out to South Africa for Julia's birthday as planned. But Julia was worried about the pain that Betty was clearly in, and Betty's doctor decided that she should go into hospital for a scan.

On arrival in South Africa, Julia had a call from her sister Marion to say that the scan had revealed a large tumour. Marion told us not to be overly concerned – there was more than a 50 per cent chance that it was benign. The subsequent biopsy, however, diagnosed the tumour as malignant. Treatment proved very painful and it was not clear that it would work. Betty chose to discharge herself from hospital, knowing that she would be going home to die.

While receiving palliative care, Betty mentioned to Julia that she did not want a wake to be held after her death but wanted a party while she was still alive. Somehow she summoned up the strength and willpower to get dressed for it and was able to receive her guests. Almost all of her family were there and most of her friends. And we had a musician sing her favourite Elvis songs.

After the party Betty's condition deteriorated rapidly. She finally passed away late in the evening on Saturday 4 June, at home as she had wanted, with her family around her.

That week I had gone back to Guernsey. I returned to the UK for the trial the day after Betty's death. Julia had not had time to start grieving but wanted to be there for me. We spent that evening together, with our younger son joining us for dinner. Nothing seemed real. Those at Terra Firma, as well as the non-barristers in our team, tried to persuade our main barrister, the QC Lord Grabiner, not to put me on the stand that week. They wanted him to explain to the judge that I was in no state to be cross-examined. At the very least, they wanted the order of witnesses changed – so that I would appear last rather than first. Lord Grabiner worried that that would suggest weakness and insisted I go on as soon as the opening statements had finished.

I couldn't sleep that night. Nor could Julia. There was so much rocketing around our heads, and it was impossible to process any of it. However much we felt compassion for each other, we also needed time individually to process what had happened and personal time was the one thing we weren't going to have.

On Tuesday 7 June, I was back in court again, poring over the EMI transaction once more. I took the witness stand and realised immediately I was in no condition to present my case. I needed to be with Julia and the family, not in a courtroom. I remember feeling sick, my sugar levels being so out of control I was close to seizure. I had medicine from my doctors to use if I approached the danger zone and I was taking it. My diabetes – and my body generally – does not react well to stress. My mind seems to be able to take it. My yoga teacher, as well as my GP, says that I internalise stress to an extraordinary extent. It becomes psychosomatic, having physical as well as mental effects. Throughout this period, I was having problems sleeping, thinking and focusing my eyes.

The judge, Mr Justice Burton, could see I wasn't in a good state and kept asking me if there was anything wrong. I wanted to disobey my legal counsel who wanted me to appear strong and say nothing to the judge. In the end, I couldn't disobey him. He was the expert. However, the one thing I wasn't in the witness box was strong. I was a nine-year-old schoolboy again. My vision was badly affected as my sugar levels soared and I couldn't see clearly.

On top of that I was struggling to process information. Mark Howard – the very bright, very pedantic cross-examiner – attacked from the very beginning, suggesting I was only going forward with the trial in order to look good to my investors. I said I didn't think I would look good to them when this was over. The judge looked as if he wanted to ask why, but then moved on. I'm not sure what I would have answered – perhaps the truth, that I was in no state to give evidence and would not be able to speak sensibly.

As my time on the stand went on, I began to feel increasingly stupid and inadequate. It was like being toyed with by the class bully. The five hours spent on both Wednesday and Thursday giving evidence felt like the longest of my life. Some of the questions Mark fired at me required such perfect memory on my part that I was never going to be able to respond adequately. I should have said as much, but I felt too vulnerable to make that admission. During repeated questioning over whether Eric Nicoli rather than David Wormsley had seeded in my mind the idea of bidding for EMI at £2.65 a share during our meeting on 6 May, I rebutted the idea but not very convincingly. 'I would accept my memory is fallible, but I do have that memory,' I said.

I could see that the judge was puzzling over what was wrong with this person – a person who was meant to be so bright but was answering the questions so badly. Eventually, in desperation, when he realised that I couldn't even read what was being put in front of me, he asked if it would help if someone read the papers to me. I agreed, but it was the final humiliation: I was completely broken. Money and reputation were at stake, and yet I simply couldn't be relied on to remember every detail or even read the papers being handed to me.

'I'm sorry, I can't follow any of this. I apologise,' I said as we adjourned early on the Thursday. The judge, in an attempt to help me, suggested I do some homework over the weekend. 'At least you can take the opportunity before Monday, without talking to anyone, to look at these paragraphs in your own time,' he said of the last, very complicated points we had been discussing. 'So, can you jot down the paragraphs, so that you understand the question and assimilate it?'

In truth, I was done. The papers ran to thousands of pages. I knew I had no chance. I couldn't focus on a single sentence. I wanted to disappear. I asked Lord Grabiner if there was any way out. He could see it was destroying me and he had his own legal issues to deal with in relation to one of his highest profile clients. For both of us the trial finishing quickly was a blessing and on the Thursday afternoon I asked Lord Grabiner to withdraw the case.

We unreservedly withdrew the allegations of fraud and offered to pay Citi's legal costs. I felt I had let everybody down: my family, my investors, my firm, my friends and myself.

The press wasn't as bad as my Terra Firma colleagues feared it would be. The journalists felt that Mark Howard had completely destroyed me in the witness box. They didn't know about Julia's mother's death, my diabetes, or how Howard had taken me back to feeling like a nine-year-old failing in a classroom. They could, however, see a broken man and they couldn't see the relevance of any of the questions, which of course there wasn't – except to break me as a witness. Howard had done that very successfully.

I didn't attend the formal closing of the trial the next day. Instead, Julia, our son and I went back to Guernsey. Julia needed time to grieve by herself, but given the state I was in, she was worried about me and felt she needed to be with me.

My friends had been telling me to take time off. My family felt we needed to get away for a bit. So Julia, three of our children and I flew to Las Vegas to meet our eldest son, who was flying in from New York where he was studying. It seemed a good idea, particularly as the family had so few opportunities to be all together at the same time. And Las Vegas seemed the right destination. It's a ludicrous place in lots of ways but it offers great accommodation, food, drink and entertainment. We stayed for three days, during which we visited the Grand Canyon, attended a Mariah Carey concert, saw Cirque du Soleil, ate well and drank extraordinary wine in a number of great restaurants and the kids went sky-diving.

As therapy, though, the trip was less successful. There's a line in 'Hotel California': 'Some drink to remember, some drink to forget.' I wanted to forget. Instead I dwelt on everything that had gone wrong or that I was unhappy with, from the EMI saga to my enforced absences from my family. Flying back to London on Thursday I wrote some poetry. I read it back in Guernsey and ripped it up – just as my mother had ripped up my teenage writing for its desperate negativity. But then I had been angry with the world. Now I was angry with myself.

My family and friends were right. I needed to take a break and regroup. Instead I went straight back to my usual routine. Here I was at fifty-seven, overweight, diabetic and mentally broken, but I carried on acting as though I was someone in their thirties at the top of their game. My schedule remained as crazy as ever. My diary continued to be packed. I felt I had to get back on the horse and the only way I knew how was through doing deals.

CHAPTER 12

Pain Plus Reflection

Having it all
Having it all
You'll never stop me
From having it all

EIGHTH WONDER,
'Having It All'

Being an entrepreneur rarely gives you bragging rights at the sort of dinner parties attended by the great and the good. Working at Goldman Sachs, McKinsey or a top law firm provides kudos. Being an entrepreneur – unless one is really successful – is just seen as being in trade. The fact is, though, it takes a lot to be an entrepreneur – ambition, the ability to take risks and superhuman drive are all key factors along with a willingness to work hard and make sacrifices. Goldman might have involved eighty-hour working weeks, but once I was running my own business I was going 24/7, 365 days a year: public holidays, birthdays, anniversaries . . . nothing was sacred. Work came first, second and third.

Hard work and drive aren't the whole package, though. Many people have the stamina to put in long days, weeks and months but are not successful. To get that crucial edge you need the qualities Chuck Davidson told me about back in 1982 – greed and balls of brass. Then you need creative ideas, innovative strategies and achievable but tenacious goals. You also need to be good at execution, or, at least, make sure you have someone in your team who really understands it – something I learnt the hard way. Above all, to be a really great entrepreneur you need to follow the advice of Ray Dalio, the founder of Bridgewater, the world's largest hedge fund, who says that the key to effective goal-setting is 'pain plus reflection'. You need to adjust your business principles each time you fail, and after failure, you need to set yet more audacious goals.

That's what I did now. I didn't limit my ambitions. Instead, I went for it. I was going to set goals beyond what would seem rational to 99.99 per cent of the sane world and go for it, full tilt. After the trial, I wrote down my high-level objectives for the future.

First, family. I had missed them enormously over the past years. I felt I hadn't been there during my children's formative years and had been too geographically distant from Julia. I needed to spend more quality time with the children. And I needed to give Julia a reason to move to Guernsey.

Second, legacy. I wanted to create one for my family. To do this, I needed to invest in businesses that wouldn't necessarily be sold after a few years but would be there for generations. One such was Villa Saletta, nearly 1,800 acres of prime Tuscan countryside with a twelfth-century village and a collection of more than forty derelict properties, which we'd bought as a family back in 2000. Wine has been made there for 3,000 years and there are written records relating to it that date back to AD 980. The Vatican's map room contains a fifteenth-century document that shows Villa Saletta as a major centre between Pisa and Florence. Back then it belonged to the Riccardi family (originally from Kent, where their name was Richards), who were bankers to the Crusaders and subsequently to the Medici in Florence, and who not only looked after the Medici's money but their land and – it's widely rumoured – the keys to their chastity belts. Over the years, they accumulated considerable wealth from their banking activities and from the funds left with them by those who failed to return from the 'Holy Land'. The Hands are just the fourth family to own the estate in 800 years.

Third, Terra Firma. I wanted it to be as successful as it had been in 2007. The company could be reborn. I could learn from all the lessons of the previous twenty-odd years of private equity experience and make Terra Firma better.

Fourth, purpose. The world had been good to me, I owed it something and wanted to repay the debt.

In looking at these four objectives, I considered what my friend Jon Moulton, who had introduced me to my Guernsey house back in 2008, had achieved. He had left the private equity firm he had founded – Alchemy – and formed a public company called Better Capital. He launched it by taking out an electronic billboard in Leicester Square, listing from A to Z how Better Capital would be more successful than Alchemy, much to the chagrin of his former team. Jon is known for his willingness to give the finger to anyone he disagrees with, regardless of status, power or authority. Like me, he grew up without family wealth, went to state schools and suffered from a disability as a child. In his case, his physical health had been severely damaged by exposure to coal smoke in Stoke-on-Trent. If Jon could succeed with Better Capital and make it more successful than Alchemy, then I could make Terra Firma 2.0 even better than the original.

Jon is less well known for his extraordinarily generous philanthropy, support of think-tanks that aim to get accurate information to people and his encyclopaedic knowledge of medical developments. I wanted to focus my attention on making the world a better place by getting people to engage with it. I can't exactly claim to be a communist, but I do believe that decisions in society should be made from each according to their ability, and to each according to their need. Everyone should be involved. Julia and I had been successful with our various educational projects that sought to help with access to good education, whether at a local school level or Oxford University. I wanted to do more of that, and I also had a hankering to do something for the environment. In fact, Julia and I had already invested heavily in tree-planting programmes that were already at a level that meant they were sucking more carbon out of the air than that produced by 700,000 people.

I threw myself into trying to achieve all four objectives simultaneously at breakneck speed. During my first week back from Las Vegas, I caught six planes, ate out at restaurants nine times, held thirty-one meetings, took a boat to Herm and back, attended a birthday party, began the process of buying McDonald's in the Nordics, went to see *The Barber of Seville* at Glyndebourne, cooked dinner for myself and a friend, went to a school open day and conducted several interviews for a new CEO for Terra Firma.

The McDonald's project was particularly close to my heart. If I could become the master franchisee to run the Nordic region's McDonald's business I could build a legacy business for my family, funded by my family, that would be far more long-term than the usual private equity enterprise.

McDonald's is one of the most famous brands in the world and I have eaten at its restaurants on many occasions when I have been out on the road visiting investors. From a financial point of view, its 'Golden Arches' nickname is very appropriate; indeed, the official company name in China changed from 'Maidanglao' meaning McDonald's, to 'Jingongmen,' roughly translated to 'Golden Arches'. McDonald's consistently outperforms its competitors across different countries and through economic cycles. To me, it's one of the great entrepreneurial success stories – beginning in 1940 with brothers Richard and Maurice and a single restaurant in California and that, thanks to their entrepreneurial flair, culminating in an empire that's still flourishing more than eighty years later. Back when we owned Tank & Rast, our motorway service station company, we entered into a franchise agreement with Burger King to introduce its restaurants along the German autobahn. But I was far more impressed by McDonald's' offering and how well its system worked. It was a slicker operation and customers loved the product more. In 2015, we started to switch Tank & Rast from Burger King with the aim of becoming exclusively McDonald's.

So, when I discovered that the corporation was seeking a development licensee across the Nordic countries, I was immediately interested. McDonald's wanted to find an investor that could sit between the company and its franchisees in Sweden, Denmark, Norway and Finland to improve the trading performance in its 433 restaurants in the region. What is little known and of little interest to the customer buying their Big Mac and fries is that McDonald's operates a sophisticated franchising system that means many of its restaurants are owned by local operators.

The company sets the tone from the top with guidelines on how to advertise the brand, hygiene standards, food preparation procedures, the standardisation of kitchen equipment and purchasing of products, service standard objectives, delivery timings and staff training. Franchisees contribute essential local knowledge. They, after all, are the people who know their market and how best to cater for it. They determine variations to the product, pricing and opening hours accordingly.

We knew that if we were able to secure the Nordic deal it would represent the first time McDonald's had carved out a region of the world where the majority of the restaurants were owned by franchisees and put those franchisees under somebody other than McDonald's themselves. Effectively, they would be making us the master franchisee, and the franchisees would be sub-franchisees. Steve Easterbrook, who was McDonald's chief executive at the time, had approved this new departure for the company. But I still had to prove that I was the right partner. I had to persuade McDonald's that they were taking the right step in selling me more than 400 restaurants in the Nordics along with the franchise for Finland, Denmark, Sweden and Norway, serving nearly 200 million meals a year.

I was quizzed eleven times during the year-long due diligence process. It was as though I was twenty again and going for my first job interview. Julia for her part was interviewed by various senior officials at McDonald's six times while our younger son, who has worked at Terra Firma for a number of years, was interviewed thirteen times. When we finally heard that we had been awarded the master franchise for the Nordics, I felt I had got the best job ever, even if I had to pay my interviewers over €400 million to secure it. The Hands family was there for the long haul. At the end of seventeen years, McDonald's will let us know if they will give us an extension of another twenty years or ask us to sell the business to someone else, or themselves. This, as a single commitment from my family and me, is the largest we have made.

But before I could give my new job the attention I wanted to, I realised that I needed to get Terra Firma to be independent of me. At the time the company was costing me personally £45 million per year. I felt it needed new blood and a new direction.

A key player was Justin King, who had joined us back in January 2016. He had run Sainsbury's for a decade, transforming the supermarket group from an underachiever into a strong performer that grew like-for-like sales for nine consecutive years. I could see that Justin could not only focus on improving the financials of the companies we owned, he could also inspire their workforces. He would also be a major presence in our London office while I continued to be based in Guernsey or travelling the world. I could see him helping us to attract new investors in the same way that another well-regarded corporate name, the former Tesco chief executive Sir Terry Leahy, had done at the buyout firm Clayton, Dubilier & Rice.

We had also long been courting Andrew Géczy, a senior

financial services operator, and reached the point where we were prepared to make him an offer. I knew Andrew from his days at Citigroup, where he had spent fourteen years in a variety of roles, most notably as global head of structured corporate finance. We had bumped up against each other on deals from 1996 onwards and I knew he was a class act. Andrew had since run wholesale banking and markets at Lloyds Banking Group and I was convinced he could bring some discipline to Terra Firma's organisation as well as help the talent we had inside the firm flourish.

Andrew made it clear that he had strong views about how he wanted to transform the firm, operationally and structurally. He would manage Terra Firma and take control of the deal flow. Justin, meanwhile, would take control of the portfolio businesses and work out how to get them working better. The two of them would run Terra Firma day-to-day. I would be its most active investor and travelling salesman.

Within weeks of the second EMI trial ending in June 2016, we announced Andrew's appointment. This was a new departure for me. I had not just acknowledged that trying to do everything myself was beyond me, I had also acted on that knowledge. The 'Guy Factor' was important for Terra Firma, but in the future it had to be about more than me. The trio of Andrew, Justin and I represented a new governance structure for Terra Firma. As we set about relaunching the firm, I experienced a profound sense of relief.

We gave ourselves twin objectives: to extract as much value as possible from Terra Firma Fund III's remaining assets, and to persuade investors to invest money in a new fund based on the management structure I had put in place. The three of us started to introduce Terra Firma 2.0 to investors and the rest of the company, explaining how we hoped to move forward together.

First of all, though, I needed to apologise officially for EMI.

My presentation at our annual investor conference in September 2016 therefore included an expression of my regrets and 'three lessons learned'. First, I said, we would never again invest 30 per cent of a single fund in one asset. Second, we would not use equity from two funds in one investment. Third, we would cap our deals at no more than €500 million of equity. My apology went down well. Our investors also welcomed the arrival of Andrew and Justin.

One of the first businesses we turned our attention to was one of those in Fund III – Four Seasons Health Care, the largest chain of nursing homes in the UK. We had acquired it for £825 million in 2012 and it was Terra Firma's biggest deal since EMI in 2007. Four Seasons operated 500 care homes with 20,000 residents, plus sixty-one specialist care centres with 1,601 beds. And it was haemorrhaging money.

We reasoned that as the UK came out of recession, spending on elderly care would at least keep pace with inflation. The government, after all, would surely feel compelled to ensure that there was support for the most vulnerable. We also felt that there was plenty of scope for improvement. The nursing homes were not particularly well run. We could make savings in procurement and food costs simply through better management. We could also strike a better deal to buy medicines from Boots and train our own nurses.

And the price was attractive. When we had first bid back in 2006, our offer of £900 million had been beaten by the £1.5 billion offered by a Qatari fund (of which £1.3 billion of debt was provided by the Royal Bank of Scotland). Now we had the opportunity to buy Four Seasons Health Care for less than we had bid the previous time, while benefiting from the fact that the company now had an additional 140 homes in its portfolio that it had acquired from one of its largest rivals, Southern Cross. Growth in the sector had been steady. Four Seasons, however, had been over-leveraged and breached its banking covenants. RBS had therefore taken control and was now looking to find a new owner.

While the team considered the Four Seasons opportunity on economic grounds, I focused on the public relations challenge. This was a deal where we would be directly responsible for vulnerable people's lives and welfare. We would need to achieve the right balance between offering quality care and ensuring a level of profitability that would guarantee long-term financial health. The stories in the press about badly run care homes did not make the decision any easier for me. I don't think we have ever gone back and forth over a deal so many times. We had ten General Partner board meetings over four months and considered 437 pages of presentations. The team were convinced that Four Seasons could become the 'IBM of care', a trusted provider to local authorities all over the country. I eventually agreed, with the proviso that not only should we not cut standards in any way but that we should try to improve them.

It turns out I was right to be anxious. Even though the recession lifted, government austerity continued and local authorities felt the squeeze. The Southern Cross homes that had been handed back to the Care Quality Commission before being passed on to Four Seasons were not good facilities. Moreover, the synergies weren't there, so we had to spend more than anticipated and increase staffing levels. And while the majority of Four Seasons homes were run spectacularly well, there were some that simply weren't viable and others that operated to standards we were not prepared to accept. We therefore had to close some properties.

Ultimately, Justin was asked to make a decision – did we let the business go and cut our losses, or continue to support it? The decision was complicated by the fact that the care homes were really two businesses – one serving the public sector and one serving private customers. The private care business was doing well. Demand was increasing and better off individuals could find the money to pay for care. The public care business, on the other hand, was struggling, dependent as it was on funding from cash-strapped local authorities. The decision needed to be made quickly as H/2 Capital, an American vulture fund, had begun buying the company's debt, which was trading at a sharp discount (vulture funds typically invest in companies or properties that are performing poorly and may therefore be undervalued).

Justin – and a number of members of my team – felt that there was still a substantial upside in Four Seasons. They also believed that H/2 Capital had no desire to take over the day-to-day operations and would therefore be open to a deal. They felt H/2 Capital would be willing to sell the debt they had bought at a sharp discount for a quick profit brought on by the restructuring of the company. The numbers they produced on what could be achieved were very encouraging. Overall, Justin's conclusion was that Four Seasons could be very profitable. It just needed time for our changes to feed through and ensure a successful enterprise with the best reputation in the market.

The other business that was crucial to relaunching Terra Firma was Wyevale Garden Centres, which we had bought in 2012 in a deal that valued it at £276 million. The retailer had 129 centres across England and Wales with a property value of around £400 million. However, it was a business that was not producing a lot of profit relative to its asset value, hence the reason why we had been able to buy it at the price we had. Our view was that we could run the business better. We also thought the real estate component was very attractive, certainly in the longer term. Most of the centres were located on former farmland on the edge of towns and so offered the potential to be developed over time for housing and retail. All we had to do was wait patiently to get planning permission from the local authorities. Since there was considerable pressure from central government to build more houses, we were optimistic. In the meantime, we felt we should get the business working better.

Wyevale had suffered from underinvestment because Lloyds Banking Group, who had taken control of it in 2009 in a debt-for-equity swap after Wyevale had failed to keep up with interest payments, was interested in getting its money back rather than owning the business long term. We felt that the business was not maximising its sales; it could do better with its homeware, and restaurants and food concessions were also possible. With that in mind, we brought in a new management team and for the first two or so years things moved in the right direction. Earnings were £27.1 million in 2012. A year later they were £42.7 million and they rose again – to £56.1 million – in 2014. The management team under the chief executive, Kevin Bradshaw, was clearly on a roll.

Some of us began to wonder whether we should simply sell the business and take our profit. Others, however, felt there was more mileage to be had in our current strategy and even thought that it would be worth turning Wyevale into a national brand. They had become close to Wyevale's management team and felt an emotional commitment.

That should have been sufficient to ring a warning bell. When dealing with management, the role of a private equity team is not to establish a comfortable relationship; it should challenge, challenge and challenge them. Every management team believes it's doing a good job: if things are going wrong, it's always someone else's fault. I've never had a member of management come to me and say, 'I'm sorry, I mucked up.' It just doesn't happen. For the most part, they have no sense of risk, only of upside. You can give them incentives but there is no real alignment of goals. If the business is successful, they get paid well at the exit. If the business struggles, most private equity firms pay the existing team well to stay on so that there's someone there to pick up the pieces. That's not to say that management don't work hard or don't care. But they're on their own side, not yours, and they tend to believe their own propaganda. Hence the reason why private equity firms have constantly to challenge, challenge, challenge.

In 2014, with the management team at Wyevale having doubled profits, we got complacent and stopped challenging them. I can torture myself for hours by digging out 'The Garden Centre Group Operational Review, Paris, 25 April 2013', thirty-two pages; 'The Garden Centre Group Strategy Presentation, Paris, 25 April 2013', eighty-four pages; and then, if I really want to upset myself, I read through 'The Garden Centre Group Strategy Presentation Appendix, Paris, 25 April 2013', fifty-nine pages. Combined they constitute a brilliant piece of work. They evaluated what the management team was good at and what it was bad at. They analysed the customer base. They segmented the portfolio. They looked at the systems. They considered the potential of a national brand rather than a local one. And their conclusions were simple. The business didn't have the skill sets to develop a strong food and beverage offering; it needed a third party to do it for them. The sites were too diverse and different to be run in the same way and the customer didn't want a national brand in any case. The company did not have the skills or the technology to introduce digitalisation for the customer or a centralised warehouse distribution system. And the company currently lacked the discipline to determine the correct allocation of space between the core business and the various concessions. Put together largely by Terra Firma analysts, these brilliant reports were conveniently forgotten once the management team had decided it could walk on water.

Instead, supported by us, the management team set out on a journey to get to profits of £100 million. It introduced a national brand, a national food and beverage concept and a centralised warehouse. It gave the best spaces to concessions and pushed the core business to the fringes. By the time Justin arrived, Wyevale's earnings were heading south towards £27 million. The one bright spot on the horizon was that, despite the company's woes, we had an offer from a large investor to take it off our hands for £700 million.

In the same way I had with Four Seasons, I asked Justin what he thought we should do. Three months later, having studied the situation carefully, he came back with his assessment. The existing management team needed to be completely replaced, he said. They didn't have the skills to implement the current strategy. Whether that strategy was the right or wrong one, he couldn't be sure, but what was clear was that the cost of unwinding it at this juncture would be too great, given that it had already eaten up £200 million and committed the business to some long-term liabilities. Justin brought in a new management team, led by Roger McLaughlan, a veteran retailer who had most recently been in charge of Toys 'R' Us in the UK. Their diagnosis was optimistic. Most of the cost of implementation had already been met, they pointed out. The recent decline could be reversed. To sell the company at this stage would be a mistake.

Meanwhile, Andrew was working on deal flow. He had managed to get us into a number of transactions including what was known as Project Ford (a chain of Italian motorway service stations), was bringing in new people and had arranged meetings with investors in Asia and Australia to help raise a new fund. Technically, this should have been Terra Firma Fund IV but since four is a very unlucky number in Chinese and Japanese – in both languages it's similar to the word for death – we decided to count two other funds we had raised and skip to Terra Firma Fund VI.

I was aware that, according to this logic, Terra Firma Fund III should have been called Terra Firma Fund IV, but given likely resistance to the number four among Asian investors shifting the numbers seemed the best solution.

Together, Andrew, Justin and I presented a new image for Terra Firma. As I travelled around the world meeting hundreds of investors, I apologised for the long-drawn-out drama of EMI, pledged not to repeat the three mistakes we had made and explained how a one-man band had become a triumvirate. Andrew focused on asking investors to remember three numbers: 1.6, 2.8 and zero. Terra Firma had returned and multiplied all investments by 1.6 over twenty years. It had multiplied our return on infrastructure and real estate by 2.8 – this number excluded EMI and demonstrated how devastating that had been to our investment. Zero was the technical breaches, FCA sanctions, auditor opinions and quarterly reporting deadlines we were guilty of or had missed.

Andrew also neatly characterised the members of the triumvirate: Guy the Investor, putting his money where his mouth is; Justin the Operator, utilising his thirty-plus years of experience in the operations of business; and Andrew the Manager, overseeing the day-to-day of Terra Firma with an extraordinary blue-chip background in major banking companies. Finally, Justin presented the individual portfolio companies and how they were doing. He ran through the management plans for them, which were ambitious but, we all thought, achievable. If we did achieve them, we wouldn't just redeem ourselves – things would be 'better', and Terra Firma would be reborn.

By November we had put together an ambitious plan to show what €25 billion under management could look like. We called it twenty-five by twenty-five, the aim being to have €25 billion under management by 2025. If we achieved this Terra Firma would be receiving €375 million in annual management fees and everyone in Terra Firma would receive a very significant carry pool. People were making their own calculations as to what they could do with this wealth in 2025. Expectations and optimism were high.

Meanwhile, as I pitched what we were now calling Terra Firma 2.0 and our new fund around the world, taking in Tokyo, Taipei, Seoul, Beijing and Hong Kong, I found investors keen to do further due diligence on the firm and, potentially, to invest. At the British Private Equity and Venture Capital Association annual gala dinner in December, Andrew hosted blue-chip investors such as the Wellcome Trust, Goldman, USS, Hermes and Stepstone and found them all receptive to backing a new fund. They could have sat at anyone's table, but they chose ours.

The only thing I could see that was going to stop us achieving €25 billion by 2025 was if something went badly wrong with the businesses currently sitting in our portfolio. We had hung our reputations and our futures on returning our investors' money. Throughout my career, I had seen new joiners mark down the positions they had inherited and blame their predecessors' decisions. Andrew and Justin chose not to. Rather than practising a scorched earth policy post-EMI – they had looked at the portfolio and felt confident that they could reinvigorate it. I believed, along with the rest of my investors, that if they thought they could do it then they almost certainly could, since they had no need to justify anything at this stage.

As we came to the end of 2016, I was very aware that Terra Firma Fund III's ten-year life would be coming to an end on 4 May 2017. The fund was valued at 71 per cent of the original funding investors had put in. To ensure they got their money back, we needed to increase the value of the portfolio by around €2 billion. This would have to be done through six investments – in addition to Four Seasons Health Care and Wyevale Garden Centres, both based in the UK, there was AWAS, our global airline leasing company based in Dublin; Consolidated Pastoral Company (CPC), our cattle station business based in Brisbane, Australia; EverPower, our wind power business based in Pittsburgh; and finally RTR, our Italian solar business in Rome. It was a ragbag collection of deals, located all over the world in totally unconnected industries, which had only two similarities – first, they were in industries under extreme pressure and going through enormous change; second, they all had a sponsor in Terra Firma who really believed in them.

In my case, it was the green energy businesses and the cattle stations that seemed most exciting. They were, I felt, businesses that, if run correctly, were capable of making a great difference to the world. They were also businesses that would do better in ownership that was long term in its thinking rather than in a private equity firm whose fund was running out. Both my second son and elder daughter have worked on the cattle stations, getting stuck in to the day-to-day business, with my son also doing an extended stint as a jackaroo.

For his part, Justin thought that Wyevale and Four Seasons were only starting their transformation. So far as AWAS, the biggest of our enterprises, was concerned, we knew we needed more time to sell it: it was possibly too large for just one buyer. Everything pointed in the direction of trying to get the fund extended. We therefore put a proposal to our investors asking for additional time in order to hit what seemed to us the very achievable objective of returning between 80 and 90 per cent of the originally invested money to them. It wasn't what I wanted – my goal was to get my investors all their money back. It would also have involved me personally making a huge financial loss as I was Terra Firma Fund III's largest investor, owning approximately 10 per cent of the fund. But it promised a better outcome than if we wound up the fund in just a few months' time, and for Justin and Andrew it would represent real success – a substantial increase in the value of the portfolio from when they joined and more than enough to allow the launch of twenty-five by twenty-five.

Fortunately our investors agreed and we were able to put in place a one-year extension to the life of the fund with support from over 80 per cent of them. They were also willing to pay us full fees even though we had lost them 30 per cent of their money and kept their investments for far longer than expected. They were willing to give us a chance.

With Justin responsible for the portfolio and Andrew running Terra Firma day-to-day, I turned to my first priority: family. We were very conscious that this would be our first Christmas without Betty and wanted to do something special. With my love of nature in mind, I organised a trip for the six of us to Punta Arenas, Chile, just before Christmas to join a cruise ship anchored in Drake Passage – known as one of the roughest crossings in the world. Since Julia gets seasick at the best of times, we caught a charter flight at 4 am from Punta Arenas, landing at King George Island two and a half hours later. The first thing we noticed was the wreckage of a plane that had crash-landed some years before and had been left to rot. Not an auspicious start. We had to walk a mile and a half across the island to find a beach where a dinghy would take us to the boat. We trooped in a military line across the island with our luggage following behind in an open trailer, dragged by an ancient tractor.

As we walked, we saw various countries' research centres, each trying to look like something from back home. Most impressive was the Russian base, which could have been a church transplanted from St Petersburg. Having made our way to the beach, we were then taken two at a time to the boat – a former icebreaker. The captain headed south to chase the good weather and the more interesting icebergs, and when we woke up the next day we were in a new world of pristine white ice, blue sky and a clear aquamarine sea as far as the eye could see. I felt alive. Our boat, the *Hanse Explorer*, was the first ship that season to go through the Lemaire Channel, reaching as far south as Antarctica at 65°07'12.0"S 64°00'36.0"W, and as we penetrated ever further over days of twenty-four-hour light, we saw an extraordinary collection of birds and sea life. It was the beauty of the ice, however, that struck me most. I loved the sounds it made. I loved the complete feeling of isolation.

It was impossible, though, not to be aware of the darker side of all this beauty. We saw icebergs that had broken away and were melting slowly over vast distances. We saw penguins that would now have to swim miles and miles to reach their fishing grounds. We saw an icy world in retreat. And we saw piles of human waste and plastic strewn around. The trip served as a reminder for me of the world beyond work – a world of family and of wider humanity. When we got home again and celebrated my mother's eightieth birthday early in March 2017 at the Sevenoaks house, that sense of family and humanity was joined by a powerful sense of mortality. Looking around a room full of friends and family, and realising that some of my mother's grandchildren were now older than Julia and I were when we were married and had children, I realised how easy it is to forget how precious time is, and how little one has.

Fortunately, there was at least now one area of my professional life that I could tie in with family. My younger son had worked at Terra Firma for a number of years and had been involved with projects that included Odeon Cinemas, AWAS and Annington Homes. Now he was an integral part of the McDonald's business, even spending two weeks at a branch in Glasgow where he did everything from a night shift to cleaning out the kitchen. After the picture-selling episode, Julia had made it clear that she would never work with me again, and given what a tough taskmaster I am – particularly with family – it can't have been easy for my son. But I came to admire his excitement to do deals – which he shares with me – and his ability to focus on smaller details and empathise with management – which he shares with Julia. And, while I could never make up for the seven years I had lost to EMI, it was great to be getting close to the family again.

2017 was looking promising in other ways, too, thanks to Annington Homes. I had first become involved with Annington – which owns privately rented houses in the UK – back in 1996 when Nomura purchased 57,000 houses that were rented out to the Ministry of Defence, which in turn rented them to service families. In 2012, along with twenty other investors, we purchased Annington from Nomura. However, it had been a heavily leveraged buyout, involving £450 million in equity and £550 million in debt. It became clear to me in 2016 that the Ministry of Defence had been advised that Annington was hopelessly overleveraged and could, as it were, be starved of funds if the ministry did not give back to Annington the houses it did not need. One could see why they might think this: they were paying a fraction of the rent that the houses would rent for on the open market, with a review not due until 2021. While they would continue to pay a nominal rent on the houses they kept empty we would struggle with our debt situation without getting houses back, which we could then sell to reduce our debt, and get ourselves in a position to refinance it when the chance arose.

The one option we were left with was to raise more equity. But that was easier said than done. Raising more equity on a business that had never paid a dividend – and had the balloon repayment of over £3 billion debt in 2022 and 2023 hanging over it – was a challenge and a half. It couldn't be done unless we could win the agreement of the senior co-investors, and the objections of two of them would be sufficient to scupper our chances. We duly went out to four banks for advice on how to restructure the debt from being a repayment of £1.4 billion in 2022 and £1.8 billion in 2023 to a staggered repayment over the next two to thirty years. If we pulled it off, it would be the largest transaction ever done in the UK sterling debt markets.

Secrecy was essential. One might assume that the Ministry of Defence would want its landlord to be in a good financial position. But if the great quantity of empty, deteriorating properties was anything to go by, such an assumption seemed misplaced. Obviously, what we wanted (and what, it seemed to us, was in everyone's interest) was houses returned to us in good condition that we could then sell or rent to young couples – an ambition very much in line with government policy. However, in love and war – and this felt increasingly like war – there is no such thing as logic. The Ministry of Defence seemed determined simply to destroy the enemy, and that enemy was Annington.

Over the next few months, the Annington team, representatives from Barclays – the investment bank that Terra Firma's team had ultimately selected to run the process – and I travelled to see the major accounts whose support we needed. Initially our approaches were rejected. By April, however, we had their support. In May, we kicked off raising the equity and in June we went out to raise the debt. The official announcement of the restructuring – the biggest ever done in the sterling market – was made on 5 July. It gave me some satisfaction that we'd managed to do all this without alerting the Ministry of Defence. To say that their advisers were annoyed would be an understatement. Some months later, and with the advisers now out of the picture, we agreed with the Ministry of Defence to go to binding arbitration to try to solve our differences over future rent levels.

At the end of 2017, as I sat on a chairlift in Whistler, I thought about the last few years. It seemed things were finally going well. It had been a tough nine years, but Julia and I were building our dream home in Guernsey, the construction of which may be completely over the top but would provide masses of employment on the island, including for skilled craftsmen, and indeed keep a number of specialist trades going for a few years. At least, that's how I justified it to myself. I was seeing my parents, brother and sister more than I had in years. Friends were coming to Guernsey more often. My son and I were finding it difficult to work together, as any son with a demanding father who is also the boss would, but we were managing it. The children were growing up, and while I was probably a little too controlling if not smothering, we were at least spending some holidays together. All I felt I needed was Julia to agree to move to Guernsey and, if she did, then maybe having it all was possible.

But the business world doesn't allow you much breathing space. After the victory with Annington in July came the disappointment of Four Seasons Health Care, which, thanks to government cost-cutting, was yanked from Justin's control and taken over by H/2 Capital in December. And then there was Wyevale and its continuing problems. We'd approached various potential investors, and had been turned down. In June, I offered to put my own money in to support the company, but the advisory board rejected it. Now I turned my attention to finding out why third-party investors, having done their own independent due diligence over the last six months, had decided to turn the opportunity down. And what I heard was not good.

The ambition to turn a collection of local businesses into a nationwide operator had proved to be massively misconceived. Britain is a conglomerate of micro-climates and different weather patterns. The assumption that you can buy perishables such as flowers centrally and then sell them all at the same time across the nation is a wholly false one. Numerous Wyevale stores bore testimony to this in terms of unsold stock. To make matters worse, when we had tried to ramp up orders with local suppliers we hadn't seen any economies of scale. Local suppliers viewed selling nationally not as an advantage but as an additional cost. The whole model was wrong.

Issues were also arising with our new management structure. Potential investors from around the world who had sat through one of my pitches and decided to come to London to do on-site due diligence were clearly detecting a certain lack of chemistry in the new triumvirate. They had been presented with a single vision by one person, but now they were in London to spend perhaps two days with us, their barrage of questions to lots of different people elicited answers that suggested lots of different narratives and even some internal tensions. And, of course, these investors were talking to each other about their experience.

It all reminded me of the 2000 film *Almost Famous*, in which a kid who has been given an assignment by *Rolling Stone* magazine to write about the band Stillwater follows them on tour and so becomes witness to various mishaps and relationship clashes. Inevitably, he wants to include them all in his article. Bad things are normal in any firm – as in most marriages. As long as no one knows, most companies and most marriages survive. But when all the investors – or, in the case of a marriage, the family and friends – are watching 24/7 as things go wrong, there is no escape. Our internal tensions were losing us our cornerstone investors. Without them we would not have the momentum to raise more money and the fundraising process would freeze up and die.

As 2018 dawned, Justin, Andrew and I reflected on the six deals we'd done that could demonstrate to investors our track record of working together. We had bought the German hotel group Welcome Hotels. Terra Firma's Support Capital initiative had injected money into a French jewellery company and a sports surfaces company that manufactured artificial grass. Our joint venture – Naga – had invested in a German jewellery business and a French cosmetics company. Finally, we had bought the McDonald's operations in the Nordics and created Food Folk. All in all, we had spent less than £400 million on these six deals – a sum less than a third of the size of the average deal in Terra Firma Fund III. Such deals were not directly comparable to the type of transaction I was used to, but they did reflect what the triumvirate were capable of.

On the other hand, we were losing money, and the amount we were losing was increasing. Costs were going up as we hired new people and as the existing funds reached the end of their life. Potential earnings were going down. Andrew had reduced the costs of the existing operation, but he had also brought in new people and we had to pay for them. Reducing costs had sometimes involved dispensing with the services of longer-standing, loyal supporters in the old guard. I missed them, and it was sad to see them go. But I also knew that it was something we'd had to do with every business we had ever bought and turned around – and if we had to do it with other organisations, we had to do it to ourselves. In other words, we were making necessary changes and it all felt exciting, but the transformation was not proving cheap. I didn't have a bottomless pit of money I could draw on to keep the company alive while we tried to raise Fund VI. At the same time, I needed to prove to myself that the money I had spent over the past ten years to keep Terra Firma alive had been spent wisely. Terra Firma 2.0's twenty-five by twenty-five didn't just have to work for Andrew, Justin and the team – it was also important for my sense of self-worth, my pride and my pocketbook.

I had always said to the team that it didn't matter precisely how well we did. What mattered was that we didn't have another failure. Our investors could take EMI. They could take Four Seasons. But they would be far less understanding if Wyevale, an operational real estate business for which we had a clear plan, failed, particularly given Justin's successful background at Sainsbury's and our earlier decision to turn down a £700 million bid.

March 2018 in England turned out to be one of the coldest months in recent times. The 'Beast from the East' – as meteorologists dubbed the cold front coming in from Siberia – froze the country. Garden centres had few customers. At our portfolio business meeting in Milan in the middle of March, I was told that Wyevale couldn't meet its wage bill that coming Friday without a cash injection. To say I was livid would be to put it mildly. The management team explained that they hadn't predicted or allowed for the Beast from the East. My view was that they should have had a contingency plan. In the end I put my hand in my own pocket and bailed the company out so that suppliers and wages could be paid. But I knew that this could only be a short-term solution to a far bigger problem.

It didn't matter that by spring 2018, retailer after retailer had gotten into trouble and many had gone under. It didn't matter that many other private equity firms had the same problem. What mattered was that if Wyevale failed, our investors would not take the risk of investing in us, not because of this specific local problem or because of what had happened with Terra Firma Fund III but because if anything went wrong with our next fund, they would be asked why on earth – given Wyevale, given EMI – they had still gone ahead and invested in us.

Top-performing funds very rarely beget top-performing

funds. Indeed, there is a negative correlation between how a fund manager performs on one fund and how they perform on the next. But investors always tend to back managers whose last fund showed a strong performance – not because it predicts good performance, but because it gives them an excuse if something goes wrong with the next fund.

If Wyevale was proving a massive problem, then President Trump's bearish comments on green energy sources wasn't helping EverPower. When Terra Firma acquired the US-based wind energy business in 2009, we saw the opportunity to scale up an operating and development business with the support of state and federal incentives. By 2018, however, we ended up selling the business in two separate transactions at a 0.8x gross cash multiple, rather than the almost 3x multiple we thought the business was worth prior to the 2016 election. In a few short months we'd moved to operating what was probably the world's worst performing fund. Justin and I realised that our hopes of getting our investors' money back had disappeared. We would be lucky if we got them back two thirds. The chance now of raising a new fund had also completely disappeared. Over the next year, first Justin and then Andrew would leave. My hopes of passing Terra Firma on as a fund management business to someone else had been dashed in three months, and my hopes of having it all had evaporated.

CHAPTER 13

Hell Has Many Forms

Bye bye happiness
Hello loneliness
I think I'm gonna die

ALL THAT JAZZ,
'Bye Bye Life'

In January 2018 Julia gave me a late Christmas present, announcing rather suddenly that she had decided she would be moving to Guernsey in March. She was prepared to sacrifice her friends and home in Sevenoaks to be with me. I, however, continued to work. I clocked up nintey-hour weeks and travelled on more than 300 planes during her first 240 days in Guernsey.

We were building our dream house together in Guernsey, but how many days would I spend in it? I missed having dogs around, but if we got them, would I ever walk them? There were 200,000 photographs I'd taken over the years that I had never looked at. My record collection continued to expand, but I didn't listen to any of it, and I hadn't viewed a TV programme in years – Arsenal, England or Man United football matches (which I would watch with Julia) and the news were the only exceptions. I still went to the opera, but that was a social thing for the company. Julia usually had to kick me to stop me snoring during the performance as I took every opportunity I could to catch up on sleep.

Eventually my body decided it'd had enough. In May 2018 I was at a McDonald's conference in Vienna. We'd had meetings all day, followed by a large drinks party in the hotel's sky bar in the evening. Most people were then planning to go to bed so as to be fresh the following morning, but I'd arranged to go out for dinner. At the reception, however, after the second drink and the third canapé I started to feel dizzy and unwell. I made my apologies and said I'd have to skip the dinner – something I'd never done before in the whole of my career. My decision to turn in was seen as so strange that one of the Terra Firma team, Pasquale Nazzaro, offered to walk me back to my room when I said I needed to lie down.

Apparently, I was lucid enough as we walked to my room, but once I'd got there and closed the door behind me, I fell on the bed. I immediately realised something was very wrong. For once keeping my mobile in my breast pocket proved a good thing. I dialled Julia on the autodial and put her on speaker. By the time she answered, my speech was almost impossible to make out. Luckily, her best friend Yvonne was there, who happens to be a doctor. She asked me various questions. Can you lift your right arm? Do you have a headache? Can you see clearly? Can you sit up? Grunt once for yes, twice for no. Through the fog, I was able to respond.

Julia kept talking to me while Yvonne rang the hotel. Receiving no answer when they first knocked on the door, the staff went away. Julia managed to make contact with Andrew Miller, the Terra Firma managing director helping with the McDonald's business, who was in Vienna with me, and he persuaded them to unlock my room. They discovered me there semi-conscious. I had been violently sick. An ambulance was called; doctors, nurses and paramedics stuck so many plastic wires on my chest that to Andrew it seemed as though they were plugging me into something. And then we were in the ambulance, with Andrew next to me and Pasquale – who had come up to see what was wrong – in hot pursuit in a taxi.

Once the ambulance had arrived at the hospital, I was rushed on a gurney through what seemed endless corridors while doctors shone lights into my eyes and asked me questions in German I didn't understand. That worried them. It's not clear whether or not they had been told I was English. Finally, a doctor who could speak English materialised and rattled through questions to

Andrew and Pasquale before putting a drip into my arm and telling them to wait with me.

I don't remember anything from the instant I collapsed on the bed to the moment I was prodded awake by Andrew and Pasquale, who had slept most of the night on plastic chairs in the waiting room. The doctor told them that I'd had a mild stroke – with any luck, he said, a transient ischaemic attack, or a TIA, which is a stroke that doesn't usually have long-term effects. However, only time would tell. Meanwhile, I was starting to come back to life. The doctor measured my blood sugar – I had eaten nothing the day before. Stress, an empty stomach, lack of sleep and alcohol were, he said, not a wise combination for a diabetic. I can't say I took much notice.

By the time I was discharged, it was daylight and I was already worrying about the next day's meetings. We reached the hotel at 5 am. Andrew and Pasquale sent me to bed. They took the 8:30 am meeting themselves, but I was at the table for the mid-morning session and went through the rest of the conference as though there was nothing wrong. Only my slightly slurred speech would have given me away.

Once back in Guernsey I went to see my doctor. She was concerned. I wasn't passing the cognitive tests she gave me, which showed that I hadn't fully recovered. Until I had undergone a battery of tests, she couldn't be sure whether I had suffered a TIA, the effects of which would pass, or a stroke. Regardless of the diagnosis, I needed to do something about my lifestyle. I was overweight, diabetic and chronically stressed. Given all that, and the fact that I had just had some sort of an attack, my chances of reaching sixty-five were at best fifty-fifty if I didn't take the appropriate steps.

Over the next two weeks they put me through a mass of tests. They couldn't find anything wrong – my sugar levels were fine for a diabetic, and my heart was fine for someone my age. The doctors I saw after the tests thought I was simply putting myself under too much pressure and needed to make some changes. My life insurance company agreed with them. At the end of the year my policy was not renewed. I could no longer get keyman insurance.

Even so, despite the doctors and the insurance company, I continued to work ninety-hour weeks and took more flights than there were days in the year. I knew I wanted to be healthier and spend more time with my family. But I felt a compulsion to keep going. These priorities were not compatible. As every newspaper agony aunt would say, my work-life balance was shot to pieces, but I wasn't listening.

As 2018 went on, it became clear that Terra Firma was not going to be able to raise another blind pool fund. I had no idea what the way forward was, or indeed if there was a way forward. All my life I had never had a mentor, nor been close enough to anyone I worked with to build the sort of relationship that many successful men and women have, that allows them to ask for advice or bounce ideas around. Now, for the first time, and years after I should have done so, I decided I needed to look for one

I found two. Glen Moreno had spent four years as the chief executive of Fidelity International and eighteen years at Citigroup, where he was a group executive. Tom McKillop had formerly been CEO of AstraZeneca and chairman of the RBS Group, which he helped steer through the early days of the financial crash in 2007. Glen understood family firms, extremely dominant personalities and the City. Tom knew what it was like to reach the pinnacle of success, experience a public failure and then pick oneself up and move forward.

We soon worked out what questions and issues I needed to address. Business-wise, what should I do with Terra Firma? What should I do with the money I had invested? What should I do with those investments and third-party investors? In terms of my private life, how should I approach family and friendships? What should I do about my health? Should I become more involved in philanthropy? Should I take more of a practical interest in politics? Should I re-engage my creative side? Above all, should I try to be happy or continue to just focus on striving to be successful?

Tom told me there are three determinants of change. First, how bad is it if you don't change? Second, what's the prize if you do change? Third, how difficult is it to change? My judgement on the first count was that I would probably die early if I didn't change – but then death, if it appears to be some years away, doesn't seem real. On the second count, it was difficult to achieve the prize unless I knew first which prize I was aiming for. On the third count, I knew how difficult it would be for me to change. I was booked a whole year ahead. Over the next twelve months, according to my diary, I would have just four free days, including weekends. I was even having to schedule my phone calls with Julia to make sure I checked in with her. I knew pretty much what I would be doing every hour of every day for the foreseeable future. I also knew that I would always be late because the schedule I had set myself was impossible, and that I would always be tired because I wasn't getting enough sleep.

A good mentor never tells you what to do. Instead, they ask you the questions most people don't have the guts to ask and they make you question yourself. Sometimes their questions are uncomfortable. Why should Julia come to Guernsey if all she's able to do is to sit in the house while you work? What are the odds on someone with your weight and fitness living to eighty?

When I looked this up, I discovered that eighty was a pipe dream. Mid-sixties was far more likely.

The trouble was, though, that even with my mentors there to help me, I still didn't want to give anything up. I wanted to do more deals, give more to charity, have a bigger involvement in politics, spend more time on photography, socialise more, eat more and drink ever better wines while spending more time with Julia and my family. If I'd taken drugs or gambled, I would have been seen as an addict and people would have distanced themselves from me. Because what I was doing was socially acceptable, it was the reverse and everybody wanted my time and my attention. Meanwhile, 22-year-olds joined Terra Firma and couldn't keep up with the way I worked, often turning up to meetings late because they were too tired after working till the wee hours then struggling to make the 7 am breakfast meeting. I would not only make the meeting but would have done an hour of work beforehand.

Then, on holiday that summer, I started to feel awful again. This time, however, it was nothing stroke-related. It was my blood sugar levels, which were averaging above 250 by US readings and above thirteen by UK readings – more than twice the normal level. I was given further diabetic medicine, a daily injection to help get my sugar levels down.

I still didn't want to make a radical change to my lifestyle, so I tried hypnotism to see if it could help combat the poor eating habits I had developed over the course of a few decades spent constantly on the move. In the process, I established that the great motivating force in my life was fear, not the desire for reward. My hypnotist proposed doing some regressive therapy to help me establish where my fears came from and why I had them. But I drew a line there: I felt I had demons enough without going out of my way to discover new or old ones. In any case, I had no desire to open up to anyone. I was willing to tell her that I was scared of boredom, of failure, of not doing enough and of letting people down. But otherwise I proved to be a difficult patient. Everything that motivated me seemed to come back to fear, and I wasn't prepared to explore where that fear came from.

That left me with a temporary success in one small area of my eating habits: roast potatoes. Quite simply my hypnotist made me fear them as the great evil that would make me unwell and kill me. This could scarcely be a healthy long-term weight loss solution, though. As she herself pointed out, she would have to keep topping up the fear. She was right. After a while, potatoes became less scary. At first, I would slip in the odd French fry. Then it was a baked potato with all the trimmings. Hypnotism wasn't going to be a long-term solution to my state of mind.

Justin, Andrew and I never really came to a formal decision not to raise another blind pool fund. However, Justin went part-time in September 2018 and Andrew left seven months later in April 2019. The rebirth of the firm hadn't worked. It's easy with hindsight to look back at Four Seasons and Wyevale and say they were never going to work, but it wasn't insane to believe that a Conservative government would support payments to nursing homes in order to provide dignity to their most loyal voters in the last days of their lives. Likewise, buying garden centres wasn't stupid. Planning permissions were becoming easier to get and many garden centres are worth more today than they were in 2012 – since we sold them most of the garden centres have increased sales and profits dramatically.

I've often wondered if it was right to try to rebuild the firm. Our ambition to have €25 billion under management by 2025 was a good dream to have. Had it worked, Terra Firma could well have been worth between €5 billion and €10 billion (private equity management companies have traded over the years on a percentage of assets under management; in 2007, Terra Firma was valued at just over 25 per cent of the assets it had under management). Justin, Andrew and I would have been billionaires, and other colleagues would have been multi-millionaires. But it didn't work and instead the nightmare years continued. The question for me as I approached my sixtieth birthday was – what could I do? After twelve years of what I saw as complete failure, was there anything positive left to come? I'd been nicknamed by some 'The Phoenix' because of my ability to rise from the ashes, but now I wasn't sure I had the energy to get off the ground. I felt more like Icarus.

Despite my personal mental state, the firm continued to move forward. In October 2018 Terra Firma led a consortium to acquire Parmaco, a Finnish company specialising in building and renting high-quality, flexible and modular buildings for schools, day-care providers and nursing homes. As a fast-growing business with an ambitious aim to more than double its size in three to five years, Parmaco appealed to us as an investment and complemented our track record of investing in asset-backed operational leasing, real estate and infrastructure businesses. I was also interested in the company's forward-thinking approach that put it at the front of the trend towards using modular solutions as long-term alternatives to fixed buildings. Entrepreneurs are impressed by creative solutions and love building businesses. Here was a company that ticked both boxes and was also increasing the number of school places available. It touched my head and my heart, metaphorically, just as both were being examined quite literally.

At the beginning of 2019, I was still feeling unwell, even though my diabetes was now under control. I therefore decided to see my doctor to see if she had a magic pill she could prescribe. She didn't. Instead, she started to talk about stress. I had always resisted such conversations in the past with anyone but Julia: I was anxious not to appear weak. But Dr Abigail, unlike the hypnotist and my previous doctors, didn't back off. Gently and persistently, she asked questions I had been asked for years but never answered honestly. Are you depressed? Do you ever feel it's too much? Are you enjoying life? Do you have close friends that you see on a regular basis? Can you share your fears with your family? Is the stress affecting your diet, energy, sleep, sex life, etc.? And finally, do you have suicidal thoughts? By the end, much to my surprise, I found myself agreeing that I would see someone.

In February I met with a psychiatrist at University College London. He asked me, 'What would you like to hear me say?' I explained to him that at times I felt very depressed, and I didn't feel completely safe, but that I didn't want to take any form of medication. I also explained that while I was interested in hearing what he had to say, as I would be interested in any academic debate, I wasn't intending to take his advice. It was my life, not his, after all.

We chatted for an hour, at the end of which he repeated his initial question: 'What would you like to hear me say?' He pointed out that throughout our session I had talked about myself in the third person. It was as if I had been discussing another person. He then said that he was happy to tell this 'other person' what he felt they should do, and I could either treat all this as an academic exercise or choose to act on his advice. Either way, having spent an hour with me and my other self, he would like us both to listen. He told us – told me – that he wouldn't recommend therapy. He said that I had managed to cope with my demons reasonably well for the past fifty years, and he didn't think it was sensible for me to release them at that time. He recommended that I take a mild anti-depressant. If nothing else, at least it would enable me to feel safe again.

An hour later, I collected a prescription for a very low dose of anti-depressant. It did for me exactly what he said it would: it took the edge off my depression and make me feel safe again. At times, he has suggested increasing the dose but I don't feel the need. It's enough to make me feel safe. I just wish I had sought such help back in 2007, when EMI started to go wrong. Out of curiosity I took a number of personality and aptitude tests that we use when recruiting people to Terra Firma before I started taking anti-depressants and after taking them for three months. The results were eye-opening. After three months, people around me were saying that I had become more thoughtful, calm and patient. I still wasn't the perfect boss by any means. But I was a little more tolerable. For me personally, life was also becoming a lot more bearable.

Back in 2007, Terra Firma had been one of the top ten alternative asset managers in the world and I was making good decisions. Over the next twelve years, my decisions had been driven as much by fear as they had by logic, and a lot of them, in hindsight, were poor. By June 2019, I hadn't raised any blind pool fund money. Since the EMI appeal verdict in 2013, I had spent €279 million keeping Terra Firma alive and my investors had given me fees of €256 million to meet that cost. With the lack of fear and clarity of mind that the anti-depressant gave me, I could finally face up to the fact that I was never going to be a Stephen Schwarzman. My dreams of an earthly kingdom created by wealth were over.

Our investor conference in September 2019 was a muted affair, conducted entirely over the phone. No one was making any estimate on what the recovery would be on Terra Firma Fund III now. I didn't attend as there was no need. We weren't raising a blind pool fund and I certainly wasn't going to give any predictions. People responsible for the individual deals gave a brief update. It was sombre, and over in forty-five minutes. The year-end mark indicated that the fund was now worth €2.9 billion, just over 50 per cent of what had been originally invested.

There was, however, some good news so far as the remaining businesses within the fund were concerned. Back in April, the Four Seasons Health Care group had gone into administration, adding another layer of complexity to the sale process for the twenty-four Brighterkind-branded care homes that we still owned. In a worst-case scenario, this would have left the Brighterkind care homes without a management team and with no operational oversight. However, by September, we had started conversations with a trade buyer that was one of the largest British care home operators. The negotiations were brutal but when we closed the transaction in January 2020, we had managed to safely and responsibly hand over the care of 1,400 residents to another sensible care home operator, and returned 2.2 times the capital that investors had put into the business with us.

We also successfully completed the break-up sale of Wyevale Garden Centres. Terra Firma's original investment thesis had been underpinned by Wyevale's asset backing, and we decided to pursue an exit strategy that gave the market – local and national – an opportunity to price these assets on an individual, portfolio and whole-business basis. We did something private equity funds normally hate doing – we attached an asking price to each of the garden centres. The combined asking price was £405 million; we achieved £404 million. We sold 145 garden centres in fifty-seven transactions. This exit allowed Wyevale to fully settle its enormous debts, pay off the pension liability, treat employees fairly and recover over £80 million in equity value.

We applied a similar approach to Consolidated Pastoral Company (CPC), our cattle station based in Brisbane, selling eight of the fifteen cattle stations on an individual basis to a broad set of local Australian and global buyers. In the autumn, I started to put the wheels in motion to buy the seven remaining stations from the fund. The prospects of this generational investment and its long-term growth potential made for a nice addition to my personal portfolio.

This personal portfolio, which some of my investors had joined, was, to the surprise of many, beginning to do really well. Whether this was because of me or in spite of me, I don't know. But there was certainly a clarity there when it came to aligning people's interests and ambitions, no doubt helped by the fact that rather than having to deal with 200 investors, I was now working with less than a dozen. It was beginning to feel a bit like the old days at Nomura.

Other businesses were going well, too. Annington paid its first dividend of £132 million, and the business entered into an arbitration agreement, accelerating the resolution of differences with the Ministry of Defence. Parmaco increased its portfolio to 243,000 square metres from 192,000 square metres the year before. Welcome Hotels completed a strategic assessment of each hotel and executed successfully on the operational improvement and capex plan, while EBITDA (a company's earnings before interest, taxes, depreciation and amortisation) increased by over 10 per cent compared to 2018. We were in the process of selling Welcome Hotels and, if we sold it at the price we were discussing at the time, we would have doubled our money in less than two years. Finally, at Food Folk, just two years after the initial acquisition the business was performing much better than anyone could have reasonably expected, and sales across our 425 restaurants had grown over 7 per cent and we were opening new stores at pace. From having purchased the worst performing restaurants in Europe, we now had restaurants performing in the upper quartile worldwide.

Meanwhile, the real estate in Hand Picked Hotels was proving valuable. Hendon Hall Hotel was sold for sheltered accommodation for £12 million, approximately three times what it was worth as a hotel. It sold on Julia's birthday. She had been born just a few miles away in Colindale – in the front room of a semi-detached three-up, three-down house, which her family shared with an Indian family who also had two children. The families became good friends, with the eldest son continuing to see Julia's family right up to Betty's death. The economic change in Julia's and indeed my life from our childhoods to now had been extraordinary, but at the same time, while we had moved financially a lot, we both felt most comfortable with the people who had known us prior to our wealth.

If the first half of 2019 was filled with uncertainty, by the year's end we were celebrating Terra Firma's twenty-fifth anniversary. And as we moved into 2020 I was optimistic again. In fact, I think I always am optimistic when a new year beckons. Maybe it's the Christmas spirit. Maybe it's having a day's holiday. Maybe it's because I love Christmas pudding. Or maybe it's because I first met Julia on New Year's Day. For me, as it was for the pagan festivals that predate Christmas, it's about rebirth. It's about a clean slate. It's about a new chance.

My aims as 2020 dawned, like the future, looked clear and bright: wind down the blind pool funds, focus on the big Hands Family Office deals (the individual businesses that I had been acquiring since 2012 that were not part of the blind pool funds), work with a small number of highly aligned investors, shrink the firm to a size where I could know everyone and be able to see them in person regularly, and travel around the world, staying close to my management teams and my co-investors, while delegating more and more those parts of the business I didn't like and wasn't good at. Things were looking up. My ambitions were a little less twenty-five by twenty-five, more about buying six or seven businesses over the next ten years – businesses that I would really love. After completing twelve lean years since June 2007, maybe the thirteenth year, 2020, would finally be a successful one.

We were already well along with one key deal. Welcome Hotels was going to be sold to a consortium of Middle Eastern investors led by an Omani family. Things had to be put on hold when the Sultan of Oman died suddenly: the Omanis felt that signing too close after his death would be disrespectful. But after a suitable pause, I travelled to meet them in Florence and we agreed to go forward.

Final negotiations involved some classic price chipping. I wanted £120 million. They haggled me down to £112 million. I was trying to secure the hotels' paintings, having discovered most of them were borrowed from the previous owner's daughter. We were even arguing over who paid for the costs of breakfast on the day of completion and who received the income from the break-fast that day. We had spent in the hundreds of thousands on lawyers, a register of assets, accountants' fees and so on. The Omanis must have spent in the low millions. But finally the deal was effectively done, subject to documentation and bar some unimaginable catastrophic event.

With the notary booked to complete the sale on 31 March, we celebrated with bottles of Italian wine over an excellent Italian meal. Selling Welcome was essential to the business plan for 2020, and the Omanis had proved to be very decent people. We had shaken hands and broken bread. What could go wrong? In any case, I had already spent the money on my other businesses.

CHAPTER 14

Heaven Is a Place on Earth

You say you want a revolution
Well, you know
We all want to change the world
You tell me that it's evolution
Well, you know
We all want to change the world

THE BEATLES,
'*Revolution 1*'

The first real intimation I had of an impending global health crisis came in a series of alarming texts and emails from my eldest son in January 2020. He had seen mobile phone camera footage of Wuhan, where the authorities were sealing off apartment buildings, and had quickly realised that this clearly wasn't just another strain of flu. At the start of February, he began buying FFP3 respirator masks for the family. Even so, Julia and I decided to fly out to Hawaii on 12 March to celebrate her sixtieth birthday.

The world, though, was rapidly changing. People on Guernsey were going around in masks, and restaurants, hotels and even beaches were being shut. Julia's grand birthday with lots of guests became a small gathering held outside a beach club one of our friends belonged to. Back home in the UK, as lockdown took hold, we closed our office in London and advised colleagues to work remotely.

The business impact was immediate. Just a few weeks before, with the sale of Welcome Hotels virtually in the bag, everything seemed set fair for 2020. At a stroke, despite the fact we'd finally agreed on a price with our Omani buyers, despite the fact that we had broken bread with them, despite the fact that both sides had spent vast sums on legal fees and liked and trusted each other, the deal was suddenly off. Oman had gone into lockdown. Given the circumstances our buyers felt they had no option but to 'postpone' the transaction. I had been just two days away from having sufficient liquidity for the next twelve months. Now the £110 million I was banking on had vanished.

I asked my CFO, Vivek Ahuja, and the team to undertake a full cash flow analysis, to examine every eventuality and suggest strategic ways forward. Were there steps I should be taking now? What would happen if I did nothing? How long could each of our businesses survive before more cash was required? How would we fill the £110 million gap? Could it in fact be filled? Vivek was ideally suited for the task: as CFO of wholesale banking at Standard Chartered Bank, he'd lived through the financial crisis of 2008 and so understood both risk and the need for urgent action in difficult times. He was also my ideal foil: calm and analytical when I was emotional and impulsive. In April he became our CEO.

The prognosis that he and the team came up with was apocalyptic. I only had sufficient cash across all my businesses, they concluded, to keep them going until June, but that assumed that things didn't get any worse, that we'd run our various enterprises at minimal cost and that we'd massively reduce the headcount. Once we reached the half year, we'd have to start selling assets. Images arose in my mind of a fire sale, with hedge funds and vulture funds picking over the family assets and my co-investors lucky to get back a few pence in the pound. I could foresee bankruptcy. Given my diabetes, weight problems and compromised immune system, I could also foresee a level of stress that might prove fatal. For her part, Julia could see twenty years of work on Hand Picked Hotels disappearing before her eyes and her loyal staff losing their jobs and livelihoods.

The businesses I've always been involved in aren't the ones governments love. We're not going to come up with the next tech innovation. No one will give us a Nobel Prize or bang the government gong because we've served a burger quicker or made a ploughman's lunch tastier. Likewise, no one will give us an award for ensuring the well-being of a bull calf as it grows into a steer.

And while they'll pay lip service to healthcare, they're not really that concerned about all the essential tasks – such as turning someone in the night so that they don't get bedsores – that make healthcare a reality. Our businesses, quite simply, are not glamorous. On the other hand, they are businesses on which millions rely and that employ many thousands.

Fortunately, this time the government threw us a lifeline: furlough. When the initiative was first announced, we had no idea what it meant, and the details regarding how it would operate would change fourteen times in the course of the next ten days. But once it became clear that a basic principle had been established that an income would be provided to employees whom the lockdown had denied work, we realised that the fragility of great swathes of the economy had been recognised. Furlough would help ensure the survival of businesses that millions relied on, just as government intervention had saved the banks in 2008.

Stuck in Hawaii, I focused on getting fitter and on looking beyond June. Governments might have been assuring us that the Covid-19 crisis would last only a few months, but I was more persuaded by my elder son's view that the pandemic was here to stay for at least two years. That meant hoping for the best but planning for the worst. That in turn meant that we needed to focus forensically on each business, stress-test each one and decide whether change was necessary and, if so, how radical that change should be. My life ceased to be the thirty or so in-person meetings a week I had been used to, and became an endless succession of Zoom calls.

I introduced two basic principles that could be applied to all our businesses. First, so far as was possible, any decisions had to be made with 'no regret' – in other words, they had to be decisions that we would be happy to have made regardless of how serious the pandemic turned out to be. Second, if we thought we might have to cut into a business, we first had to inform ourselves thoroughly by amassing as much information as possible, and then give ourselves the time – and the man power – to analyse it and debate it. Given that we had eight businesses located in twenty countries, employing more than 23,000 people, with a turnover the previous year of more than €2 billion and a profit of €377 million, any steps we took had to be thought through to the final detail. We not only wanted to make sure our businesses survived and were able to withstand anything that the new reality might throw at them, but we also wanted to make sure that they continued to develop.

To oversee this we created the Scenario, Contingency and Planning Committee: a quick reaction force – consisting of Justin, Vivek, Iain Stokes (a senior member of all of our General Partners in Guernsey) and me, supported by one of our deal managing directors, Dave Browne – to address critical issues across the portfolio and make strategic decisions. Among the first 'no regret' moves we made was to cancel our 2020 Analyst Programme just two days before the eight potential analysts – out of 2,000 original applicants who had made it through numerous tests, the assessment centre and interviews with Terra Firma senior staff – were due to meet me. And we also suspended our deal origination activities and curtailed the search for investment prospects.

We then ran four different scenarios through a cash flow model. In the case of the worst possibility – the world shutting down for more than fifteen months – we concluded there was little we could do. If the pandemic followed the path of previous flu epidemics but was mitigated by modern medicine and the introduction of a vaccine before the end of 2020, then we could certainly survive beyond June 2021, assuming we sold a reasonably-sized business and cut expenditure wherever we could. We would also need to borrow where possible from our banks and where we couldn't, extend the length of our loans for as long as possible. And we would have to make use of the various government liquidity lines available in the countries in which we operated, along with such national support for businesses as was made available to us.

Each decision we took and enacted involved some tough choices. On the one hand, we wanted to be as sympathetic and supportive to each of our businesses as possible. On the other hand, we knew we could not afford to be the lender of last resort. Sentiment would count for little if the end result was that no one emerged on the other side.

Our experience with our McDonald's business Food Folk and the cosmetics company Talika illustrate both the range of challenges we faced and people's extraordinary ability to be flexible and to respond well under pressure. The two concerns couldn't be more different in scale. Food Folk has our largest pool of employees and is responsible for our largest single chunk of turnover. Talika is the smallest on both counts. It's also hard to imagine two businesses operating in sectors more dissimilar than high street fast food, and cosmetics available principally via duty-free shops and on planes. Yet both responded equally robustly and imaginatively to the pandemic.

Food Folk felt the immediate impact of Covid-19, with sales falling 22 per cent in March alone. Not surprisingly, therefore, many of our franchisees wanted immediate financial support and some even wanted to close. I said no to both. It was important for us, the brand, the employees and the franchisees to stay open and to serve our customer base, even if we didn't know when profits would return. In any case, I pointed out, if we closed we would struggle to survive past June. So far as financial support was concerned, it was true that in some parts of the world McDonald's was offering local help, but my argument was that it would be absurd to give loans and rent relief as a matter of course at a general level or indeed at the level of individual restaurants. Not all franchisees were suffering equally: those who had a mix of restaurants, for example, might be struggling with their shopping mall outlets but were doing well with their drive-through restaurants. I also said that such financial support as we did agree to provide to a franchise should take the form of a partnership payment, rather than a loan, and that we would get our return by sharing in the earnings from the restaurant over a period of time.

In other words, I felt we should be helping franchisees who, through no fault of their own, actually faced bankruptcy, but not enterprises experiencing tougher than usual trading conditions. In the end, we found that roughly 10 per cent of franchisees needed financial support, and we gave each of them on average ten times more than each of the franchises in the global McDonald's loan plan. This made us popular with that 10 per cent. It also made us unpopular with the remaining 90 per cent, some of whom were very vocal with me about their unhappiness. But then business is not about winning popularity contests, and I believed our approach was the right one. In fact, as the year wore on and the dividends for remaining open became apparent, the 90 per cent came to believe it too. Ultimately, we gained market share in all four countries in which we operated (sales in Finland were the highest of any quick-service restaurant chain there), and we ended the year with sales flat on 2019: an impressive result in the circumstances. Some might argue that this was because Nordic countries as a whole withstood the pandemic reasonably well. Given that many of our local competitors recorded sales down 40 per cent and that some went bankrupt, I'm not so sure.

Talika was a very different proposition. My involvement here was as a passive investor who had loaned money to Naga – a joint venture between Terra Firma and a brand management team – to acquire a minority share of the cosmetics business. Naga had been aiming to pay off our loan and buy out our equity at the beginning of 2020. Unfortunately, when Covid-19 hit, their investors disappeared.

In the course of Zoom meetings with majority shareholder Alexis de Brosses we thrashed out a strategy for a company whose traditional customers – air travellers – had more or less vanished overnight. First Alexis cut costs by reducing the labour force as quickly as possible. Then he substantially reduced new product development. He concentrated sales and TV advertising on eye make-up, arguing that with face masks mandatory in most countries, eyes had become the new smile, and that in the current environment mascara would score over lipstick.

His approach was tough but extraordinarily effective. By the end of the year, the number of employees had fallen from thirty-five people to fourteen, and budgeted turnover had fallen by nearly a quarter. But at the same time the business had become more efficient and the new online focus was paying dividends: one infomercial alone brought in sales of more than 16,000 units. By September the business was making a profit again.

Food Folk and Talika weren't our only challenges. With Parmaco, our Finnish company specialising in building and renting high-quality buildings for schools, we had a business that was actually doing really well but that threatened to run out of money if we continued to build new schools at the rate the management team wanted. We could have looked to recapitalise the company and increase the amount of debt it had. But that would have come at a cost. And since, in any case, we needed to raise a substantial amount of money for Terra Firma as a whole by

June 2021, I felt that far from looking to find the additional sums Parmaco required, we should actually be selling it as quickly as possible. The timing was far from perfect, given Covid-19, the fact that Parmaco's CFO was leaving and that the CEO, Ossi Alastalo, had decided, after thirty-two years, that he wanted to go part-time and become a non-executive chairman. But while the general view of others at Terra Firma, the management team and our co-investors was that we should get the business refinanced as quickly as possible and put it up for sale later in 2021 when we had a management team in place and settled in, I felt instinctively that this simply wasn't the right path to take.

Covid-19 demonstrated to me how lucky Finnish society is to have what many people regard as the best school system in the world. It's a system that concentrates first and foremost on helping children assimilate into society and become useful and positive members of the community, and only secondarily on academic results. Not that academic standards in Finland are poor – the country is consistently rated as one of the top three in the world for literacy (the UK, by contrast, ranks seventeenth). Whenever I looked at the schools we built in Finland, I was struck by just how much space was given over to activities that were not related to the academic curriculum. There were special surfaces that younger kids could play on. Classrooms were equipped with pull-down beds to allow children to have proper rest periods. I was also impressed that all pupils in Finnish schools receive free school meals up to the age of sixteen and that these meals are of an excellent nutritional standard (Finland was the first country in the world to offer this free service to children). I am convinced that the emphasis placed from an early age on co-operation and community helps explain why Finland managed to avoid lockdown during the pandemic and yet record very low death rates. People pulled together.

Had circumstances been different, I would doubtless have taken a different path with Parmaco. It's a great business. As it was, I rejected the refinancing option, and set to work getting the business ready for sale. My own view was that it was worth more than €1 billion and so we set that as our target. I was acutely aware, however, that my valuation and that of the market might well be very different things.

With the decision made, we started on four separate pieces of work – all of which we knew would be essential for a successful sales process. First, we needed to find a new CEO and CFO. Since the plan was to sell the company, there might have been a temptation to look for individuals who would simply come across well. But I wanted to hire people I would be happy to leave as long-term custodians of the business. When we briefed the head-hunters I therefore made it clear that we would only consider people who had passed Terra Firma's psychometric and aptitude tests – tests that only around sixty-five of the 2,000 graduates who apply to us each year pass. I was warned we risked not making an appointment in time. No matter. So far as I was concerned, this just meant that the headhunters would have to work harder for their money. And it worked. We had a CFO, Marina Ruohonen, in place in the summer, and a CEO, Sami Laine, in November. Alongside Ossi Alastalo, I felt they made a dream team.

Our second task was to explain the cash flow of the business to potential buyers, to outline any potential risks and suggest how those risks could be mitigated. I knew that potential investors would examine the business forensically. If they didn't understand something, or were concerned about it, a deal would become that much harder to strike. Since the mathematical and analytical skills to do such work are very specialised (I had drawn on them during my securitisation stint at Goldman Sachs and also Nomura when I formed the Principal Finance Group, but they didn't really exist in Terra Firma), I decided to bring in an old colleague who had worked with me at PFG and now ran his own advisory firm. It proved a gruelling experience for the Terra Firma and Parmaco management teams, who found themselves subjected to tough questioning from an expert number-cruncher who possessed the mindset of a sceptical and hard-nosed investor. But it worked. By the end of the process the numbers were clear. They also happened to demonstrate that the business was indeed worth more than €1 billion – €1.1 billion, to be precise.

Our third task was to see what the business could do to maximise its profits, whether this involved launching initiatives to extend the modular school approach, building modular care homes or expanding the business to other countries. The challenge here came not so much from the need to generate new ideas as from the requirement to produce a simplified business plan for each initiative. We brought in the consulting firm McKinsey to help us and had the necessary documents in place in early 2021.

And finally, we needed to choose a bank to run the sales process and start presenting to potential buyers. The first part of this two-stage process went smoothly enough. By the end of October 2020 we had Deutsche Bank in place to kick off the sales process and by February 2021, after two rounds of indicative bids, we were down to four prospective buyers. But then we hit a problem. Just before we were due to move on to the next stage, I watched a dry run of the presentation that management would make to prospective buyers and immediately got very cold feet. I felt the team were presenting as individuals, not as a cohesive unit, and that there was no emotion there. Worse still, it was very boring: a lecture, not a passion pitch.

When I expressed my reservations, I was told that I had got it wrong. The Finns are reserved people, colleagues said, and what I was asking for was too Anglo-American. I was unconvinced.

People are people. Americans sell well, not because they're born with the skill but because they're trained to sell. In any case, three of our potential buyers were not Finnish. There was a real danger that the presentations – which would have to be done over Zoom in English – would fall very flat.

I delayed the presentation and turned to an old friend for help. Julia Goodman at Personal Presentation had previously helped me hone the public-facing skills of the head of our McDonald's franchise in Finland; taking a shy accountant and turning him into a brilliant front man who could own the room in meetings with large numbers of Finnish franchisees. His new-found confidence and energy were, I believe, largely responsible for the turnaround of the Finnish business. When he projected self-assurance, the franchisees picked up on his positivity. They stopped bringing up petty issues and worked together to drive the business forward and provide a great customer experience. Confidence is infectious.

The four Finns slated to give our sales pitch to potential buyers were not keen on the idea that Julia Goodman would give them the Personal Presentation treatment. I could understand why, having myself been on the receiving end twenty years earlier. It's painful to be told that something you think you have been doing well every day for years, is something that – via Zoom with three other people – you are actually doing terribly. But I felt the medicine needed to be swallowed. True to form, Julia did not mince her words with the team and a very painful few days followed. But, working through the weekend and late into the night, they eventually got there. And I at last felt confident that we would not fall at the final hurdle.

When bid day, on 24 February, came round, we received three bids at over €1 billion, with a top one close to €1.1 billion. When they heard that they were the underbidders, two of the potential buyers asked if they could increase their offer. In both cases I said no. We had made it clear that we were not going to accept further bids and people should put their best foot forward at the outset.

In the end it was Partners Group, a fund based in Switzerland with €100 billion of assets under management, that bought the business. I believe they will be good owners and I rolled some of the money that I earned from the sale of Parmaco back into the business. It will be good to stay connected and see the company go from strength to strength. At the same time, the successful conclusion of the bid process had given me enough money to support my remaining businesses. I no longer had to fear for their survival.

If the Covid-19 pandemic presented huge challenges to our fast food business, it posed an existential threat to Julia's Hand Picked Hotels. Founded by her in 2001, the company had won AA Hotel Group of the Year twice, countless awards for food and service and had just been voted Conference Hotel Chain of the Year. But no hotel chain – or hotel for that matter – could cope with a national lockdown.

If you are a Premier Inn with modern buildings, you can at least cut your costs by closing your doors. Hand Picked Hotels, however, comprises Grade I and Grade II listed historic buildings set in great swathes of countryside. Just keeping the buildings safe, watertight, and well-maintained costs millions. Closing the doors and waiting for the crisis to pass was not an option. Over the course of the next fifteen months, I was to pump £60 million into the company to keep it afloat.

For Julia and me the challenges posed by Hand Picked Hotels presented another dimension too. When Julia first agreed to manage the business, she made it very clear that she was not going to work for me. The Hand Picked Hotels were her baby, and she wanted to run them with minimal input from me. Now that I was injecting so much money into the business, however, that hands-off approach no longer seemed in order.

As with every other business in which I was involved at that time, I wanted to take the opportunity the hotel chain's enforced period of downtime afforded to run a strategic review of the business. This was going to be a painful process. When you subject a management team to a transformation process, you need to get them to accept the need for change, the prize for successfully changing and the methods for achieving the change – just as I did following my mild stroke in 2019. The meetings that I hold with management during a programme of change occur once a week and last two hours, at the end of which everyone is exhausted, angry and frustrated – myself included. Generally, I'm angry with myself because I feel I haven't explained clearly enough what it is that I want done, and I'm frustrated with management for not just getting on and doing it. The management team becomes similarly angry, frustrated and exhausted after two hours of hearing why they need to change and why what they've been doing for years no longer works. I normally end up asking management to reconsider the problems or opportunities that we are focusing on that week as part of the change programme, and come back to me with alternative solutions. Normally it takes at least two or three rounds for me to be satisfied with the solution. I also supplement the existing management team with outsiders who come from different businesses to act as 'devil's advocates' and challenge existing management or, in some cases, replace them.

Nine times out of ten when I have bought a business and gone through this process, the existing management teams do indeed depart. This ultimately makes life easier for everyone. With Hand Picked Hotels, however, this was hardly on the cards. Nor could I really suggest to Julia that we meet once a week for two hours and then leave my team to work with her by themselves. Instead, conversations at bedtime became arguments about IT systems, brand and room rates – she had been charging rates that put her into the top three value-for-money hotel chains in the UK for a number of years. I could hardly blame Julia for never wanting to work for me; she knew my work style better than anyone and knew how I put myself and those who work for me under extraordinary pressure in order to achieve the best result possible. Covid-19 forced me to take the time to work out how all my businesses could be challenged, improved and transformed. I was going to do whatever was necessary to transform my businesses so that they would survive. This was about survival, and all businesses and their stakeholders had to come above personal sensibilities.

Julia had already decided to make changes, particularly in Hand Picked's use of technology, its deployment of specialist skills, its room rates and its brand. However, Covid-19 meant that these changes needed to be done far quicker and more extensively than anyone in Hand Picked was prepared for.

Inevitably, Julia and I didn't always agree; I can't remember ever fully agreeing with a CEO during a change process. The closest I ever got was with John Brown at William Hill, who offered his resignation at his first meeting with me, though it did take us about a year to reach an agreement. At times we must have appeared like two naughty schoolboys fighting. This approach wasn't going to work with Julia. But we were of one mind when it came to the values we felt Hand Picked should espouse: a sense of family, local engagement, welcome, heritage, sustainability, quirkiness, service, comfort and individuality. Whether or not future customers will value having their breakfast sausages sourced from a nearby farm, the art and sculptures reflecting the heritage of the building in which they are staying and the staff wanting to tell them everything about the local community while doing everything they can for their families, we don't yet know, but Julia and I believe strongly they will. We also believe we can persuade people that rather than travel to Rome, Milan, Paris, Stockholm or Copenhagen for a break, they should try the wonderful British countryside. Hand Picked Hotels will emerge post-pandemic having had over £100 million pumped into the business with Julia's vision executed in a far shorter period of time than I think she or her management team could have expected.

One other casualty of Covid-19 was the public launch of Engage Britain, a charity that acts as a vehicle for political change. In recent times I have sought to re-engage with political life and try to make a positive contribution – attempting to apply some of the business lessons I have learnt during my career in a wider context.

It's certainly not a straightforward proposition. Leaving aside Julia's consistent threat to leave me if I venture to actually become a politician, the simple fact of the matter is that I don't like the British political scene. When Britain voted for Brexit, for example, my first response was – perhaps inevitably – an emotional one. I felt depressed and I experienced a sense of anger with the Remain campaign leaders who had handled the issue so catastrophically. However, the businessman in me reacted more rationally. I could understand why people chose the path they did, and why they had effectively wanted to put two fingers up at the political status quo. When you look at failing businesses, you find that engagement, empowerment and a sense of belonging have disappeared. Post-Brexit, you didn't have to be a genius to realise that those three qualities were under threat in the UK. So many people felt disengaged from government and politics – from those who wielded power. If British politics had been a business, I would have immediately prescribed a radical operational overhaul, brand refocus and a replacement of the senior personnel.

I started a series of conversations about a way forward with moderate figures among the great and the good. I was disappointed by the outcome. Their solution, I felt, seemed to repeat the mistakes of the past – the only difference this time apparently being that they thought that they could do it all better. I found this hard to believe. There are only three things you can change in a business – the people, what they do and how things are organised. When buying businesses in trouble, those are the things I focus on and it's the people I almost invariably end up changing – not because I blame them, but because they are part of the problem and they find it hard to become part of the solution. I felt the same about the great and the good; they could not be part of the solution.

As I re-engaged publicly with politics I set out my principal beliefs as succinctly as I could: 'Our politicians are not delivering for our country. Political and policy paralysis is increasing. Many of the biggest challenges we face – such as poverty, the environment and how people live alongside one another – are not new issues: they are ones that have not been properly addressed. Britain is a country fizzing with talent and ideas, but too often those who have the keenest first-hand experience of the issues we need to solve and those who are most affected by decisions made in Whitehall aren't listened to. This needs to change.'

As 2016 became 2017, I discovered that no one in the establishment agreed with me. After all, I was asking them to trust communities across Britain, and to accept that they were the servants of the people, not the other way round. It was like getting turkeys to vote for Christmas. I was told that I was crazy, that the public wasn't bright enough to make good decisions. 'People are bigoted and nasty,' some added, evoking a notion of the 'rabble' that takes us right back to the Peasants' Revolt.

I responded by saying that I'd never seen a connection between education and good decisions, though I do believe knowledge is important. I also pointed out that, in any case, politicians try as hard as possible to stop the public thinking about issues in depth. Instead, they combine them into a single package and expect voters to buy into it like football fans choosing a team. As for the accusation that people are intrinsically bigoted, I felt sure this was incorrect, but I did fear that they might have become as divided and extreme as the press made out.

Lord John Birt, who had been a loyal confidant through the process and who had slowly moved from regarding me as crazy to being only half-mad, suggested that I meet with Julian McCrae at the Institute for Government. I was sceptical. According to his CV he'd read PPE at University College, Oxford, worked at the Institute for Fiscal Studies, then at Whitehall and gone on to take up a role in the prime minister's strategy unit. In other words he had spent over two decades in the establishment. To me he seemed to be part of the problem, not part of a potential solution.

I met up with Julian in a panelled room at Churchill Court, our home in Sevenoaks. We made an interestingly contrasting pair. Julian had a beard and looked like a classic Islington left-winger. I have been told that I look like Jerry Springer (an Indian restaurant in Sevenoaks once refused to believe I wasn't him and insisted on taking photographs of me with the staff to prove that Jerry Springer ate there).

I started out by expressing my view that if you could remove politicians and the media from the picture, you'd be left with a nation of decent people who share similar beliefs. The divisions we see in society, I argued, are largely down to miscommunication. Julian seemed to concur with the gist of what I was saying and agreed to organise a survey that would put my hunch to the test. From these conversations, Engage Britain – a charity that acts as a vehicle for change – was born. Julia and I provided the funding to get it off the ground and Julian McCrae came on board as the director.

The results of the survey Julian arranged confirmed my gut feeling. Politics might be broken, but the British people most definitely aren't. The vast majority emerged from the survey as fair-minded individuals, with a great belief in social justice, community, working together and doing the right thing. I felt hopeful for the first time since the referendum. Maybe there was a way forward for Britain if we could find a way to get the voices of the 'silent majority' heard.

With Julian in charge, Engage set about a further test to see what would happen when we introduced, say, conservative old ladies to tough kids from the wrong side of the tracks. We set topics for them to discuss, provided facilitators, put a video camera in place to record them and then left them to it. It was the sort of social experiment that no politician would dare to try.

The results were incredibly moving. Groups of people who in everyday life might well be scared or resentful of each other were realising for the first time that they hadn't really seen or heard each other before. I particularly recall watching a grandmother engaging with a kid in a hoodie. Guarded at first, they bonded when she noticed that his facial tattoos were similar to the ones her grandson had.

The arrival of Covid-19 forced us to put our plans on hold. We couldn't launch Engage Britain in person, and a virtual launch via Zoom seemed out of place; we will have to wait until normality returns. But on the upside, as contact with community leaders around the UK has increased, our connection with local communities has become stronger. I feel very privileged to have been able to join the bi-monthly meetings in which local people discussed the impact of lockdown on them, their families and the wider community.

My vision for Engage is that it should give people both a better understanding and a voice. I've become acutely aware of the fact that the vast majority of us have little knowledge or comprehension of just how desperate life can be for many in our society and how marginalised minority groups can feel. If Engage can heighten people's awareness, I am sure that they will come to demand change and that a better society will emerge. I say this not least because I feel that many of the problems that various sections of society face – poverty, for example – are so far removed from others' experience that in the current environment there is little chance of them being addressed. This is not a question of getting the more fortunate to condescend patronisingly to lean in or help, as I feel can be the case with 'luvvies' from Islington or 'paternalistic' conservatives. It's a question of bringing together human beings who share so much but whose life chances have been very different.

My work with my old Oxford college, Mansfield, is part and parcel of this philosophy. Getting an Oxford college's intake to more closely reflect UK society was a small success in creating a fairer and better country. The next project Julia and I are planning is to get the privileged students at Oxford to spend some of their time at university connecting with a community that they would never come across unless they make a conscious effort to do so – but to do it at a time when they are still open to different thoughts and don't yet totally believe that the fact they can do well in an exam makes them better than others. In other words, we want to catch them before they become set in their ways and upholders of a status quo that offers little in the way of genuine happiness and self-fulfilment.

As I have widened my focus, I've also recalibrated my approach to business. The realisation that I was never going to raise another blind pool fund freed me up from having to be an asset manager acting on behalf of investors and allowed me to return to doing what I love best: doing great deals. With the full power of Terra Firma behind me – now focused on sourcing, executing, operating and ultimately exiting assets – I became its cornerstone investor, and the Hands Family Office has turned into the chief vehicle for my business ambitions.

Not only have I returned to my entrepreneurial roots, I have also shifted my philosophy of business. Transformation for economic value isn't enough. Each business in which I am involved needs not just to be a leader in its field but should set itself targets that involve making the world a better place. This is not the same ambition as simply saying we will 'do no harm' or that we will only invest in businesses that are deemed 'good' or 'ethical'. I want to be involved in transforming existing businesses that may be neither, so that, for example, they no longer pose environmental dangers and are active in reducing carbon emissions and in carbon capture. They must also support a positive social agenda, focusing on the communities in which we invest and promoting diverse representation, social inclusion and a safe workplace. They must drive transparency, accountability and sustainable business practices across all stakeholder groups, including employees, customers, suppliers, investors and communities. They should also ensure they secure active engagement across the whole value chain in each of our businesses, from suppliers to investors, explaining to everyone if they do not meet our standards, why they did not. That also makes us accountable for monitoring the sustainability practices of the parties we do engage with.

At one stage having strong environmental, social and governance (ESG) credentials was a nice-to-have. Today, I believe, it's a must-have. It's about baking ESG into everything we do in business, making the mantra 'leaving the world a better place' a rule for every single day. I say to my colleagues all the time that if ESG is the elephant in the room, our job is to get the elephant to dance. And speaking as a man whose dancing skills require intense concentration, I know the only way to do this is to make it very, very simple. We don't have time for excuses. I won't pretend to have all the answers. But I'm not scared of failing as I attempt to find them. I'm far more scared of not giving it a go.

If all this sounds completely out of character for someone who has been portrayed as a hard-headed businessman, I'm not surprised. But my guess is many business people reach a point in their lives where they realise that succeeding at business hasn't brought them happiness and they've realised just what they have given up for success. In my case, it's a bit like going through the five stages of grief: denial, anger, bargaining, depression and acceptance. Having reached acceptance and realising I can't change the past, I'm busy re-evaluating my approach to business and what business should entail. I'm seeking a wider engagement with society. And I'm reforming myself as I do so in everything from my eating and drinking (which I used to indulge in far too heavily) to my involvement in the life of my family, which I feel I neglected for too long.

During the summer of 2021, as I looked out to sea over the Pea Stacks – beautiful granite rocks that Renoir had painted during his time on Guernsey, rocks that Victor Hugo had brought to life in *Toilers of the Sea*, rocks like many around Guernsey, beautiful to look at, but rocks that have wrecked hundreds of boats and drowned thousands of sailors over the years – I decided I could give myself the freedom to leave the 'Under Toad' behind.

I will have no one to blame but myself if I don't grab the moment and for once follow my own advice. My purpose in life when I was six years old was to leave the world a better place. Fifty-five years later, I have no excuse for not doing so. If I work on that, then I have the chance to find satisfaction and achieve a sense of fulfilment. If on the way I enjoy myself and spend some of my money on material things or presents for the people I love, or helping out people I feel for, or on being extravagant, or burning too much carbon – not everything I do is altruistic – then I will just be human. No better and no worse than anyone else, and with no need to feel guilt for being me. If I stick to this, then the 'Under Toad' will finally disappear.

Looking out to sea I feel that I am six years old again, with all the enthusiasm of youth. At the same time I can now draw on the experience of age. My passion for life is returning. After everything I have seen and done, this has to be the best feeling in the world.

ACKNOWLEDGEMENTS

Like Shaka Zulu, I have around me a tribe of people who have helped me and shaped my life beyond what could have possibly been expected. My story's making would not have been possible without the tremendous efforts of hundreds, if not thousands, of people, to whom I am eternally grateful.

It would be impossible to thank everyone who has contributed to my life, but my first debt of gratitude must go to my family: my wife Julia; our four children; my parents, Sally and Chris, and Julia's parents, Betty and Joe; my brother and sister, Philip and Alison, and Julia's sister, Marion.

I would also like to extend my thanks to those who have helped bring the book to life:

The production team: Nigel Wilcockson, my editor; Caroline Michel, my agent; the writers Stephen Armstrong, James Ashton, Tim Bouquet and Andy Silton; Louis Waite, who helped with the photos; Susie Campanella, who helped with the layout; and Nick Caley, my trusty PR man.

Then the Terra Firma staff who have patiently worked alongside me on this for the last ten years: Sara Little, Paulina Fruth, Lizzie Edwards, Laura Oxley, Schuyler Clemente and Christen Thomson.

My thanks to those who refreshed my memory and provided anecdotes: Tim Pryce, Vivek Ahuja, Mike Kinski, Bill Miles, Julie Williamson, Justin King, Lord John Birt, Jenny Dunstan, Jerry

'Melch' Melchionna, Paul Spillane, Anthony D'Souza, Billy Mann, Carol Dunseith, Tim Short, Andrew Miller, Pasquale Nazzaro, Riaz Punja and Mayamiko Kachingwe.

My thanks to those who kept me out of trouble, before, during and after the EMI trial: Terry Revere, Trudy Cooke, Denelle Dixon, James Oldnall, David Thomas, David Wolfson and Chris Duffy.

And, finally, my gratitude to those whose guidance over the years has helped me avoid even more mistakes than those I made: Sir Tom McKillop, Glen Moreno and Patrick Allen.

Thanks to each and every one of you for helping me on this journey.

LIST OF EPIGRAPHS

PICTURE PERMISSIONS

Oxford University Conservative Association hustings; Guy Hands speaking at the Oxford Union © Jon Collinson.

Guy Hands selling pictures © Billett Potter.

'Contract chaos kills dome deal' newspaper clipping, 2000 © Telegraph Media Group Limited 2021.

Millennium Dome, 1998 © PA Images/Alamy Stock Photo.

The Rolling Stones EMI cartoon © Robert Thompson.

Guy Hands EMI cartoon © Joe Cummings/*Financial Times*.

Guy Hands arriving at an EMI meeting © Kieran Doherty/Reuters.

Guy Hands arriving at court in New York © Louis Lanzano/Bloomberg via Getty Images.

All other images © Guy Hands.

The author and publisher gratefully acknowledge the permission granted to reproduce the copyright material in this book. Every effort has been made to trace copyright holders and to obtain their permission. The publisher apologises for any omissions and, if notified, will make suitable acknowledgement in future reprints or editions of this book.

INDEX